THE SYNDROME OF SPECIFIC DYSLEXIA

Edith Klasen, currently Head of the Child Welfare Department, The German Caritas Association (Freiburg), conducted the major part of her research for this book from 1963 through 1971 as Director of Child Guidance and Testing at the Ellen K. Raskob Learning Institute, College of Holy Names, Oakland, California, where she also served as instructor of graduate courses in Special Education.

Dr. Klasen holds diplomas in Social Work from the Women's College of Social Work, Cologne, and in Clinical Psychology from the Friedrich-Alexander University, Erlangen-Nuremberg. Following graduate study at Boston College and at the University of California, Berkeley, she obtained her Ph.D. *(summa cum laude)* in Clinical Psychology from Fribourg University, Switzerland.

An American citizen since 1967, Dr. Klasen is the author of *Audio-Visual-Motor Training With Pattern Cards* (Peek Publications, Second Edition, 1970), as well as numerous articles.

THE SYNDROME OF SPECIFIC DYSLEXIA

WITH SPECIAL CONSIDERATION OF ITS PHYSIOLOGICAL, PSYCHOLOGICAL, TESTPSYCHOLOGICAL, AND SOCIAL CORRELATES

Edith Klasen, Ph.D.

UNIVERSITY PARK PRESS

BALTIMORE • LONDON • TOKYO

UNIVERSITY PARK PRESS

International Publishers in Science and Medicine
Chamber of Commerce Building
Baltimore, Maryland 21202

Copyright © 1972
by University Park Press

Printed in the United States of America

Library of Congress Cataloging in Publication Data

Klasen, Edith.
   The syndrome of specific dyslexia.

   Translation of Das Syndrom der Legasthenie.
   Bibliography: p.
   1. Dyslexia.   I. Title.
RJ496.A5K5813   618.9'28'553   72-3743
ISBN 0-8391-0704-8

To those to whom I am indebted:
Friends, teachers, colleagues, and students

CONTENTS

III. Conclusions

IV. Trends in Literature Published between 1969 and 1971

Appendix

PREFACE

It was not only empirically gained knowledge and interest in research that motivated the compilation of this volume, but mostly the need of dyslexic students for increasingly discerning treatment of their learning and adjustment difficulties. Encounters at the Ellen K. Raskob Institute demonstrate daily and with impact that the longer a specific learning disability goes unrecognized and untreated in an individual case, the more internal balance and social adjustment are jeopardized. The greater the factual knowledge of parents, educators, physicians, and all others involved, the greater the chances for early and specific diagnostic, educational, psychological, and medical help.

A particular contribution of this book, in comparison with other contemporary publications, is its broad empirical and statistical base, involving the dossiers of 500 individually and thoroughly investigated dyslexics. The wealth of observations and data simply suggested itself for investigations of relationships, causal or merely associative, between dyslexia on the one hand, and physiopsychological symptoms, psychopathological factors, test profiles, and social aspects on the other. Years of experience indicate that specific learning disabilities are primarily and most frequently associated with neuropsychological symptoms, such as disorders of speech, lateral dominance, spatial orientation, perception, coordination, motor activity, etc. Emotional disturbance, frustration intolerance, behavior difficulties, social maladjustment, characteristic psychometric test results, family background, and related variables seem to be of secondary and less frequent occurrence. This hypothesis, developed by casual observation and knowledge, had to be tested statistically.

Findings—and therein lies another unique feature of this investigation—were not only presented and discussed, but also compared with those obtained by other researchers, in the United States as well as in several European countries. English, French, and German language literature was perused and the pertinent data condensed and utilized in this book. Of the nearly 200 publications listed in the bibliography, approximately two-thirds are American, the rest various European writings.

A number of professionals have facilitated my work, and I am
pleased to record my acknowledgement. To Sr. Eileen M. Cronin,
Ph.D., Associate Professor of Education at the College of The Holy
Names in Oakland, California, founder and director of the Ellen K.
Raskob Institute, I am grateful for permission to use student files, for
provision of technical aid available in the Institute, and for constant
interest and encouragement. I also gratefully acknowledge the valuable professional counsel of my colleagues who gave generously of
their knowledge, experience, and time. I am happy to express my
indebtedness to Mr. Robert Raskob. His personal involvement and
interest in the work of the Institute provided valuable assistance and
secured financial support through the Bill Raskob Foundation. Finally,
my sincere appreciation is offered to Dr. Eduard Montalta, Professor
of Psychology, and founder as well as director of the "Institute for
Special Education, Applied Psychology, and Social Science" at the
University of Fribourg, Switzerland. His constructive criticism and his
emphasis on scientific exactitude as much as on a fully human view
greatly stimulated and improved my work.

Edith Klasen

I. INTRODUCTION

1. DESCRIPTION AND ANALYSIS

1.1 The Concept of Specific Dyslexia

In 1877 Adolph Kussmaul, a German internist, translated the neurologic-psychiatric term "alexia" as "word blindness." Since that time the terminology has grown more confusing, rather than clearer. Hopefully this can be taken as an indication that today we know much more about the subject and are more aware of its complexity, although we have not yet reached the degree of clarity which would allow simplified, precise concept formation.

The word dyslexia is hardly used any more in German-speaking countries; it has been replaced by the widely known term "Legasthenie" = *legasthenia*, or reading weakness. It is synonymous with such English descriptive terms as "reading difficulties," "reading problems," "specific reading disability," "reading retardation," or "reading-spelling disability." It does not seem judicious during the present, unsatisfactory state of affairs to add yet another term; thus, we will use here the expression "specific dyslexia," meaning reading-spelling and various other language disabilities, observed in students of normal intelligence who are otherwise at least average in academic and social achievements. In this definition we agree with Linder, who defined specific dyslexia as a special weakness, not present in other areas of learning, in the acquisition of reading skills (and indirectly also of independent and accurate spelling skills) and despite otherwise normal or — as compared to the reading facility — relatively high intelligence.[1]* Busemann similarly states that specific dyslexia is clearly present in cases in which intelligence shows normalcy in other areas, despite the obvious failure in reading.[2] To let yet another au-

---

thor speak: Bleidick considers specific dyslexia an isolated
reading weakness (usually combined with a spelling disability)
in spite of an otherwise normal degree of intelligence.[3] A more
detailed definition was given by Tomkins, "Reading performance markedly inferior to performance in other areas of learning ... and also inferior to ability indicated by nonverbal IQ
tests, a tendency to have trouble in other language skills, such
as speech, spelling, penmanship, and the ability to express
ideas or to organize a story ..."[4] The Swiss author Kocher
bases his definition on an analogous concept, "The notion of
specific dyslexia is more restrictive; it is a question of difficulty
in learning to read which manifests itself in a child normally
developed in areas where the written language is not particularly involved."[5]

It must be emphasized that the term specific dyslexia, as it is
used here, is not synonymous, as some authors claim, with
congenital reading disability. Kobi, for instance, wrote that dyslexia (= reading disorder) and congenital reading disability
(= present at birth) were to be considered synonymous.[6] We
cannot agree. The term dyslexia is still widely associated with
the original concept of a clinically diagnosed brain lesion and,
therefore, a more severe degree of reading disability.[7] We
know today, however, that lesions are by no means ascertain-
able in all cases. Therefore both concepts, that of dyslexia as
well as that of word blindness (originally having meant
alexia = reading inability), are no longer very common.[8] In the
United States wherever the term dyslexia is used, it is more
exactly specified, as in specific dyslexia.[9] Denmark seems to be
an exception in adhering to the expression "word blindness,"
as, for instance, the "School For The Word Blind" in Copenhagen, founded by Edith Norrie, indicates.

Specific dyslexia does not necessarily imply a congenital origin. Although the findings of this study coincide to a large
extent with those of researchers who consider constitutional
and hereditary factors as important causes, it is apparent that
specific dyslexia is not always congenital. There exist also exogenous and emotional forms. As long as the etiological factors
cannot be scientifically and definitely determined, there is no
justification in reserving the word dyslexia for congenital forms

alone. Only to avoid repetitious language are we going to use interchangeably such terms as "reading-spelling weakness," "reading retardation," "reading problems," etc. They all stand for "specific dyslexia" as defined above.

How little agreement exists in the terminology today becomes obvious when we take a look at publications in the field. In addition to the terms mentioned above, we find: "visual" and "auditory dyslexia," "literal" and "verbal," "primary," "isolated," or "pure dyslexia" (as opposed to "secondary"), "dysphasic dyslexia," and "linear dyslexia." As this enumeration demonstrates, the terminology is not based on equal principles, but rather on various points of interest; etiology, symptomatology, degree, etc. Moreover, not all assumed causes can be considered clinically amenable to diagnosis.

Thus, it should be mentioned once more that in the study presented here we use the term specific dyslexia without etiological implications and without considerations of degree. It is simply a descriptive expression for a reading-spelling retardation which exists despite otherwise satisfactory performance in the classroom, normal or better than average general intelligence, and adequate senses.

1.2 Specific Dyslexia as a Social Problem

Nearly 100 years of research have done nothing to diminish the significance of the phenomenon called specific dyslexia. Our highly developed, mechanized, and specialized civilization requires more and more knowledge and skills. Children have more to learn[10] and reading has become the sine qua non of all learning. It is well known, however, that a high percentage of children in Europe, North America, Japan, and other highly developed countries do not at all or only partially acquire reading facility. All learning depends on reading ability.[11] Any degree of reading retardation today has grave consequences, not only for the dyslexic, but for society as a whole, and therefore deserves all possible effort in terms of research as well as better preventive or curative measures.

Several years of diagnostic and therapeutic work with dyslexics and their parents and educators at the E. K. Raskob Learning Institute of the Holy Names College in Oakland, California, provided a wealth of observations, information, experience, and leading questions. In time the impression grew stronger and stronger that dyslexia, despite many individually different characteristics, appears to have certain basic features which are present in all of its manifestations.

1.3 Dyslexia as a Scientific Problem

Although the various manifestations of reading problems are known in the field, especially among teachers and educators, science still has not been able to answer all the questions they pose. The concept of a dyslexic "syndrome" can be found here and there in the literature, but it appears that usually only special, single aspects are included. Thus, the seemingly representative reading-spelling errors of dyslexics have been intensively researched: in Germany a statistical analysis of typical errors of 1099 students was made by Ferdinand,[12] and Biglmaier devoted the larger part of his book to a discussion of quantitative as well as qualitative analyses of reading performance.[13] Both authors also describe related work of other researchers and suggest further readings about this subject. It appears that this aspect of dyslexia, namely the typical errors, has been more extensively researched than any other aspect.[14] Aside from that, however, dyslexia is still an incomplete and not at all scientifically clarified concept. Nevertheless, should a common dyslexic symptomatology exist, it would have to be derived from a study of a large population in which certain characteristics would have to keep reappearing. Thus it is the objective of this study to analyze statistically the dossiers of 500 children with reading-spelling disability. Should this analysis arrive at the recognition of a specific and recurrent syndrome, it would certainly become a valuable contribution toward earlier diagnosis, better preventive methods, and more effective therapy.

2. SURVEY OF THE LITERATURE ON SPECIFIC DYSLEXIA

2.1 Existing Publications

Today we already have an almost inexhaustible supply of literature on dyslexia. In 1968, in the United States alone there were 4000 research publications and nearly 50,000 books and articles on various important dimensions of normal as well as impeded reading processes. In Switzerland, Germany, Norway, Denmark, France, the Netherlands, and Japan much has been written on the subject also. It would be impossible to discuss all these publications in depth. Emphasis will be placed on studies which were based on statistical and objective methods. These studies seem to form a minority and, furthermore, many of them seem to focus on only one angle or on only a few partial aspects. In addition, as far as we were able to ascertain, there were no studies – with the exception of the one mentioned earlier, on typical spelling mistakes – that had utilized samples containing more than 125 subjects with reading retardation. These limitations constitute certain dangers. If a hypothesis is verified with regard to only one particular feature or a few narrowly defined aspects of dyslexia, it may be that the researcher found, and considers proven, what he had wanted to find. Thus error is built in from the start, in the design, in the method, or in the question to be investigated. The result is predetermined; the study pushed in a certain direction. In cases of small samples there is also the danger of unjustified generalization of conclusions.

The following case illustrates this point of view. It will be discussed in some detail because it is relevant to our study in several other respects also. It is a publication by Weinschenk, summarizing his five case studies of dyslexics. He remarks on the "amazing similarities"[1] to other cases reported in neurological writings. As to the symptomatology of his cases, Weinschenk emphasizes that none of them showed positive neurological signs and that electroencephalograms as well as pneumoencephalograms, as far as they were applied, failed to indicate any remarkable findings.[2] Perusing his cases, one realizes that the EEG's were given in only two out of the five cases; and in one of these the EEG showed waves considerably slow for the patient's age and would have to be considered slightly atypical, though not enough to be of diagnostic value.[3] Weinschenk might have added that these findings were not yet diagnostically significant. We know today that so-called mild or minimal neurological signs are more frequent among disabled readers than among average readers with regard to the slow waves mentioned by Weinschenk. Money suggested that the so-called theta waves (4 to 7 per second) are relatively slow and not unusual in children up to 14 years of age, but that they are considered abnormal if present in the EEG of adults.[4] Neurologists are currently researching these minimal signs, confident that some day a key will be found to make them diagnostically valuable.[5] Weinschenk considers the absence of neural signs as part of the definition of congenital dyslexia,[6] and bases this opinion on the five case studies he made as well as on "cases published by neurologists."[7] By contrast, the English neurologist Critchley writes: "The occasional impurity of the syndrome is shown by the elucidation at times, on appropriate testing, of various minor deficits, or 'soft' neurological signs, as they have been called in the USA. Some of these are virtually 'minimal' and may elude superficial examination, coming to light only after more searching techniques."[8] Two of the five disabled readers examined by Weinschenk were only 11 years old. The others were 16, 17, and 21 respectively. Thus, at least theoretically, there is the possibility that neurological factors did play a part in the etiology of their reading failure but were no longer diagnostically apparent because of the normal physiological maturation of the brain and nervous system.[9]

We have discussed neurological implications here at such length to point out that it would be an unacceptable overgeneralization, considering the number of cases and their ages, in Weinschenk's sample, to make the absence of neurological signs a criterion of definition and diagnosis for congenital reading disability. We cannot concur with Weinschenk's request that one exclude cases with positive neurological signs from studies designed to develop the concept of hereditary dyslexia.[10] The sample on which he bases his conclusions is not only too small but also too unilaterally selected: all five came to him as juvenile delinquents. Considering the views and research findings of a number of other neurologists, we can only conclude that we have no final answers as yet. Therefore, dogmatic statements and overgeneralizations are better avoided.

As much as we share Weinschenk's desire to come to a clearer conceptualization and a distinct terminology, to restrict the term "dyslexia" to the congenital form alone appears a precipitous simplification of the situation. Even choice of the word "congenital" precludes distinctness. Weinschenk understands it to mean an "inborn weakness to learn reading and spelling despite otherwise normal intelligence and regular neurologic condition,"[11] but Hinshelwood, for instance, employs the term "congenital" to mean that the reading disability stems from a localized brain lesion which could be either inherited or acquired.[12] Schilder writes: "We do not doubt that the congenital reading disability can and must be interpreted from a neurological point of view."[13] The word "congenital" implies only "present at birth," it does not, by definition, specify whether the problem is the result of a weakness, an injury, a delay in maturation, a temporary or permanent, partial or total arrest of growth, a dysfunction, an inherited constitution, or a prenatal trauma.

There are no indications that reading disability will ever be traced back to a single etiological factor. The complexity of the reading process itself makes this most unlikely.[14] The observation of the German neurologist Kleiner, who attended the convention of the German Psychological Association 1965 in Berlin, is interesting in this connection. He told the convention that, as a physician, he could neither readily nor easily join in their very differentiated discussion concerning the etiology and educational rehabilitation of dyslexia, but that he had noticed with interest that they seemed to understand dyslexia as a polyetiological syndrome and would soon come to speak of a "group of dyslexias," just like psychiatrists who use the labels "schizophrenia," "epilepsy," and "psychopathy" as collective terms. "Just as we do in forensic psychiatry, you too seem to come to understand the syndrome under discussion here as a group of factors strengthening one another in the sense of sequels."[15]

After this very insightful commentary we return once more to Weinschenk who dismisses psychologists and educators summarily (only Linder's study is excepted) for not having selected their research populations according to the etiology of their reading disability.[16] This raises the question, whether the hereditary indications observed in the families of his five cases, and the claim that other neurologists have published similar cases, are sufficient reasons to consider his sample as selected according to etiology? This sample does not seem to justify the etiological classification "congenital." Weinschenk himself admits the almost insurmountable difficulties in ascertaining "heredity" and the nature of the disability, and he is not certain by what age dyslexia can be diagnosed with some degree of certainty to be "congenital."[17]

Since congenitality itself cannot be diagnosed with certainty and since it cannot be proved that all dyslexia is inherited, for there is not even a clear conceptual distinction between "inherited" and "congenital," we prefer to use the term "specific dyslexia" as we defined it. Whether eventually the terminology will be determined by etiological or phenomenological criteria must await future research findings.

As we have seen in the discussion of literature on reading retardation, there are many publications, but little agreement with regard to terminology and etiology. It is therefore interesting to note how some authors, ignoring all the futile attempts at precision made so far, base their studies on a descriptive or working definition.

Two French psychologists and coauthors have presented a new approach to the study of dyslexia: Mucchielli and Bourcier look at the problem not as previous researchers have, as observers, but rather from the point of view of the dyslexic himself. Through empathy they try to experience and to describe his world as he experiences it. According to these authors the world of the failing reader is neither "chaotic" nor "senseless," but it is instable and full of double meanings. He lacks a steady orientation in time and space, his perceptions are labile, unreliable, and changing; consequently there is also some "disorientation" in his emotional experiences.[18] As possible causes Mucchielli and Bourcier suggest difficulties in verbal communication, debility, problems of body schema, uncertain lateralization, infantile behavior patterns, and deafness or partial hearing loss.[19] According to these authors specific dyslexia is not an isolated learning problem existing despite normal general intellectual potential, but rather a disturbance in social, spatial, and temporal relationships. Unlike most other writers, the authors fail to distinguish "manifestations" (verbal communication problems, disorientation in space, etc.) from "causal factors" (deafness, mental retardation, etc.). Here we are confronted directly with the still unanswered questions of which are the causes and which are the consequences, which of these factors are primary and which are secondary? One might ask whether it is necessary or indicated to seek an organic correlate to the reading-spelling defect, whether it is sufficient to concentrate on a psychological-conceptual reduction. Although Mucchielli and Bourcier leave this question open, other psychologists assume primary psychological defects in such phenomena as "gestalt differentiation weakness" or "right-left confusion,"[20] "weakness in perceptual interpretation,"[21] "conceptual shortcomings,"[22] "spatial disorientation, acoustical or visual discrimination problems,"[23] and "weakness in memory storage."[24] Such primary conditions are thought to cause the reversals, inversions, substitutions, and omissions of letters, and words, and the confusion in reading direction so often observed in dyslexics.

In addition to endogenous causes of organic or psychological origin there are a number of potential exogenous sources: reading teaching methods, family background, sibling rivalry, etc. In regard to methods of teaching reading, we distinguish, in agreement with most educators, the synthetic method which starts with the whole word or sentence, from the analytical method which begins with the letter or syllable and builds up. The current confusion with regard to their terminology is probably the result of different emphases. When definitions stress the point at which the methods begin, then "synthetic" is correct for the whole word method and "analytic" for the letter approach. When emphasis is placed on the methodical process, however, we would have to call the whole word method analytical and the letter method synthetical. At the 1965 convention of the German Psychological Association participants discussed whether the synthetical or the analytical teaching method contributed more to the genesis of writing-reading deficiencies. Linder stated that it is less important whether one or the other method is employed than whether or not each was taught during first grade, conscientiously and fully in accord with teaching rules.[25] By contrast, Bleidick, another participant, felt certain that the synthetic or whole word method was responsible for the origin of reading retardation.[26] This point of view is frequently presented in the United States, too.[27]

Despite the strength of the opinions held by individual educators, the problem remains open and controversial, and further research is needed.[28]

The family situation of the disabled reader, more than any other component of the dyslexic syndrome, remains uncertain and open-ended, especially with regard to the distinction between cause and effect.[29,30,31]

What we have said so far about exogenous and endogenous causation and about primary and secondary symptomatology, shows that the phenomenon of specific dyslexia, like its research, is extraordinarily complex and difficult. The current state of research indicates that we have a great deal of knowledge but little agreement and even fewer positive dependable results. Thus, it may be quite rational, to work, like Mucchielli and Bourcier, for the time being, with a pragmatic, functional, or operational definition, without attempting to presume or to find either organic or psychological substrates at the base of reading and spelling failures. Not only French- and English-speaking countries, but German-speaking countries as well are making an effort in this direction.[32] Fortunately, we may add, we have reliable and successful teaching methods and therapeutic approaches even though etiological issues are still controversial. For the interested reader we list here at least some of the existing publications in various languages on the therapy and prevention of specific dyslexia.*

The discussion of publications based on statistical research will take place later, in connection with the presentation and interpretation of our own findings.

Before closing this chapter it should be pointed out once more that today there is an increasingly strong tendency to consider specific dyslexia in its relation to neurological correlates. Several studies show that a high percentage of dyslexic children do display certain neurological signs. These may become manifest as awkwardness of movement, incoordination, lack of fine motor control, directional confusion, incomplete knowledge of body laterality, distorted body image, speech defects, visual or acoustic perceptual difficulties, concentration problems, sensory or motor disinhibition, etc. Such symptoms, according to many neurologists, must be traced back either to structural or functional disorders or to delayed maturation of the nervous system. In the United States there is much talk about "soft neurological signs" or "minimal brain damage."[33] Recent studies along these lines were published by Clements et al.,[34] Cohn,[35] Myklebust[36] and Whitsell.[37] Although neurological research is quite advanced in the United States, interest in this area is growing in Europe now, too.[38] In this connection we should mention here the American physician Doyle who speaks of an "Organic Hyperkinetic Syndrome,"[39] and the German

---

*Ingenkamp, K.: Lese- und Rechtschreibschwäche bei Schulkindern, pp. 139–338; Kobi, E.: Lernhilfen Für Legastheniker, in: Heilpädagogische Werkblätter 33, 1964, pp. 276–289; Hunger-Kaindlstorfer, M.: Die psychologische Behandlung der Legasthenie, in: Zeitschrift für exp. una angew. Psychologie 10, 1963, pp. 187–196; Cronin, E. M.: For the Problem Reader of Any Age; Gillingham, A. and Stillman, B.: Remedial Training for Children with Specific Disability in Reading, Spelling and Penmanship, 5th ed.; Smith H. P. and Dechant, E. V.: Psychology in Teaching Reading, pp. 296–353; Kocher, F.: La Rééducation des Dyslexiques; Bourcier, A.: Traitement de la Dyslexie; Chassagny, C.: Manuel pour la Rééducation de la Lecture et de l'Orthographe; Lückert, H. R.: Behandlung und Vorbeugung von Leseschwierigkeiten, in: Schule and Psychologie 7, July 1966, pp. 193-207; Critchley M.: Developmental Dyslexia, pp. 81–90; Delacato, C. H.: The Treatment and Prevention of Reading Problems.

It is interesting that most publications concerned with the early diagnosis and prevention of reading disabilities have been written by physicians and are mostly limited to medical measures.

author Lückert who remarked in a recent article that the more
recent studies on specific reading problems stress their neurological basis.[40]

Lückert was influenced by the writings of Delacato and Doman, whose Institutes for Achievement of Human Potential in
Philadelphia have become widely known for their treatment
methods with spastic children, many of whom prove also to be
poor readers. Their treatment, known as "patterning," consists
of physiotherapeutic exercises for the development of neuromuscular movement patterns. It must be added that this method is still controversial and is considered scientifically unsound
by many American physicians. It has been pointed out that the
basic premises on which the patterning practice rests cannot be
proven scientifically, that it is not certain, for instance, that, as
Delacato and Doman assume, language is localized in the brain
and that the dominant hemisphere controls the verbal and the
subdominant hemisphere the tonal abilities. During treatment
periods, Delacato and Doman insist, all tonal abilities, receptive
as well as expressive (music, singing, etc.), are to be avoided.

The English neurologist Critchley, in his chapter on "Minor
Neurological Signs" discusses a number of neurological symptoms observed in dyslexics and he concludes: " . . . that these
findings are by no means integral. Many a dyslexic—perhaps
even the majority of cases—show no such disabilities . . . perhaps they should be regarded as important epiphenomena—
significant when they occur, but not essential in any consideration as to pathogenesis or aetiology."[41]

Despite the variety of opinions about the significance of neurological involvement in the case of reading-spelling disability,
we are confident that further research in this direction will
significantly contribute to a still better and more effective
knowledge in the diagnosis, treatment, and prevention of the
problem.

2.2 Prevalence; Relationship to Special Education

The discussion up to this point has already implicitly shown that
several scientific disciplines are involved in the research on and

the treatment of dyslexia: education and special education, psychiatry and neurology, ophthalmology and audiology, to name only the most important. Where, however, is the "home base," the center where all information, all findings, experiences, and open questions should be gathered, coordinated, and applied? In order to answer this question it would seem appropriate first of all to think of the dyslexic himself. Where do we usually meet him? In the schools. With what frequency do we find dyslexics? One cannot expect to find an exact answer to this question as long as the concept of "dyslexia" remains somewhat unclarified and controversial. As long as various researchers base their work on different concepts, no dependable percentages can be arrived at. If the range of the findings published to date seems wide, we must keep in mind that a variety of diagnostic means and criteria are used in research. Findings also seem to differ somewhat according to language. In English speaking populations, for instance, the reading-spelling weakness is apparently slightly more prevalent and noticeable since English pronunciation rules are varied and complex. For German speaking countries Bleidick estimates that about 5% of the school population are dyslexics,[42] but Kirchhoff thinks that between 2% and 20% are.[43] Hallgren speaks of 12% in Sweden.[44] Kretschmer in Switzerland believes there are 4% with severe and 18% with medium degrees of dyslexia.[45] Schomburg says that in England one out of four students at the age of 15 cannot read fluently, and that 21% of the 12-year-old students are "backward readers," reading at the level of normal 7 year olds.[46] In Copenhagen, Denmark, according to Ellehammer, there are 150 reading classes for severely retarded readers and 100 reading groups for lightly retarded readers.[47] Kirchhoff estimates that Copenhagen has 3.5% dyslexics.[48] According to Cronin, 15% to 25% of the regular school population of the United States is unable to read properly.[49] Gray states that in 1956 11% of all American citizens had a reading efficiency lower than the fourth grade level.[50]

Estimates of the prevalence of dyslexia in today's Western Civilization range from 2% to 25%. More important than such percentages, it would seem, is careful consideration of each case in its particular individuality. What do we know about the dyslexic? Is he mentally retarded? Certainly not; this is excluded by definition alone. (It is regrettable, therefore, that Hanselmann in his widely used textbook on special education debates dyslexia under the heading "The treatment of mentally retarded children."[51]) The disabled reader is intelligent enough to realize his shortcoming and to suffer deep frustration. Neurotic reactions are not at all rare, and if reading retardation is allowed to persist into adolescence, it not infrequently leads to delinquency and related maladjustive developments. Only a few are so extraordinarily talented that they are able to automatically compensate for their difficulty. The slow reading child suffers internally and externally. Peers, teachers, and parents criticize, ridicule, and press for better performance. It is doubtful that he will find an adequate vocation or position in life. Reading and writing skills have become the basis in any training today, even in vocational classes. Parents are usually not in the position to perceive the child's problems objectively or to find the right treatment. Rey describes especially vividly the dead end road on which the dyslexic finds himself in today's society.[52] Just as we cannot expect parents to adopt an objective attitude, so we cannot expect that every teacher can have the background knowledge, material, and time necessary to recognize, evaluate, and treat each dyslexic in his regular classes.

Who then will help? An answer can be found in a statement by Montalta: "Special educational help is needed in each educational situation in which we encounter unexpected obstacles, or unusual complications which cannot be surmounted by means developed to educate the normal child. Special education is education in the face of complicated (physical, emotional, social) circumstances."[53]

It is clear, then, that it must be a purpose and goal of special education experts to develop and redevelop, to collect and screen, to interpret, distribute, and apply any findings, teachings, and methods that might be of help to the retarded reader. In view of all that has been said here so far, we cannot expect this to be easy, but it certainly is a challenging and rewarding task.

3. AIM AND METHOD OF INVESTIGATION

3.1 Ellen K. Raskob Learning Institute

The data and experiences utilized in this study were gained at the Ellen K. Raskob Learning Institute in Oakland, California. The Institute was founded in 1953 when its present director, Sister Eileen Marie Cronin, Ph.D., professor of education, opened a summer reading course to 35 students, ranging from grades three through eight. It was the first special reading class offered in the area and turned out to be highly successful.* The number of students grew rapidly; in 1960 137 were enrolled per quarter; in 1966 there were 700 students in all enrolled throughout the year. They attend usually three to four hours per week. In addition to the specialized therapeutic teaching at the Raskob Institute, a program is offered at the College for the training of reading specialists. Licensed teachers with at least two years of classroom experience are eligible and take eighteen units of theory and practicum. The Institute furthermore offers workshops for parents or teachers, parents' nights, public addresses, parent counseling, child guidance, group therapy, speech correction, and physical education. A new wing is planned in which a full-time school could be housed for the

---

*The following are only the most important milestones in the further development of the Learning Institute: in 1958 the summer reading workshops were incorporated into the curriculum of the Education Department at the College of the Holy Names of whose faculty and order Sister Eileen Marie is a member. The College of the Holy Names is a four-year Liberal Arts College. In 1960 the Institute moved into a building of its own, erected on campus through a grant by the Raskob Foundation. Thus the name: Raskob Institute. The faculty and staff of the Institute consist at present of the director, three psychologists, a consulting neurologist, a consulting psychiatrist, a social worker, a child guidance expert, a teacher for dance and physical education, a coach, two librarians, thirteen reading specialists, a receptionist, two secretaries, and several volunteers.

more severely dyslexic to whom the regular classroom has become a place of frustration and failure. They would return to their regular schools as soon as they were able to function at grade level.

3.2 Working Hypothesis

All observations and data collected on students at the Institute were kept in individual files and in time these contained a wealth of information for research. Sufficient objective data became available by which to examine objectively general and personal impressions gained in the daily routine of testing, observing, interviewing, and data collecting. In accordance with the methods of exact science, personal hunches and intuitive perceptions were transformed into the following working hypothesis:

There exists a syndrome of specific dyslexia which can be shown empirically and statistically and which suggests certain theoretical as well as practical conclusions.

Thus the aim of this study was clearly defined; the hypothesis was to be verified scientifically.

3.3 Method of Verification

The first question was how to arrange the data so that they could be most purposefully investigated. This meant that the questions had to be formulated which were likely to be answered through the observation material. They were not to be simply listed but to be grouped. An order of the classifications was derived from the procedures at the Institute. They include investigation of the following: (1) neuropsychological factors, (2) psychopathological findings, (3) potential intelligence and the degree of its realization, (4) environmental factors. After the specific questions had been categorized into these four groups, the data could be collected from the files accordingly. In a punch card type operation each question was given a key and each child was represented through his own card.

3.4 Subjects and Documents

3.4a) Selection Criteria

Selected were the files of those children who applied at the Raskob Institute during the past two years, and which contained as completely as possible data that were to be investigated. Thus it was possible, for instance, to study comparatively the verbal, performance, and full-scale Wechsler-IQ scores of 488 children; in addition, all subtest scores were available for 466 subjects. According to Institute policy, children with IQ's below 90 are not admitted. This is a well-considered cut-off score, set according to our experience and a realistic chance of success for the child. The Hamburg psychologist Tamm apparently had similar experiences.[1] Kirchhoff, also in Germany, excluded children from his sample whose IQ's were below 95; he assumed that they had other deficiencies in addition to reading-writing deficiencies.[2] It must be said, though, that a specific reading disability can exist in combination with a low general learning potential. Such cases are, however, quite rare.[3,4] At the Raskob Institute the cut-off score was fixed below that used by Kirchhoff because many slow readers are unable to demonstrate all their abilities on a Wechsler scale. To avoid test results and admission policies, individual testing must be extremely rigorous. However, should observation and differential diagnosis reveal discrepancies between quantitative test findings and apparent potential, exceptions have to be made. Thus a case in which the total IQ is below 90, but either the verbal or the performance IQ is above 90 would be included. Two important criteria were adhered to in the selection process: first, children who were referred to the Institute because of general learning and/or behavior problems were excluded; second, the file was accepted only if individual professional evaluation confirmed a disparity between general intellectual potential and actual achievement level in the language areas. This last criterion corresponds with Raskob admission policies.

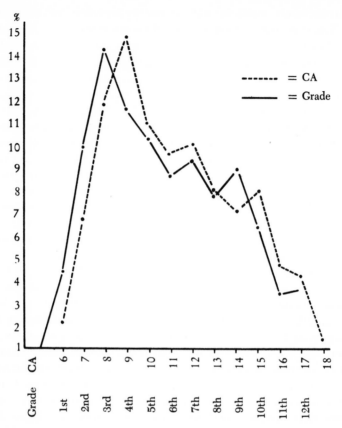

Fig. 1. Age and grade level distribution of the 500 dyslexics contained in the study.

3.4b) Age Distribution

The children in the sample are between 6 years 0 months and 18 years 11 months old. The graph in Figure 1 provides an overview of the distribution of age groups as well as grades. It is immediately apparent that the third and fourth grades are most frequently represented. It seems interesting that for the third grade the age curve is relatively lower than for the fourth grade. This may indicate that the promotion from third to fourth grade is a hurdle many students cannot take. In the fourth grade more reading is required, more independent work, math includes word problems—some parents and teachers hesitate to promote a child if he does not seem to be ready, others might promote him to the fourth grade and then make him repeat it after he has failed to cope with the increased scholastic demands. For the eighth grade the two curves come closely together. As students enter high school, another selective process seems to take place and the age curve again rises above the grade curve. The first and second grades form only 4-10% of the whole group. This is probably because of the tendency of educators and parents to "wait and see"; the problem may disappear with maturity and some degree of the typically dyslexic error patterns, such as spatial, temporal, or directional confusion, is still normal at this point of development. For these reasons and because we lack tests for early diagnosis, specific reading-writing problems are difficult to detect at this early stage.

After the fourth grade the percentage declines progressively; this, too, is understandable. If the learning disabilities are severe and lasting, the student will be placed in special classes or else will lose hope, go unnoticed, and just be passed through the grades. Only a few find their way to a reading clinic. Many develop serious emotional, mental and/or social problems, many drop out, others are expelled. A broadly based investigation is needed, to find out how many inmates in criminal, correctional, and mental institutions are disabled readers. We found a few statistical indications that this is the case and we will discuss these in connection with secondary emotional and adjustment problems (see the table on p. 22).

3.4c) Sex Ratio

The ratio of boys to girls is 2.5 : 1, slightly lower than that reported by most investigators.

Money mentions Newbrough and Kelley who found a ratio of 3 boys to 2 girls and Prechtl who arrived at a 2 : 1 ratio. Money also points out that delinquency presents a similar picture, that life expectancy is shorter for males, and that sexual deviation is more frequent among females. He concludes: "Evidently it is

Distribution of ages and sexes

Subjects	Number	Percentage
Boys 6 to 13 years old	283	56.6
Boys 14 to 18	75	15.0
Girls 6 to 13	102	20.4
Girls 14 to 18	40	8.0
	500	100.0

or

Subjects	Number	Percentage
Boys	358	71.6
Girls	142	28.4
	500	100.0

more hazardous to be male . . . ," and goes on to explain that at this time dyslexia cannot be correlated with any of the male hormone dysfunctions or hormone imbalances currently known to endocrinologists. Even the newer methods of chromosome research have provided no clues. Money recognizes the fact that males react more readily to erotic stimuli than females and thus he thinks it might be that males react in a particular manner to verbal visual stimuli also. He adds that this is a "wildly conjectural" theory, but then he goes on to present another, possibly even farther fetched one, derived from Lynn, who pointed out that girls learn their female roles by direct identification with the mother, while boys — because of the frequent absence of the working father — learn their male role through abstraction, or second-hand. Since reading supposedly requires more inventory than abstraction girls might thus be better equipped than boys.[5] In a later publication Money suggests a somewhat different hypothesis to explain the large male proportion among deficient readers: the development of a male embryo is more complicated than that of a female embryo, thus it might easily be that two important, typically male characteristics remain underdeveloped, i.e., the territorial and the directional instincts.[6,7]

These explanatory attempts are presented here to demonstrate how little we know about the reason for the uneven sex ratio among dyslexics. European and American findings show close correspondence with regard to the sex ratio. Critchley constructed a table representing the figures compiled by 15 researchers on a total of 1685 retarded readers. These figures allow the calculation of an overall ratio of 4 to 1. Critchley quotes Vernon who stated that boys were more often represented only because they tended to be more aggressive in their reactions, thus drawing more attention and causing more management problems and that parents are more anxious for their sons to learn to read than for their daughters. Critchley, like Money, mentions that so far chromosome research, investigation of the influence of position among siblings, blood relations, etc. have remained unsuccessful.[8]

Kobi remarked that dyslexia occurs four to five times more frequently among boys than among girls and that three-quarters to four-fifths of the children brought to child guidance institutions are boys. He says that boys, because of their slower speech development, are more susceptible, especially if they enter school prematurely.[9] Siersleben has no findings of his own but quotes those of several other authors: Paulin emphasized that the generally slower development of boys delays their reading readiness, and that only for the girls are chronological age and school beginning well coordinated; Argelander mentions that boys perceive the environment through analytical abstraction rather than through gestalt as girls tend to do; Jarwis, a psychoanalyst, emphasized that the highly symbolic content of reading-writing symbols could easily bring to the surface hitherto repressed aspects of the Oedipus conflict.[10]

Lückert, strongly influenced by Doman, reports that reading problems occur four times more often among boys than among girls. He adds that birth traumata are more frequent among boys too, because of their larger heads, and because of the longer duration of their birth processes.[11] He also points out that birth injuries first affect the evolutionarily younger cells, the carriers of communicative, specifically language, skills.[12]

Despite general agreement with regard to the sex ratio among poor readers, there is little evidence of a scientifically sound explanation for this disproportionate phenomenon.

3.4d) Reports and Tests

Finally each child's dossier contains two questionnaires, filled out by the parents at the time of application, and giving information about the child's family, school, health, and social background. A parent conference later confirms and completes this information. If reports from teachers, of former psychological testing, from physicians, etc., are available, they too go into the folder and add to the overall background information, facilitating diagnosis and treatment plans.

To avoid one-sided conclusions, each child at Raskob is seen by at least two different testers. Of the 500 dossiers studied here 480 were compiled by three different Raskob psychologists, 20 came from other agencies. As much as we would have preferred to include more reports from the outside, it was impossible because too few contained the data needed in this investigation.

In addition to questionnaires and outside reports, all test data gained during initial evaluation, a full interpretation and report, including observations and data from the parent conference, go into the folder. A clear grasp and presentation of the disparity between potential and achievement are needed for the designing of individual treatment programs: these include behavior observation, background information, personality assessment, summary, and recommendations.

The following tests, selected according to age and/or achievement level of the child, are used at the Raskob Institute in the initial evaluation: the various Wechsler Scales of Intelligence, Goodenough Draw-a-Man Test, Koch's Tree Test, Bender Visuo-Motor Gestalt Test, Frostig Developmental Test of Visual Perception, Peabody Picture Vocabulary Test, Huelsman Word Discrimination Test, Wide Range Achievement Spelling Test,

Harris Tests of Lateral Dominance, Wepman Auditory Discrimination Test, Keystone Visual Survey Test, Bond-Clymer-Hoyt Developmental Reading Test, Durrell-Sullivan Reading Achievement Test, Iowa Silent Reading Test; projective tests such as TAT, Sceno, World, Rorschach, etc., are not routinely employed but are used only for purposes of differential clarification, if necessary.

In summary, all the findings discussed in this study stem from the test batteries mentioned, behavior observation during testing, history taking, questionnaires, parent interviews, and reports released from outside agencies (the latter, naturally, never obtained without parental consent).

II. PHENOMENOLOGY AND ETIOLOGY OF THE DYSLEXIC SYNDROME

1. PHYSIOPSYCHOLOGICAL FINDINGS*

1.1 Speech

1.1a) Speech Disorders

Of the 500† dyslexic children observed, 112 had speech impediments; that is equivalent to 22.4%, almost one-fourth of the
whole group. The following symptoms were considered indicative of impediment: stammering, stuttering and other signs
of interruption in the flow of speech, lisping, pronunciation
difficulties with certain consonants, vowels, words, etc., the
omission or substitution of words or syllables, displaced emphasis, rhythm disturbance, and poor articulation; in other words,
only disturbances of the speech mechanism, not of the language
level, of expressive language facility nor of the age of onset of
speech. The latter will be discussed in a chapter by itself. The
main concern here was to identify and isolate speech imperfections related to physiopsychological rather than mental and
environmental influences. Language, in contrast to speech, depends on cultural rather than physiological factors. To what
extent the speech defects under consideration were of central
or peripheral origin could not be discerned, but apparent structural causes, such as cleft palate or similar deformities, were
extremely rare.

The high percentage of dyslexics with speech impairments is
not a new or unique finding. Quantitative data are not available
in the German literature, but the question was touched on at
the Psychological Convention in Berlin 1965.[1,2,3] Bleidick point-

---

*Summarized tables of all results discussed in this chapter can be found in the
appendix in Tables A–1 and A– 2.

†In regard to the physiopsychological findings, totals are not always 500 because in some dossiers information on this particular aspect was not available.

ed out that only that which is known in the spoken language
can be read.[4] Kobi declared: "Speech disorders are frequently
associated with reading-writing weakness."[5] Kocher mentioned
that some authors consider speech impediments the cause for
reading retardation; at his speech clinic many children also had
reading difficulties.[6] Biglmaier observed that reading is closely
related to speech and is, therefore, easily influenced by speech
disturbances. He found that many investigators repeatedly observed a great number of slow readers among those with
speech impediments.[7] Lückert counted reticence and stuttering
among the typical symptoms connected with reading disability.[8,9] Lory drew attention to the interdependence in perception of auditory and visual language signs.[10,11,12]

English-speaking authors provide some exact data on the
frequency with which speech and reading difficulties exist simultaneously. When Critchley quotes the figures of several
authors it must be kept in mind that no differentiation is made
between speech distortion and delayed development of speech.
According to Critchley, Kagen (1943) found speech difficulties
among 30% of those with reading problems, Hallgren (1952)
found 41% among his retarded male readers and 32% among
his poorly reading girls, Ingram (1959) reported to have observed a certain number, while Hibbert (1961) diagnosed 16 out
of 23 retarded readers as also having speech impairment.[13]

The Americans Smith and Dechant quote Monroe (1948) who
found 27% of 415 disabled readers to have speech defects; in a
control group of 101 average readers the percentage, by contrast, was only 8%.[14]

Weinschenk arrived at a different conclusion in connection
with what he terms "congenital" reading weakness; in this
condition, he emphasizes, speech defects play no part.[15,16]

The quantitative data derived from our own sample
confirmed the observation by Hallgren, that speech impediment
is more frequent among male dyslexics. We found a statistically
significant disparity, using the chi-square test and the 5% level
of probability.* That boys should be the more frequently
affected is not surprising, if one considers that more boys than

*All statistically significant disparities observed in the physiopsychological
findings are summarized and presented in the appendix in Table B.

girls are dyslexic, and that more boys have birth injuries, emotional disturbances, behavior problems, etc., as indicated in the
previous chapters.

In summary then, most authors from a variety of countries
and scientific disciplines agree that speech impediments occur
in a large proportion of retarded readers and that boys are
more often affected by these impediments than girls.[17]

A discussion of the etiology of speech disturbance is beyond
the purpose of this study, but, briefly, there is no simple, valid
answer to the question of which came first, the speech impediment or the reading-spelling deficiency. Quite possibly both go
back to a common origin, and are different aspects of one basic
disorder. It appears that German speaking authors emphasize
causation or at least cocausation through speech impediment,
whereas Anglo-Saxon and Swiss writers stress the high frequency of their associated occurrence and from there suspect a
common causation. Those who suggest a single etiological factor are primarily neurologists and psychiatrists, regardless of
their country of origin. They point furthermore to the relationship between speech functions and cerebral dominance, and to
the frequency with which these two factors are associated. The
New York psychiatrist Mosse, for example, stresses that many
areas of the brain must be intact and must interact flawlessly.[18]
Cohn mentions Dreifuss who in 1963 tried to prove that delayed
speech development resulted from underdeveloped cerebral
dominance, caused by bilateral brain traumata.[19]

Lückert, in agreement with Doman and Delacato, also discusses the cortical zones in connection with reading disabilities.
However, he emphasizes that human speech potential is localized in the brain so that the dominant hemisphere controls all
speech functions, while the nondominant hemisphere regulates
the tonal qualities of speech. Stutterers, he says, can sing without stuttering because the disturbance lies in the dominant
hemisphere, the tonal abilities are intact. Lückert emphasizes
even more than Mosse that, nonetheless, localization is neither
rigid nor exclusively determining.[20] Kocher is another researcher who sees a connection between cerebral dominance and
speech, as well as reading-spelling problems, stressing a possible physiopsychological origin.[21]

Smith and Dechant, American coauthors, make the general observation that speech defects are often accompanied by reading problems and that speech impediments can hamper reading ability in many different ways.[22] Harris noticed that two kinds of speech defects occur most frequently in connection with reading disability: lack of articulation and paralalia.[23] Monroe found a relationship between stuttering and reading weakness: 9% of 415 retarded readers, but only 1% of the 101 normal children in the control group were stutterers.[24]

A large proportion of our own sample (the exact percentage could not be calculated because of inexact observational data) showed poorly articulated speech patterns, not only in reading and in other stressful situations, but even in the most casual conversation. Many parents are surprised when their child's speech is characterized, by a tester, as inarticulate; they are so used to it that it takes an outsider to draw their attention to this very common cosymptom of reading difficulties. For this reason, data furnished by parent questionnaires on this subject are not reliable for research.

The Raskob Institute has amazingly few stutterers among its students. Among the 950 children seen by one psychologist in three years there were about six. This is approximately 0.6%, a proportion far smaller than the 9% observed by Monroe. It is possible that in the stutterers speech defects are so much more obvious than any reading difficulty, that they are taken to a speech clinic rather than a reading clinic. In fact, a great number of the children in our sample were said, by their parents, to have stuttered at some time during their development. But in this case too, the information was not exact enough to be used for quantitative statistical evaluation. It was also not possible to collect concrete data on the reverse question, namely, how many of the children enrolled in speech therapy are also slow readers.

Smith and Dechant are convinced that speech and reading have closely connected neurological ties because of the nearness of the locations of their centers in the brain.[25,26] Thus, it is not surprising that Betts concluded that 90% of disabled readers need medical assistance before special educational measures.[27]

Indeed the physiological aspects of learning disabilities must not be neglected or ignored by educators or psychologists. This is even more apparent if one considers how many physical conditions could conceivably contribute to learning problems: Mateer found that vitamin deficiencies were associated with reading disability;[28] Harris,[29] together with Witty and Kopel,[30] held that more retarded readers than normal readers showed endocrinological disorders; Eames examined blood samples of 30 retarded readers, and discovered that 20% of them showed abnormal cell forms and that one-third of them were deficient in hemoglobin.[31] Among 20 slow readers, Watts found six with nutritional and digestive problems, five with respiratory and heart trouble, two with glandular disorders, and two with nervous symptoms.[32] This of course, again, immediately raises the question of what is primary and what might be secondary. Smith and Dechant, after reviewing this research, warned that associative manifestations do not automatically prove causal relationships.[33]

Despite the widely observed concurrence of speech and reading disorders, the related literature mentions little or nothing about specific therapeutic measures.[34,35]

Interesting are the findings of Kinsbourne and Warrington who examined various aspects of 13 slow readers. After dividing them into two groups, they found that the six children in the first group had Wechsler scale verbal IQ's 20 or more points higher than their performance IQ's. All six of these children had specific disorders in verbalization and three also had receptive language difficulties. The remaining seven children of the second group whose performance IQ was significantly lower, had neither expressive nor receptive speech disorders.[36]

Goldiamond and Dyrud, from a behavioral point of view, stress the complexity of the reading process, dependent as it is on current as well as on former reinforcements, and on total behavior. They deny the existence of evident, consistently associated neurological symptoms, accepting only various behavioral deficits as occurring in association; these are delay in motoric speech development, inability to learn clearly articulated speech at the right time, prolonged baby talk, lisping, stuttering, stammering, specific reading-writing disorders, word blindness, etc. They emphasize that speech development depends greatly upon environment and social factors. This seems a narrow view since the factors which make behavior possible, i.e., neurological bases, and all that influences and motivates behavior from inside, i.e., intelligence, emotion, drive, etc., are simply disregarded. The authors make no therapeutic suggestion but require further analysis of reading behavior per se, so that specific, sequential programs, with their own internal logic, can be developed.[37]

Lawson offers no quantitative findings, but she is impressed that the relationship between speech and reading ability is discussed so widely both in Europe and in the United States. She points out relationships between speech and reading which are closely connected to linguistic processes that require symbolic formulations, interpretations, and expressions. She agrees with those investigators who occasionally consider the speech impediment as a cause, but who frequently see it as a cosymptom, based, like the reading disability itself, on a common causative factor. Lawson further postulates that the developmental lag which often causes speech and reading difficulties and the condition diagnosed as childhood aphasia may be the extreme manifestations of a single continuum.[38]

Although we have emphasized the neurological bases of learning to read, and although we tend to agree with Lückert who states that "everything speaks for a functional (neurological) explanation,"[39] we do not agree with his statement that "every" weakness in language functions (reading disability) is the result of neurological disorganization.[40] Lückert himself says that with today's methods not all cortical dysfunctions or traumata can be diagnosed. As long as scientific certainty is unattainable, we tend to believe, in accordance with our observations, that multiple and complex combinations of endogenous as well as exogenous causes may contribute to the picture. Differential diagnosis is difficult and can only be arrived at in individual examinations. Even then many questions remain open. It is certain, however, that we will encounter many cases of associated speech and reading-spelling disabilities.

1.1b) Delayed Speech Development

Information about early speech development was available for 414 children in our sample; 164 of them, i.e., 39.6%, did not even speak words by the time they were 18 months old. This age was chosen as a limit in accord with Bühler, Gesell, and other developmental psychologists who have established norms for normal development. Many of these 164 children began to speak only after their second birthday. Some did not speak their first words until they were three or four years of age and were still using baby talk when they entered kindergarten.

Lory was confronted with similar problems; he too found it difficult to obtain adequate information from parents with regard to their child's early speech development, yet he felt certain that the first sign of growth disparity, typically observed in poor readers, is often a delay in developing normal speech.[41] He rarely found cases in which *severely* retarded speech and dyslexia existed together.[42] This corresponds with our observations at the Raskob Institute. It seems necessary that speech and reading therapists work together more closely. Few authors make a clear distinction between speech impediment and delayed speech development. Therefore, there is little information that is suitable for direct comparison with our findings:

		Percentage found with delayed speech development
Kobi[43]		30
Linder	(quoted by Kobi)	34
Kagen[44]	(quoted in Kocher)	30
Klasen	(present study)	39

Aside from these few percentages there are a number of general observational remarks in the literature. Saunders mentions that Orton was sure, as early as 1937, that all language functions were interrelated and that dyslexic children especially tended to have had developmental delays in their speech.[45] Zangwill examined 60 children with incomplete hand dominance and found among them a tendency to have been

late to speak.[46] Schenk-Danziger remarked that the same
delay could be observed in three different areas, and that one
of them is language development.[47] De Hirsch, who carefully
studied a number of slow readers, is certain that reading-spelling disability must be considered as *one* aspect of a
complex disorder; she felt that all difficulties in spoken or written language result from retarded speech comprehension.[48]
Orton, in listing characteristics of retarded readers, names,
among others, delayed speech development.[49] The same observation was made by Money,[50] and also by Clements.[51] Johnson
considered reading difficulties the natural consequence of delayed speech development; while normal children progress
without difficulty from sound to slight vocabulary, the disabled
reader who acquired speech late, finds this developmental process extremely difficult.[52] Critchley held that those authors who
consider dyslexia as part of a total delay in language development drew attention to the coexistence of speech disorders in
retarded readers.[53]

Wepman thought it possible that both delayed speech and
specific reading disability could be traced to inadequate development in auditory perception.[54] Thus he brings a new element
into the discussion. Basically, the question as to the origin of
these conditions remains open. We considered speech disturbance and delayed speech development separately because we
had observed that apparently neurologically based learning
difficulties seem to manifest themselves in two different forms:
structural and functional disturbances. Speech inpediment appears to be related to the former, retarded development of
speech to the latter. Although a clear differentiation into two
groups of this kind is diagnostically most difficult, the educational consequences are important. The dyslexic with a general
developmental retardation does learn more slowly, but he may
eventually reach a normal, or even above average, achievement level. His handicap is less resistant to special educational
help; he is less inclined to be hyperactive, distractable, and he
is less often a discipline problem. Ideally these children should
be placed in groups by themselves.

Wepman suspects that delayed speech development origi-
nates in an agenesis of the acoustic conductive nerves, which
negatively affects speech growth. In his opinion these children,

even after acquiring normal speech patterns, still show "a tendency toward speech inaccuracy."[55] This corresponds closely with the frequently observed articulation difficulties at Raskob Institute. Myklebust further confirms that among neurologically and psychologically normal underachievers poorly articulated speech and below average reading-spelling achievement are frequent.[56]

The term aphasia has been intentionally avoided so far. Originally a psychiatric and neurological term for complete or partial loss of language after it had been developed, it has by now lost this specific meaning. Today it designates various language disorders of the expressive as well as the receptive type, independent of origin or onset of the disturbance. Many consider agraphia and alexia as forms of aphasia. Myklebust wrote that to try to hold on to the old meaning of the term would cause unnecessary confusion, especially in cases of childhood aphasia and dyslexia.[57] At a medical convention in 1964 Jacobson stated that the concept of aphasia has become a confused one which cannot always do justice to the complexities and variability of language disorders.[58] In view of the still uncertain etiology, as well as terminology, in regard to aphasia, any further discussion or use of the term is unnecessary within the context of this study.

In comparing children in the primary grades with those in high school we found that among the younger children speech was significantly more frequently delayed than among the older ones. Two possible explanations are: first, parents of teenagers no longer fully recall the early steps in their children's development, and they seem to have been less anxious and less observant than the younger generation of parents whose children are still small. The latter are flooded with psychological and medical lay literature, advertising, etc. Second, many late developers, once they have outgrown their maturational lag, are no longer in need of special help and thus are not sent to a special clinic.

1.1c) Summary

According to our findings and to those of many other investigators, a frequent coexistence of speech and reading-spelling disorders cannot be doubted even though few exact statistical figures are available yet. The correlation of these disorders and possible causative relationships are under intense investigation today. In order to find more definite answers further quantitative data and more comparative work with control groups of normal children are needed.

Hallgren found speech defects among 41% of the boys and 32% of the girls with dyslexia; our sample showed that speech disorders are even significantly more frequent among boys. Hibbert reported that 69% of 23 retarded readers had speech impediments, while Monroe found 27% among 415; 22% of our sample of 499 slow readers had speech defects.

Regarding late speech development, Kobi found 30%, Linder 34%, Kagen 30%, Ingram 25–50%,[59] and there were 39% in our sample. In other words: 22–69% of dyslexics have speech defects, but only 30–39% have delayed speech development.

Because of the close interrelationships between organic and psychological speech functions, disturbances in either one are likely to be felt in both. Lory for instance, like Myklebust and others, points out that any weakness in auditory discrimination tends to impede not only speech but also reading-spelling skills.[60] Whether causation is primary or secondary is an open question. An interesting theory advanced by Money postulates that functional developmental delays may impede the learning process by restricting intersensory transactions, i.e., the ability to transfer stimuli from one sense modality to another.[61] In short, much more research on learning processes is needed for more factual understanding and more effective treatment of language disabilities.

1.2 Laterality

1.2a) Crossed Dominance

Almost one-half (44.2%) of the children studied here did not have clearly developed laterality, but showed various forms of crossed dominance or incomplete eyedness, handedness and/or footedness. Information on ear preference, unfortunately, was not available. Of the remaining 55.8% with well-established dominance 6% were leftsided. The remaining 49.8% had well-developed right dominance.

For several reasons we did not try to treat left-handedness and ambidexterity as separate entities. First, the test data did not supply reliable enough information, which is easily understandable if one considers how difficult it is to diagnose either one. Immediately the questions arise: what is left-handedness, and when should a person be called ambidextrous? Kramer published a broadly based and complex study on left-handedness and declared herself in agreement with Wegener who defined left-handedness as "the better disposition of the left hand for complicated movements; it can be inherited, is not altered by environmental influences, but can be kept latent through self-imposed as well as external training."[1] Thus, it would require thorough history taking and extensive testing before true left-handedness could be diagnosed with any degree of reliability. That a person writes with the left hand cannot be considered a decisive criterion, although this has been done frequently in research as well as in testing.[2]

Test batteries for the evaluation of lateral dominance have been devised. The German language tests of this kind are extensively discussed by Kramer.[3] Despite the various measurements available she comes to the conclusion: "It is obvious that there can be no single test which would be applicable to all individuals and by which one could with accuracy find all left-handers contained in a given group."[4] This conclusion makes it more readily understandable that quantitative data about the frequency of left-handedness differ widely, ranging between 1% and 50%.[5] There is agreement among investigators that left-handedness is more frequent among males than among females, and, obviously, more frequent in the younger age groups where children are still partially undeveloped. Examinations reveal that at approximately seven years of age most children are clearly right-handed.

Ambidexterity, meaning equally good use of both hands, is also difficult to diagnose with certainty. Kramer holds that only the exterior manifestation is visible; the ambidextrous person may be unable to use either hand predominantly, or he may be able to do so, but prefers to switch back and forth.[6] Critchley also states that many investigators considered retarded readers as ambidextrous, when in similar cases today we would be much more hesitant to use this term.[7] Smith and Dechant consider both-handedness as the absence of dominance and they add that everybody is to some extent ambidextrous.[8] Thus it becomes clear that there are no unique norms by which a distinct demarcation between one and two-handedness can be established.

Perusal of the pertinent literature reveals that left-handedness, which is only one form of lateral deviation, has been given too much attention while researchers have neglected other forms. There is no valid reason for concentration on left-handedness since this condition is not of greater significance in retarded readers than other laterality imperfections. Hess, for instance, is convinced that left-eyedness or cross-eyedness and crossed-handedness are more negative in their effect on the beginning reader.[9] Critchley also thought that crossed dominance was a more frequent and more significant factor than left-handedness in dyslexia.[10] Critchley quotes the findings of Harris and Chesni who observed 40% and 37% instances, respectively, of crossed dominance among dyslexics, findings which correspond closely with the 44% observed in our group. Interesting in this context are the quantitative findings of Leiser-Eggert: among slow and normal learners with emotional disturbances there were 30%, but among controls only 15%; among 200 normal college students there were 13% with crossed dominance.[11] Among 101 normal children Monroe observed 27% with lack of dominance, among 150 slow readers, however, there were 38%.[12] Thus it can be seen that quantitative estimates concerning normal subjects lie between 13% and 27%, whereas the percentages for retarded readers range from 37% to 42%.

Zangwill is another investigator who came to the conclusion that crossed dominance and retarded reading are apparently frequently related.[13] Schonell's research led him to think that cross-eyedness and cross-handedness cause reading problems.[14] Harris observed that crossed dominance as well as delayed development of laterality occurred, up to the age of nine, far more frequently among slow than normal readers.[15] Kocher,[16] Smith and Dechant,[17] as well as Whitsell[18] are a few more authors who have no doubt that some association exists between reading disability and crossed dominance. Whitsell[19] believes with Brain that missing cerebral dominance is not an effect but part of the same cause that produces the speech and the reading-spelling deficiencies. Thus the various functional disturbances would all have a single origin.[20] The question of causation and effect is of less importance here than the fact that in all of these investigations there is an apparent association of cerebral dominance and dyslexia. Benton, McCann, and Larsen examined 250 children with reading difficulties and found that 93 of them had crossed dominance; 82 were right-handed and left-eyed; 11 were left-handed and right-eyed; 36 were more or less ambidextrous; 17 had no eye dominance, and 104 had incomplete eye dominance.[21] Dearborn compared 76 dyslexics with 124 normal readers and found among the former 14% more left-eyed ones and 17% more with crossed dominance.[22] Smith examined 50 slow readers, comparing them with a normal control group of equal size, age, and intelligence. Among the slow readers he found many more who had been changed or directed in lateral preference.[23] Leavell pointed out that few children with well-established right laterality show reading difficulties and that for years we have been aware of some connection between ambidexterity and speech impediment.[24] Vernon carefully estimated that youngsters with speech problems, poor readers included, do not demonstrate as clearly developed laterality as do normals.[25] Orton drew attention to these questions as early as 1937. He thought that incomplete cerebral dominance enhanced the probability that reading disturbances and mirror writing would occur; these he observed more frequently among boys than among girls.[26]

Weinschenk saw no association between incomplete dominance and congenital dyslexia; however, one of the five cases he investigated was left-handed.[27,28,29,30] Hildreth perused all studies published up to 1950 and concluded that the relationship is still unclear since the various findings are partially contradictory.[31] Spache believed that the typical reversal errors of slow readers are independent of eyedness, handedness, and cerebral dominance.[32] Along the same lines Smith and Dechant mention that several studies found no positive correlation between laterality disturbances and reading problems. In support of this they quote Woody and Phillips and also Wolfe.[33] The coauthors themselves felt that a positive correlation can be found more often in cases of severe reading disability than in mild cases.[34] Critchley also discusses research done in connection with this topic; even today he considers missing dominance an acceptable and important factor in the explanation of reading difficulties.[35] Lückert has no doubt that peripheral preference becomes a significant factor in reading disability if dominance is crossed.[36] Lory says it is no coincidence that reading proceeds from the usually weaker to the dominant side; this then presents a difficulty to the person with left dominance.[37]

Two points seem to emerge clearly from all this: the majority of investigators is convinced of at least an associative positive correlation between laterality and reading problems; second, the confirming studies seem to increase in number and are of more recent origin than those denying a positive relationship.

1.2b) Theories of Etiology

Confused laterality has been attributed to both missing cerebral dominance and delayed maturational patterns. It was Orton who observed that traumata in the nondominant hemisphere do not usually cause reading difficulties. He concluded that children who at the time they enter school have not yet fully established preference for either side will have reading problems. Confused spatial orientation, reversals, and similar mistakes are caused by the alternating use of memory engrams from either hemisphere.[38]

Although this theory was largely rejected, it is remarkable that today we seem to be coming back to a very similar neurological explanation. Orton himself was thinking not so much in terms of organic structural changes, but rather in terms of functional disturbances. Lückert emphasizes that eye, hand, or foot preference becomes significant in the causation of reading disability only if they are crossed and thus indicative of functional disorder. He is convinced that all signs suggest a neurological functional disturbance despite the fact that an adequate theoretical explanation has not yet been developed.[39] Smith and Carrigan grant Orton that his theory helps to explain the directional confusion so often observed in dyslexics, but they hold that it does not explain any of the other, also typical, weaknesses such as short memory span, poor visual learning, distractability, etc.[40] Critchley's[41] opinion of Orton's theory is also a supporting one; he too considers the theory of cerebral dominance as valid now as it was then acceptable and important.

Whether the incomplete lateralization observed in so many dyslexics is the result of structural or functional causes is still uncertain. As Lückert is convinced of its functional nature, so Zangwill is certain of its organic origin. Zangwill showed that early childhood trauma in the left hemisphere often leads to total or partial change of hand preference, delay in speech development, and reading difficulties, based possibly on the partial switch to the right hemisphere. He adds that the EEG's of many dyslexics show anomalies in the left hemisphere, that they do poorly in drawing and copying, and that they have weak spatial orientation and are uncertain about right-left differentiation. Zangwill asks for more research into the question whether such disturbances are caused by constitutional or genetic factors or by exogenous effects, such as minimal brain injury at birth.[42] Lückert holds that another problem lies in our diagnostic means which do not yet readily allow definition of minimal damage, especially in cases where motor deficiencies are not apparent. He estimates that 70% of all reading disability cases are expressions of functional disorders which are currently even more difficult to diagnose.[43] Lory also expresses regret that brain research has not been able to offer definite explanations.[44]

Vernon is an exponent of the theory of delayed maturation. She claims to have observed a disposition toward combined difficulties, such as reading disability, speech impediment, incoordination, left-handedness, and ambidexterity. In a few cases these are related to familial tendencies, she agrees, but a neurological developmental lag is the predispositional cause, and in the presence of the other factors the reading-spelling disability becomes manifest.[45] Four years later Critchley stated that the theory of delayed brain maturation was the most frequently held theory among neurologists.[46]

Of special interest here is a study performed by De Hirsch, Jansky, and Langford whose theoretical position is based on twenty years of experience with reading disability cases. These coauthors are convinced that reading problems are caused by neurophysiological maturational delay. They examined 53 prematurely born children and showed that their growth patterns were much more irregular than those of full-term babies. On kindergarten tests the latter were superior on 36 out of 37 items; 15 of these items measured oral language ability and reading readiness. Although the prematures seemed to catch up to some degree between kindergarten and second grade, they were clearly behind, in reading among other skills, well into the eighth year.[47] The authors felt that prematurely born children start life with a neurophysiological lag which is still present and not fully compensated for by the time they are expected to learn to read and write.[48] Even Zangwill, who thought primarily in terms of brain injury, admits readily that arrested development could well produce disturbances of dominance; the unspecific functional symptoms apparent in neurological examinations and electroencephalograms seem to him to support the idea of the maturational lag.[49] Geschwind advanced the idea that more efforts are needed to combine our knowledge of the function and the anatomy of the brain. It seemed to him that a faulty development of the gyrus angularis had to precede reading disturbances.[50] Zangwill, too, indicates the incomplete state of present knowledge when he writes that dyslexia might be traceable either to early brain trauma, to a constitutional defect in growth patterns, or to secondary retardation caused by stress. He contends that it might even be the result of a combination of all these. In any event, one would need a better understanding of reading disabilities before he could be certain how asymmetrical brain function comes about.[51]

Thus, it has not been determined whether cerebral dominance or maturational delay, based on organic or on functional aberrations, causes the lack of dominance and thus reading disability, or whether a combination of several factors leads to the learning problem. A causal relationship between crossed, incomplete, or missing dominance and dyslexia can be neither proved nor disproved according to current knowledge. This issue of faulty lateralization is especially important in view of the similarly frequent observed symptoms of confusion in spatial orientation and directionality in disabled readers. Does one cause the other, or do they co-exist as effects of the same cause? This question will be pursued further in the chapter on perception.

In our sample crossed dominance was significantly more frequent among younger children. This is not at all surprising and lends support to the idea of delayed development. Kramer also found more cases of crossed dominance among children than among adults; 46% among 114 subjects four to ten years old, 34% among subjects eleven years old or more.[52] Lory, noticing the frequency of left-handedness among his dyslexic students, thought in terms of genetic structure with associated effects of variable combinations.[53] Such theories of familial hereditary tendencies toward basic central nervous system disorders causing various combinations of functional disorder must be considered, for the time being, theoretical and conjectural.

1.2c) Summary

Our discussions can be summarized as follows:

A frequent correlation between disorders of lateral dominance and reading-spelling difficulties has been observed and confirmed by many investigators. In our sample we found only 49% of the subjects to have fully developed right dominance, 6% had well-established left dominance; 44% had various forms of crossed or incomplete laterality. According to various quantitative findings faulty dominance occurs in 13% to 27% of normal subjects, but in 37% to 44% in reading disability cases.

A causal relationship between anomalies of laterality and reading-spelling is suspected but cannot be proved.

Left-handedness seems less important in reading disability than the various forms of crossed dominance. Hess estimated that 30 –40% of his beginning readers preferred the use of the left over the right eye,[54] and Thibaut, also a teacher, stressed no less that eye dominance is of greater significance in reading-writing skills than hand or foot preference.[55]

Explanatory theories on the origin of laterality problems center in two major ideas: abnormalities of cerebral dominance, either structural or functional in nature, and delay or arrest of maturational neurophysiological development. More research is needed in both areas.

Left-handedness seems to occur more often among boys than among girls although our own sample did not show any statistically significant disparity in this regard. Faulty dominance, however, was significantly more frequent among primary school children than among teenagers, a finding which seems to support the theory of developmental lag.

1.3 Sensory Perception and Motor Functions

1.3a) Visual-Perceptual Difficulties

Of the 500 students in our sample 28.6% had visual-perceptual disturbances only. In 38.6% we found combined difficulties in visual perception and motor functions; this quantitative finding confirmed our general observations made while working with the individual children. In order to ascertain the true proportion of children in our sample with visual-perceptual difficulties we must combine those with only visual deficits and those with both visual and motor deficits; thus we arrive at 67.2%.

What is visual perception, and how can it be disturbed? This can be answered here only in a most cursory manner. The importance of visual perception in reading has led to a controversy between those who consider reading a sensory and those who consider it a conceptual process. This seems an unnecessary dispute if one considers that reading is a complex and continuous function, extending from simple sensation to complicated intellectual processes, all interrelated. To mention a few viewpoints: Spencer enlarged the concept so much that he called any form of perception, visual, tactile, etc. 'reading'; the decoding of visual language symbols is then only *one* type of reading.[1] Pietrowicz also presented a generalized reading concept, but recognized the aspect of cognition.[2] A modern representative of an extreme sensory position is Delacato,* whose patterning treatment has been under critical attack from the medical field in part simply because he looks upon reading as a sensory not a cognitive act, concluding that neuromuscular exercises designed to train neurological organization, i.e., crawling and patterning, will increase such cognitive functions as reading ability.

While reading is not merely a sensory process, it is also not only a mental one, as claimed by Artley, who considers reading a pure thought process, consisting of grasping the meaning of the written word.[3] Such discussions ignore other important aspects influencing reading: personality traits, interest, motivation, mood, memory, etc. Ephron stresses rightfully that reading behavior cannot be isolated from other behavior, but must be seen within the context of the total personality and its behavior patterns.[4]

Diagnosis and treatment of dyslexia are colored by our theory of what reading "really" is. It is important to keep in mind that it involves sensory as well as mental and total personality elements, that it begins as a simple sensation, necessitates perceptual interpretation, and must progress to a cognitive process if it is to reach its full purpose and value. Certainly perceptual recognition and interpretation of the visually presented letter is a key element in the reading process, as Smith and Dechant stress.[5] Biglmaier also emphasizes that reading consists of the "interpretation of visual word symbols."[6]

It is the merit of the gestalt psychologists to have shown that the perception and analysis of all the elements is not enough to recognize the whole, which is more than the sum total of its

---

*In bibliography see Nos. 29 and 30.

parts. Perception according to gestalt theory has to be completed by spontaneous insight.

It is to the credit of the behaviorists to have pointed out that the establishment of firm automatic stimulus-response reflexes is a necessity in good reading behavior. Educational psychologists place the emphasis on cognitive and conceptual aspects of the reading process. All of these studies and insights are useful and demonstrate, with or without conscious intention, the complexities of this most complicated and most recently acquired of human skills. Manifold disorders of visual perception (visual memory, visual attention span, alertness for detail, speed of visual perception, analysis, etc.) are in De Hirsch's opinion, at the very center of many reading disabilities.[7] Frostig, author of widely used visual-perceptual test and training materials, found that visual-perceptual imperfections are easily overlooked and yet are an important factor, especially since they can occur independently of each other.[8] Her test materials permit the computation of a PQ (perceptual quotient).[9]

We said, initially, that 67.2% of our slow readers showed visual-perceptual difficulties; this includes all kinds and degrees of such deficits, as long as they could be observed either in test behavior, especially on the Frostig, Bender, Goodenough, and Wechsler scales, but also through analysis of error patterns in reading and writing. The high percentage is not a surprising result since all degrees and kinds, variations and combinations are included and since, as especially Getman emphasized, visual perception is not only the most important modality in the visual task of reading, but also the most significant in the development of general intelligence.[10]

Perusal of the relevant literature yielded no quantitative figures for comparison with our findings. American literature contains older and more material on perceptual disorders than European writings. Research results lead to differing views on the correlation between dyslexia and defective perception. Some investigators deny any connection, others do not doubt it at all. The latter group includes De Hirsch who assumed it was generally known that fragmented visual perception is part of reading disability.[11] Thompson found it only natural that children of normal intelligence who suffered from reading disability should have poor form perception and other visual-perceptual deficits.[12] Frostig tells us her test materials were developed on the basis of years of observation on children whose reading difficulties were at least in part caused by visual-perceptual disturbances.[13] Money belongs to those who do not see a causal relationship, but he agrees that at least among those with neurophysiological deficits, which seem to be related to the reading disability, there are many with spatial disorientation, imperfect form perception, and poor right-left orientation.[14] Benton noticed that reading difficulties are often present in cases with form and object agnosia and that one might thus be justified in concluding that dyslexic symptoms are merely another manifestation of the same basic agnosia. Visual perception was in his opinion certainly the most frequently observed symptom in connection with reading disability.[15,16]

Application of the chi-square test to our sample did not yield any statistically significant differences, either in regard to the sexes or to the age groups. Only in the group of children with combined visual-perceptual and motor dysfunctions were the younger children significantly more often affected than the teenagers.

Birch stresses the evolutionary fact that optic perception, as the highest form, is the last developed and offers the hypothesis that incomplete development of visual perception adds to reading disability and may even allow its prediction.[17,18] Silver and Hagin examined 150 children with behavior problems and found that a high percentage of them had visual-perceptual difficulties.[19] Similar investigations were made in the U.S. as early as 1917 by Bronner. She published the results of her investigation, but refrained from final judgment, stating that reading might contain a subtle synthetic process which, if incomplete, would impede reading ability severely, but not enough was known about this synthetic process yet.[20] Six other studies have since been completed and have been discussed extensively by Benton[21] as well as by Critchley.[22] While Benton considers visual imperception as *one* factor in the causation of reading difficulties, Critchley confines himself to remarking that research results so far are contradictory.[23]

In the European literature on reading disability visual-perceptual disorders find frequent and contradictory mention also. Schomburg mentions, for instance, that the investigations carried out in Holland by Prechtl have been confirmed in similar German studies by Specht; both found the majority of retarded readers with visual-perceptual deficits.[24] No percentages were given. Most German writers take the presence of incomplete visual perception in poor readers for granted and discuss it only secondarily in connection with questions as to causation. Three authors denied any correlation: Lobrot (France), who sees only the inability of the child to make sound-symbol associations,[25] Daniels (England), who recognizes almost exclusively only auditory weakness as contributory factor,[26] and Ellehammer (Denmark), who observed only a retardation in speech and reading, not in visual perception among 21 retarded readers.[27]

While American investigators tend to think in terms of organic aberrations, European writers seem to think primarily in terms of missing psychological functions. Influenced by gestalt psychology, by Busemann's concept of superimposed layers of intelligence, and W. Stern's psychological theory of intelligence, they consider sensation, imagery, and perception intellectual functions. Biglmaier thus declared dyslexia to be an additional weakness or disorder of intellectual cognition.[28] Lory points out three critical areas of failure in dyslexics: faulty differentiation of letters and sounds, errors of reading direction in the form of right-left progression, and fragmentation of word gestalts.[29]

Bleidick speaks of an intellectual deficit in analyzing a given perceptual field ("Durchgliederungsschwäche") and expects all three kinds of dyslexia, acoustic, visual, and cognitive, to be seen in terms of a reduced ability to analyze configurations ("Gestaltgliederungsschwäche").[30] Kirchhoff also confirms that perceptual deficits in analytical as well as synthetical elective processes ("Gestaltgliederungsschwäche") impede conceptualization which takes place as a person hears, sees, speaks, or writes.[31]

R. G. E. Müller,[32] Ferdinand,[33] Linder,[34] and Schenk-Danzinger[35] differentiate between visual and auditory dyslexia, but do not say that these exist always independently. Schenk-Danziger was convinced that auditory perceptual deficits affect spelling more than reading.[36] Ingram observed that auditory perception was more frequently incomplete in children with delayed speech development.[37] Pietrowicz told the representatives of the auditory and visual groups that he would not reduce Gestaltgliederungsschwäche to either, but rather to a general anthropological factor, namely, a basic gnostic dysfunction in reading ("global-gnostische Störung").[38] Kobi called gestaltpsychological etiological theories the presently most valid ones.[39] Weinschenk reduces concept and causation of congenital dyslexia to hereditary predispositional weakness in word formation ("ererbte Anlageschwäche zur Wortgestaltung"),[40] which compels one to agree with Lory who states that such narrowness of concept makes it impossible to do justice to the complexity of the phenomenon we are dealing with.[41] Kobi stated, more factually and carefully: if we ask about the origin of the dyslexic learning deficits we enter a vast field of open questions on which investigators of various backgrounds are still battling.[42] In a similarly discriminatory manner Bleidick observed: there seem to exist quantitatively and qualitatively different forms of reading disabilities; monothematic etiological interpretations cannot be sufficient for their interpretation, it remains to discuss whether reading disorders are to be considered a disease sui generis or simply symptoms of varied origins.[43] Ellehammer after studying 21 severely dyslexic children of normal mental endowment and comparing the findings with a control group of 220 average students concluded: many uncertainties come to light, more research is needed, it seems likely that several impeding factors have to occur simultaneously before it comes to such severe manifestations of reading disability.[44]

Although the associative connection between visual-perceptual and reading-spelling difficulties has led to contradictory conclusions, and although the causative correlation remains unclear for the time being, fortunately diagnostic and therapeutic measures for their evaluation and alleviation have already been devised and are widely in use. The better known ones will be listed here for the interested reader.*

1.3b) Combined Visual and Motor Disorders

As mentioned in paragraph 1.3a, 38.6% in our sample showed combinations of visual and motor dysfunctions. In the concrete individual case it is often nearly impossible to say which of these are primary. Auditory deficiencies often further complicate the picture. Just as most students are not either exclusively visual or auditory or kinesthetic learners, so perceptual difficulties in the various sense modalities are not usually clearly distinguishable. This was also stated by Tamm who wrote that, except in the case of specific selection, groups of disabled learners will contain auditory, motoric, and visual learning disabilities.[45] Kocher drew attention to the close connections between the various sensations and perceptions even in their normal functions and believed that some perceptual difficulty is present in every dyslexic. He described vividly not only their typical misspellings and reversal errors, but also their confusion in space, time, and body image.[46] His remark, though, that these symptoms have been given too little attention, seems only partially correct. Such concepts as spatial confusion, right-left disorientation, sequencing disability, etc., can be found anywhere in European publications. However, studies on gross and fine muscle control, eye-hand coordination, dexterity, maturational level, and body schema appear to have

---

*Tests: Getman and Kephart, Advanced Tests of Visual Perception; Bender's Visual-Motor-Gestalttest; Benton, Visual Retention Test; Frostig, Developmental Test of Visual Perception; Harris, Draw-a-Person Test; Thurstone, Embedded Geometric Figures Perceptual Test; Monroe, Figurenanordnungen; Busemann's Abzeichentest; Kohs' Cubes, Wechsler's Mosaik-Subtest; Zazzo, Manuel pour l'examen psychologique de l'enfant; Rey, Figure complexe; Borel-Maisonny, Demi cercles et droites (No 391 de la Société Binet).

Teaching materials: Fernald's Kinesthetic Method; Harris' Visual-Motor Word Study Method; Gillingham Method; Kephart's Program; Cruickshank's Teaching Methods for Children with Perceptual Disorders; Strauss and Lehtinen Perceptual Methods; Gallagher Perceptual Methods; Frostig and Horne, The Frostig Program for the Development of Visual Perception; Kremer and Denk, Optisches Lehrsystem; Lory, Übung der visuellen Differenzierung.

been somewhat neglected. If motor functions are mentioned it is usually in terms of generalized awkwardness, and tests as well as practice materials aim at poorly defined motor deficiencies. American researchers have paid closer attention to fine muscle control and body related aspects of position in space, laterality awareness, etc. Recently some authors have asked whether all development might not be looked upon as the establishment of sensory functional patterns. Birch for instance speaks of the fact that intersensory functional systems are not based on visual-acoustic experiences alone, but also on visual-tactile and kinesthetic experiences. His observations indicate that retarded readers show disorders of intersensory relationships more frequently than do regular learners.[47]

If we emphasize the employment of multisensory learning experiences in the regular classroom, it becomes even more important in therapeutic teaching of reading. It is important to begin with the better developed sensory avenue of learning and to proceed from there in the training of the weaker sense modalities. This points out the necessity for individually tailored reading programs. They are imperative if success is to be attained. The methods must be selected and applied to meet the child's need; we cannot, as we often have done, expect the child to meet the method.

1.3c) Motor Dysfunctions

Almost one-half of our sample, namely 49.2% of all the children, displayed motor dysfunctions. Of these 10.6% had only motor disturbances; the remainder, 38.6%, showed various combinations of visuo-motor dysfunction.

We were unable to find comparable quantitative data from other researchers. In the German language literature we found only a few, rather general allusions to either the frequency or significance of motor functions in regard to reading problems. Kobi, for instance, wrote that he saw "here and there" children with motor disorders in the form of general awkwardness, jerky movements, contracted muscles, poorly coordinated movements, etc.[48] Later he also mentioned dysgraphia and lack of dexterity.[49] Biglmaier also observed only "a few" slow readers

with difficulties in the motor functions needed for reading, such
as eye movements, but more with difficulties in the muscle
control needed for the writing and speaking processes.[50] Hunger-Kaindlstorfer said that one of the typical characteristics of
poor readers was poorly developed fine muscle coordination,
sometimes reaching the degree of apraxia.[51] Bleidick listed
motor insufficiencies among the symptoms,[52] and Lory thought
he found especially often two types of children among the
dyslexics: "dwarfs" and "giant babies," the latter large and
heavy for their age and at the same time very poorly coordinated, showing concomitant movements reminiscent of cerebral
palsy.[53] Kirchhoff held that we should look beyond external
mobility and consider also the internal motor functions which
become apparent as total rhythm of movement.[54] Walter asked
that during diagnostic evaluations more attention be given to
deviations in motor development.[55] Schenk-Danziger is also one
of the few who indicates the importance of delays in motor
development.[56] Hohlman observed how awkwardly poor readers perform in physical education classes.[57] Kossakowski stated
that difficulties in fine muscle control lead to the characteristic
difficulties which dyslexics display in speech, reading, and writing.[58] Lückert wrote that reading disorders traceable to brain
damage, especially when it has been severe, are often accompanied by motor deficiencies.[59]

The authors mentioned above are not just a sampling, but an
almost complete count of all who have written in Europe on the
subject of motor functions and their relation to reading disability. American investigators have given the matter much
more attention. Kephart presented an especially good account
of how a child's earliest learning is based on motoric experience
and development.[60] Equally clearly, movement was identified
with learning by Getman who described how learning cannot
take place without movement.[61] Anderson emphasized no less
that experiences of movement and touch constitute a child's
earliest learning about his environment.[62]

Prechtl, stimulated by such researchers as Rabinovitch, Bakwin and Bakwin, and Cohn, investigated 50 hyperactive children without evident neurological signs who had normal IQ's
and were between 9 and 12 years old. The majority of these

children, he found, were clumsy; almost none could distinguish clearly between right and left, 58% had ambilaterality, 90% had reading problems, 98% demonstrated defective eye movements in reading, and almost all of them had poorly developed fine muscle control. The few who did not have reading problems all had IQ's of more than 130 and could thus compensate their reading difficulties.[63] The Orton Society, located in New York, requests, among other things, an evaluation of the motor functions in the initial assessment of the slow reader.[64] Johnson observed that dyslexic children need additional tactile and kinesthetic practice in order to be able to establish and retain associations between spoken and written words.[65] De Hirsch found, among eight carefully studied children with severe reading disabilities, no involuntary concomitant movements and hardly any restrictions in gross muscle coordination, but fine muscle control was poor. The majority had dysgraphia.[66]

Several authors investigated whether or not visuo-motor defects tend to be outgrown in the course of normal growth and development. De Hirsch observed little hyperactivity among older dyslexic children and stated that perceptuo-motor signs had become less obvious.[67] These findings were confirmed in our sample: the younger group, as the chi-square calculations revealed, had statistically significantly more children with motor insufficiencies than the older group. The younger children also showed a significantly higher frequency of combined visuo-motor deficiencies. Observation during testing revealed that the older the child grows the more subtle the symptoms of perceptual and motor difficulties become. De Hirsch found little correlation between IQ and spelling and concluded that specific reading-spelling disability cannot readily be compensated for by intelligence.[68]

Etiological questions concerning motor dysfunctions are still largely open, but diagnostic and therapeutic methods are available and in use.*

---

*Tests: Some of the performance subtests of the Stanford-Binet and Wechsler Scales; Benton, A., Right-left Orientation and Reading Disability; Money, J. et al., A Standardized Road Map Test of Direction Sense; Lincoln-Osteretsky, Motor Development Scale; Oseretsky, Psychomotorik, Methoden zur Untersuchung der Motorik; Heuyer-Baille, Motorische Testreihe, Tests moteurs;

1.3d) Auditory-Perceptual Deficits

Our quantitative findings showed that 10.2% of the sample had auditory-perceptual difficulties, despite normal sensory hearing ability. Acuity was not impaired, but discrimination of similar and dissimilar sounds, retention, reproduction, integration of sounds were inadequate, and the children could not correctly perceive their sequence, were not alert to sounds, showed fewer reactions, and paid less attention to them.

Kirchhoff speaks of auditory dyslexia, especially affecting the ability to analyze sounds; he found acoustic difficulties, either isolated or in combination with visual-perceptual problems, and thought that auditory imperception caused the same kind of reversal errors that are caused by visual-perceptual difficulties.[69] Kocher emphasizes the importance of auditory-perceptual problems, especially in the transfer between optical and acoustic functions and describes the resulting difficulties in detail.[70,71] Myklebust drew attention to the lack of rhythm in slow readers and felt a rhythm test should be given in each case to determine auditory ability in the reproduction of a given rhythm.[72]

Bleidick pointed to the difficulty that poor readers have in isolating or synthesizing sounds and letters of whole words or of speech.[73] Pietrowicz preferred to think not so much of an "either-or" proposition of auditory and visual perceptual dysfunction but rather of a total gnostic disorder which has an auditory component.[74] Schenk-Danziger isolated six symptoms comprising an "auditory syndrome": isolation of sounds, isolation of words, association of auditory and visual speech symbols, trans-

---

Borel-Maisonny, Epreuves motorices d'orientation (No 391 de la Société Binet); Rey, Coordination visuo-manuelle libre et directe.

Teaching Materials: Kephart's Motor and Visual-Motor Activities; Gillingham and Stillman's Remedial Training; Delacato's Neurological Re-organization (Patterning) Program; De Hirsch, Predictive Index (for kindergarten age); Fernald, Tracing Techniques; also improved and enlarged edition by Johnson, Visual, Auditory, Kinesthetic, Tactile Specific Tracing Techniques (= Vakt); Tamm's practice manual "Lies Mit Uns – Schreib Mit Uns"; a list of specific and combined methods can be found in Ingenkamp, K. (editor): Lese- und Rechtschreibschwäche 'bei Schulkindern, 1967, Weinheim and Berlin, Julius Beltz, pp. 377–385; Klasen, Edith: Audio-Visio-Motor Training with Pattern Cards, 1969, Peek Publications, Palo Alto, California.

fer of temporal sound sequences into spatial sequences of
graphic symbols, discrimination between voiced and unvoiced
consonants, differentiation of certain vowel combinations and
vowel mutations.[75] Like Pietrowicz, Lory thinks in terms of a
global or central disturbance; he found clearly distinguishable
visual or auditory deficiencies only rarely in his teaching experiences.[76] While Lory suspects that missing or weak gestaltpsychological brain functions are the basis of these phenomena,
Weinschenk is certain that we are confronted with a congenital
weakness, but he is not sure whether it exists as definite brain
damage or as functional disorder; psychologically it becomes
manifest as hereditary weakness or absence of the ability to
synthesize letters and to analyze words.[77] Schenk-Danziger
considers auditory discrimination difficulties as possibly caused
by predispositional weakness.[78]

Critchley discusses several etiological theories, but does not
consider any particular one as the true answer; rather he wants
to wait for more research findings.[79] Thus he stands apart from
most of his European colleagues who often believe firmly in just
one cause, such as Daniels who declares that the inability to
correctly perceive the sounds of a word has nothing to do with
inherited structure, but consists of a developmental delay
caused by environmental inadequacies, such as too much visual
instruction in the teaching of reading.[80]

While most European investigators have no doubt about the
presence and importance of auditory deficits, they discuss them
primarily and almost exclusively in connection with causation.
Two authors are exceptions in this respect. Tamm, who extensively investigated error patterns of dyslexic children, found
that 15.3% of all mistakes were made in connection with voiced
consonants, the students being unable to discriminate them.[81]
Müller's empirical findings led him to conclude: subjects with
reading-spelling disability tended to have much more frequently faulty perception than did normal control subjects; they
were much less able to write by dictation; they were much less
adequate in discriminating sounds, especially those which are
similar; their characteristic errors may be a result of incorrectly
perceived sounds.[82]

American scientists consider auditory perception as an important part of maturation and learning. Flower especially has pointed out how many different auditory discriminations have to be learned within the context of reading. A child must have 3000 or more words at his command when he enters school. The home is thus of greater significance than is usually recognized. Auditory functions are among the most important components of reading readiness.[83]

Durrell and Murphy, intrigued by so many children with normal hearing, good speaking vocabulary, high mental potential, clear speech patterns, and good schooling who could not analyze certain sounds within words, had to accept that this auditory deficit caused severe reading disability despite all the other assets. They also found that all children whose reading was below first-grade level showed an obvious inability to discriminate sounds.[84] Wepman also emphasizes the importance of auditory functions, especially during the early stages of language development.[85] Myklebust thinks that auditory deficits are a more significant handicap than visual difficulties and points to the phylogenetically as well as the ontogenetically greater importance of acoustic functions in language acquisition.[86]

Quantitative data, comparable to ours, seem not to exist, but nobody seems to doubt that auditory perception problems are part of the reading-spelling problem. Thus Money reports that more and more physicians are ready to acknowledge that many patients, despite normal ears and auditory nerves are unable, because of some central defect, to adequately discriminate the flow of sounds entering their brain.[87] Rabinovitch also observed inadequate auditory functions among most retarded readers.[88]

Hardy considers dyslexia a speech problem in the widest sense, which as such is directly connected with the sense of hearing and is manifested as inattention or inability to listen.[89]

De Hirsch observed among 16 severely retarded readers, 11 to 15 years old, with better than average IQ's, that their speech disorders were unusually persistent, especially those consisting of auditory memory span and auditory discrimination.[90]

Flower was certain that auditory perceptual difficulties were widely spread among dyslexics, making it difficult for them to learn to read in the regular classroom setting; in regard to causation the author points out that refined diagnostic methods have been developed only during the past 15 years and that questions of differential diagnosis cannot yet be answered with certainty.[91,92] Eisenberg believed he saw growing proof that children with normal hearing acuity can very well have auditory-perceptual difficulties which impede the ability to transfer from auditory to visual stimuli and thus to reading ability.[93] Bannatyne divided slow readers into two groups, according to his observations; one group consisted of those who were unable to associate simultaneously and in correct sequence sight and sound symbols.[94] The investigations of Smith and Dechant revealed that superior auditory discrimination directly increased sight vocabulary, and that among four quantitatively measurable components of reading readiness auditory discrimination took first place.[95] Benton calls discriminative and integrative deficits in auditory perception "cognitive disorders of a higher order" and thinks they originate from brain injury acquired either at birth or through illness. He speculates that lesions located in the cortical regions are responsible for the auditory deficiencies.[96]

As is the case with visual and motor disorders, auditory-perceptual inadequacies can be diagnosed and treated despite the still unresolved etiological aspects.*

1.3e) Summary

There seems to be general agreement on the frequent association of auditory and reading-spelling deficits. Whether this is a causal, primary, secondary, or only chance relationship is un-

---

*Tests: McCarthy and Kirk: "Illinois Test of Psycholinguistic Abilities"; Wepman's Test of Auditory Discrimination; Auditory Tests 1 and 2 in Monroe's Reading Aptitude Test; Subtests of the Wechsler and Stanford-Binet Intelligence Scales; word lists by Haskins and Borel-Maisonny (No 392 de la Société Binet); also informal tapping or rhythm tests by Kadletz, De Hirsch, Kirchhoff, Myklebust and others.

Teaching Materials: Bannatyne Color Phonics System; Progressive Choice Reading Methods by Edwards; Tamm recommends Denk-fix-Spiele and "Stille Post" as well as the use of tape recorders and his work book "Lies Mit Uns — Schreib Mit Uns; Schmiedeberg: Audio-Visuelles Lern- und Lehrgerät; Lory: Übungen zur akustischen Differenzierung. These listings do not purport to be complete.

clear, both in individual cases and for dyslexics in general. More research is needed. However, there is also agreement that manifestations of auditory deficits exist independently of intact auditory sensory and central organs.

American writers have contributed by far the highest number and the most extensive of investigations concerning the correlation between auditory and other language disabilities. They generally emphasize that diagnosis, treatment, and prevention will have to based on functional definitions as long as etiological questions remain unresolved.

French-speaking authors pay less attention to hereditary and congenital connections, but stress disorders in spatial and temporal orientation affecting the child's ability to relate to the world about him. Lobrot interprets his observations as indicative of environmental rather than congenital causation, and thinks matters can be explained through a psychology typical to the child.[97] Mucchielli, Bourcier, Chassagny and Kocher are the authors who especially vividly describe the mistakes and the difficulties characteristic of the disabled learner.

German-speaking investigators, influenced by the psychology of memory and the gestalt school, discuss missing or weak basic psychological functions as the basis of perceptual as well as cognitive disorders. Sometimes they are considered inborn, sometimes they are seen as organic defects which may be either functional or structural. Much attention has been given to the analysis of dyslexic reading-writing error patterns. The hope that new insights and new therapeutic ways could be gained from these has not been fulfilled. It is difficult to understand the certainty and exclusiveness with which some state their conclusions. Schubenz, for instance, asks: "And where does this child's dyslexia come from? I say he has a genetically weaker ability to utilize his memory in regard to details."[98] The range of explanatory theories expands from narrow or one-sided causal explanations to generalized and confused descriptive narrations. Bleidick's condensed list of existing views reflects clearly the present stage of controversy and confusion; depending on the theory in vogue, he writes, auditory difficulties are seen as psychological weakness in analytic and synthetic functions, traceable to either isolated, partial, or general central pathology, but in the concrete individual case the visual, auditory, and other, nonsensory dysfunctions are seen as having one and the same origin.[99]

In England diagnostic and teaching methods were given more attention than etiological investigations. Critchley tends toward the theory of maturational delay in the development of the cortex, but also points to the controversial findings produced by research so far.

Our own findings of high percentages of perceptual disorders among dyslexics tend to disperse any doubt about at least positive associative correlation, if not necessarily a causal one. Hopefully the figures will at least provide a new impetus to further study.

1.4 Organic Sensory Defects

1.4a) Visual-Perceptual Difficulties

In 27 of our 500 cases reliable information could not be obtained; among the remaining 473 we found 32.1% whose sight was impaired by various types and degrees of pathology. In 36.8% of these cases, however, vision was corrected through glasses to the best possible extent. Children who at the time of the initial evaluation have previously undetected vision problems are referred by the Raskob Institute to eye specialists. Which kinds or degrees of eye problems tend to contribute to reading difficulties? Weinschenk rightfully requested visual testing in every single case regardless of whether sensory defects are really either responsible for or additional to the learning problem.[1] Little has been said or done in regard to the relation between reading-spelling and sensory problems in German- and French-speaking countries. No statistical data are available on the subject. At a German psychological convention in 1965 it was stated that recent research indicated that fewer sight impediments existed among school children than had been assumed, and that there existed, in this regard, a vacuum yet to be filled in the test procedures for dyslexia.[2] Bleidick lists myopia, hyperopia, farsightedness, reduced peripheral vision, nystagmus, fusion and accommodation problems as possible contributors,[3] but no one states how these peripheral sensory deficits affect reading ability. This is true also of Biglmaier who assumes that reading, as a primarily visual task, naturally would have to be impaired by vision handicaps.[4]

Our finding of 32% with sight defects would have more significance if percentages among nondyslexics were known. Schomburg has stated that among 120 children beginning first grade, 20% were found to have impaired eyesight.[5] Our findings are high in relation to this.

Anglo-Saxon investigations arrived at contradictory results. Edson, Bond, and Cook, for instance, studied 188 children of the fourth grade and found no statistically significant correlation between reading ability, visual acuity, fusion, or depth perception.[6] By contrast, Jackson and Shye, investigating 640 ninth graders, realized that those with vision problems had better mean intelligence as well as reading scores.[7] Farris detected in a group of 1685 children in the seventh grade 44% with eye defects of various degrees, and in this connection he quotes two other studies which yielded 42% and 63%, respectively.[8] Compared to these figures our own seem low. Robinson found 73% of 22 dyslexics tested to have defective vision, but she emphasized that in only 11 of these cases the impaired sight actually contributed to the reading problem.[9]

Austin compared several studies on the relationship between eyesight and reading success and arrived at the interesting conclusion that beyond the primary grades no more significant differences are found; she thought that the older children had either compensated for their weaknesses or had dropped out.[10] Whereas Taylor[11] and Farris[12] found more farsightedness among poor than among good readers, Stromberg,[13] Swanson and Tiffin,[14] as well as Witty and Kopel,[15] observed no significant correlation among school children or among college students. Robinson even found better reading achievement in cases with astigmatism, adding that only severe degrees of astigmatism tend to impede reading ability.[16] Harris found that among the various defects those in near vision and convergence showed the highest correlation with reading difficulties.[17]

Eames also saw positive correlations; he compared 114 slow readers with 143 controls and had 44% with impaired sight among the former, but only 18% among the latter. Exophoria and farsightedness were by far the most frequent.[18,19] Bond and Tinker felt good eyesight was important to reading; the good reader with poor sight probably would be a still better reader had he good vision. Only certain cases of farsightedness, binocular disorder, fusion problems and aniseikonia had negative influence on reading ability.[20] Gruber, on the contrary, noted no connection between binocular coordination and reading.[21] Critchley remarks categorically that developmental dyslexia is independent of refraction errors, muscle imbalance, and impaired binocular fusion. Although some investigators thought they had found correlations between minor defects in color perception and color naming, he himself has seen no such relations.[22]

Unfortunately, our own material did not allow further investigation into kinds and degrees of contributing sensory visual defects. Application of the chi-square test yielded no statistically significant differences in frequency in regard to age or sex.

Studies which deal with eye movements of good and poor readers are also interesting. In German language literature one finds general remarks such as the one by Biglmaier, stating that some dyslexics have difficulty with the motor control needed for eye movements.[23] Mosse and Daniels in England believe that some cases of dyslexia are caused exclusively by functional motor disorders in eye movement. They referred to this as "linear dyslexia," a condition in which children cannot move their eyes along straight lines as is necessary in the reading process.[24]

Fixations and regressions in eye movements determine reading speed. Their measurement thus is an important diagnostic tool. Miles, for instance, cut a small hole into cardboard and let the child look through it while reading, and she meanwhile observed the eye movements, a procedure which has become known as the "Miles-Peephole-Method."[25] Bond and Tinker introduced the use of a small mirror for the same purpose.[26]

Today more and more ophthalmographic, photographic, electrographic, and tachistoscopic measures are being employed here and abroad.

Spache, after perusal of several studies, concluded that the frequency of fixations does not correlate with reading speed.[27] Buswell, studying 186 subjects, from six to eighteen years old, observed that eye movement ability develops fast during the elementary grades, but will hardly improve at a later stage. He was convinced that regressions in eye movement result in poor reading.[28] Critchley is not surprised that unusual eye movement patterns are observed in slow readers, but considers the controversy of whether they are the direct cause of the reading disorders as useless.[29] Mosse, on the other hand, thinks that faulty eye movements in the reading process may not have an organic basis but can be caused by early acquired faulty reading habits, especially since reading consists generally of a linear process of learned reflexes.[30]

The rather specific issue of eye movements in reading cannot be further pursued in the context of this study. The interested reader will find a critical evaluation of a number of studies in this field in Critchley.[31]

1.4b) Auditory-Perceptual Deficits

We had no reliable information on the hearing of 121 of our 500 dyslexics. Of the remaining 379 there were 9.2% with hearing losses of various degrees and kinds. If hearing defects are first noticed in a child during initial testing at the Institute, referrals to ear specialists are made.

It is apparent that the development of speech depends greatly on intact hearing, and that reading depends in turn on well-developed speech. However, little agreement exists, as in the case of sight defects, as to which types and which degrees of hearing loss impair reading-spelling ability. The relatively few studies published so far in this context yielded contradictory results. Bleidick stated that any degree of organic or peripheral hearing loss must be taken into account as secondary impediment to reading.[1] Biglmaier made a very similar observation.[2] Interestingly, Hoeksema found among 10,180 school children in Holland 4.3% with hearing losses.[3] This proportion is almost identical with findings by Silverman,[4] Bond and Tinker,[5] and O'Connor and Streng[6] in the United States. Our own result, 9.2%, is nearly identical with that arrived at by Robinson, who found that in 9% of the dyslexic cases reduced hearing acuity was a contributing factor. Robinson also noticed that sensory hearing loss was less often associated than auditory perceptual disorder.[7] This also corresponds closely with the findings in our study.

Investigating 34 retarded readers, at the age of 11 still reading at first-grade level, Johnson found that 17.6% had hearing losses. Although this is a higher portion than we found, other aspects of his findings correlate well with ours: 61.8% with visual perceptual difficulties and 41.2% with delayed speech development, as compared to our 67.2 and 39.6%, respectively.[8]

That hearing loss is generally considered a less significant factor in the development of dyslexia could be partially the result of the fact that many minor hearing losses go undetected. Thus Hoeksema observed among the 4.3% with impaired hearing 46.4% whose losses had not been detected by parents or teachers.[9] Kocher draws attention to the same point.[10] We have no uniformly valid definition of "normal" hearing, and little is known about which kinds or degrees of impaired hearing may cause which reading-spelling difficulties. Of course, even if reliable tools of diagnostic evaluation of hearing in cases of dyslexia were evolved and employed, the question would still remain: are the hearing losses primary factors or secondary consequences?

While Sheridan, for instance, reports that with increasing hearing loss the reading disability grows,[11] Ewing and Ewing worked with 12 deaf children who, without exception, were able to make substantial progress in reading as soon as they were provided with special reading classes.[12] It certainly seems that hearing loss and reading-writing disability are not directly related. More likely, several factors have to occur together before certain disorders develop. Kobi writes that children with relatively good hearing in the lower range often are handicapped by classroom background noise which may cause spelling mistakes.[13] Sheridan made very similar observations.[14]

Speech sounds in the higher ranges were identified as the most
critical elements in articulate comprehensible speech by Berry
and Eisenson.[15]

Not enough is known as yet about the development and the
norms of hearing. Thus Cole thought that six-year-old children
are not yet ready to discriminate consistently between certain
consonants.[16] Money also considers developmental phenomena
when he states that retarded readers only rarely have definite
sensory acuity problems.[17] Flower is convinced that the auditory difficulties among slow readers are rarely organic in origin,
but are the result of a delay in maturation. He, too, considers
high range losses as the most significant ones.[18]

In our study investigation with the chi-square method showed
that the frequency of occurrence was significantly higher
among boys than among girls. With regard to high tone losses
only, our findings were somewhat confirmed by Dahl who lists
six different studies which all showed that more boys than girls
were afflicted by hearing losses.[19] He also observed more auditory losses among younger children than high school students,[22] but our material showed no significant difference.

As was seen in relation with perceptual and sight defects, too,
more research is needed. It must be based on more unified
criteria and terms, on better diagnostic means and more modern equipment. For the reader who would like to further pur-
sue the question of correlation between hearing and learning
problems Flower[21] offers an extensive bibliography on this issue.

1.4c) Summary

Speech, reading, and writing require normal sensory functions;
certain kinds and degrees of sensory defects in the general
language area can cause various handicaps. In regard to vision
defects it seems that especially farsightedness, fusion problems,
and severe astigmatism impede reading ability. In relation to
hearing loss it appears that especially high pitch losses and
severe degrees of acuity loss hamper speech development and
thus also reading-writing ability.

Despite the fact that research results so far are inconclusive and often contradictory, it is generally agreed that both sight and hearing losses are more frequently observed among retarded readers than among good readers. Here is a table of the few quantitative data available:

Dyslexics	9% – 17% ⎫	hearing loss
Normal controls	4% – 5% ⎭	
Dyslexics	32% – 73% ⎫	impaired eyesight
Normal controls	25% – 63% ⎭	

At first these do not seem to be very significant disparities, but they do suggest a correlation. If it does not shed any light on causal relationships, at least it indicates the need for more and better research in these areas. As matters stand now, it is widely assumed that vision defects affect reading ability more severely than do hearing losses.

1.5 Neuropsychological Symptoms

1.5a) Hyperactivity

One-quarter of our group, namely 26.8%, were hyperactive, i.e., constantly in motion, unable to sit still, distractible, impulsive, overly talkative, etc. In short, they showed motor as well as sensory disinhibition, being victims of their own inner impulses and at the mercy of external stimuli.

German language literature mentions hyperactivity only in passing, and gives it little significance. Quantitative information is not available. Kleiner is one of the few to remark that he found "in a small number of severely dyslexic cases" a secondary neurotic syndrome consisting of hyperkinesis.[1] Bleidick's etiological categories list hyperactivity under the headings "environmental" and "encephalopathic" theories. He points out the vicious circle a congenitally hyperactive child finds himself in: constantly reprimanded and rejected because of his uncontrolled and difficult to tolerate behavior, he tends to become even less manageable and thus "it comes to a constant interfusing of psychological and organic components.[2] Lückert reports that among 45 slow readers, 8 to 18 years old, Delacato and Delacato observed that hyperactivity in early childhood was a most outstanding characteristic.[3] Lory writes that a classroom full of poor readers strikes the visitor as a restless, tense, hyperactive group of children.[4] Kobi is another teacher who is aware of the hyperactivity among his retarded readers and wants them to be considered as a separate category.[5] Biglmaier lists hyperactivity as one of the factors that impede reading ability.[6] Kirchhoff presents a case analysis of an 8-year-old girl whose reading-spelling disability was based on severe motor disinhibition.[7]

Critchley in England, as well as Kleiner and Schomburg in Germany, discuss the studies of the Dutch author Prechtl who describes a "choreiform syndrome"; while Critchley is not convinced of its significance in connection with developmental dyslexia,[8] Kleiner considered the choreiform syndrome *one* side of a triangular dyslexic syndrome, whose two other sides consist of infantilism and reading-spelling disability.[9] Schomburg holds that Prechtl's findings are confirmed by Spechts's investigation, the results of which are unavailable.[10]

Prechtl apparently submitted his findings in three publications: 1959, with Stemmer in German,[11] 1962 in both English[12] and American publications.[13] In his conclusion he carefully states that "some children seem to have reading and concentration problems as a consequence of the specific choreiform syndrome.[14] Prechtl's study of children with choreiform symptoms led him to the discovery that 90% of them were disabled readers. Conversely, our investigation of the reading disability syndrome led us to ask how many dyslexics showed the signs of Prechtl's choreiform syndrome. Our results were:

Hyperkinesis	26.8%
Poor concentration	39.0%
Faulty dominance	44.2%
Dyskinesia	49.2%
Visual perceptual difficulties	67.2%

Furthermore, 15.8% of the children in our sample had a combination of the first two of the above symptoms; 3.2% had combinations of the first three, and 4.2% had all five symptoms. These high percentages strongly support Prechtl's findings. All five correlates named by Prechtl are in the categories for which we found the highest frequencies in our sample.

At about the same time that Prechtl described his syndrome, Doyle, in the United States, delineated an "organic hyperkinetic syndrome," consisting of hyperactivity, unpredictability, hyperthymia, concentration problems, temper tantrums, moodiness, low frustration tolerance, poor impulse control, antisocial behavior, crossed dominance, right-left confusion, spatial disorientation, imbalance, visual-perceptual difficulties, and reading disability.

Testpsychologically, he found, these children were less adept at tasks involving visual, auditory, or motor functions; they earned better verbal than performance scores; on the Goodenough Draw-a-Man Test they generally scored two or more years below their chronological ages. According to his estimate approximately 5% of all American school children suffer from this syndrome.[15] This percentage accentuates how much our sample with its 26% hyperactivity lies above the expected norm.

Among the eight seriously retarded readers studied by De Hirsch there were no less than five with severe hyperactivity.[16] Gofman listed nine characteristics which she frequently observed in disabled readers and thought were too often missed by pediatricians and neurologists; one of these was hyperactivity, another distractibility.[17] Cohn, in a neurological study, theorized that the aggression, particularly common among older dyslexic children, is a compensation for motor disinhibition.[18]

The medical, and more specifically neurological, investigations of hyperkinesis as related to learning and behavior problems originated with Strauss,* who by the thirties had depicted a syndrome, listing, aside from distractibility and perceptual problems, reading and spelling difficulties. Strauss thought that this syndrome, today widely known as the "Strauss Syndrome," was the result of brain injury. The controversy he initiated with regard to endogenous versus exogenous causation is still unsettled. For the interested reader

---

*Strauss, Alfred: The Education of the Brain-Injured Child. Amer. J. Ment. Defic., 1951, 56, pp. 712–718.

we present a list of publications which treat the hyperkinetic syndrome from neurological points of view.*

In summary, the investigation of dyslexia frequently uncovers hyperactivity and related neurological factors, while studies of hyperactivity and brain injury frequently find associated reading-spelling disability. The hyperkinetic phenomenon occurred statistically significantly more often among boys than among girls in our sample and also significantly more frequently among younger children than among those in high school. In both cases the higher frequencies were significant on the 1% level of confidence.

This is an interesting but not surprising result, since it has been observed already repeatedly in this study that boys seem biologically as well as psychologically more vulnerable, and that many symptoms are outgrown through normal maturational processes. The prescription of psychotropic substances through physicians has proved a valuable aid to the teaching-learning process at the Raskob Institute. Pharmacological treatment often reduces the hyperkinetic symptoms, enabling the student to concentrate longer, to tire less, to cope more readily with frustration, and thus to enjoy better learning ability as well as self direction.

---

*Strauss, A., and Lehtinen, L. E.: Psychopathology and Education of the Brain-Injured Child, New York, 1947, Grune and Stratton. Pasamanick, B.: Epidemiology of Behavior Disorders. Res. Publ. Assn. Ment. Dis., 1954, 34, pp. 397–403. Gallagher, J. J.: The Tutoring of Brain-Injured Mentally Retarded Children; an Experimental Study, 1960. Charles C. Thomas Publisher. Lewis, R. S., Strauss, A. A., and Lehtinen, L. E.: The Other Child; the Brain-Injured Child—a Book for Parents and Laymen, 1960, New York, Grune and Stratton. Cruickshank, W. M., Dentzen, F. A., Ratzeburg, F. H. and Tannehauser, M. T.: A Teaching Method for Brain-Injured and Hyperactive Children; a Demonstration Pilot Study, 1961, Syracuse, N.Y., Syracuse University Press. Lewis, Richard S.: the Brain-Injured Child: the Perceptually Handicapped, 1963, the Nat. Society for Crippled Children and Adults, 2023 W. Ogden Ave., Chicago, Ill. Strother, Charles R.: Discovering, Evaluating, Programming for the Neurologically Handicapped Child with Special Attention to the Child with Minimal Brain Damage, 1963, Nat. Soc. for Crippled Children and Adults, 2023 W. Ogden Ave., Chicago, Ill. Thompson, Alice C.: Educational Handicap, 1964, Escalon, Inc., 234 S. Garfield Ave., Monterey Park, California, Cruickshank, William M.: The Brain-Injured Child in Home, School and Community, 1967, Syracuse, N.Y., Syracuse University Press.

1.5b) Hypoactivity

We had 18.4% hypoactive children in our sample of disabled readers. They were slow to react and move, and difficult to arouse. They were disinterested, vicious, reticent, unspontaneous, and retiring. No quantitative data on hypoactivity were available from other studies. But we found a number of general references to it. Bleidick, in connection with encephalopathological etiology mentions a "hypokinetic syndrome" leading to "torpidity."[19] Linder observed that many reports on these children listed, among other secondarily associated symptoms, "absentmindedness, dullness, lack of participation, fatigue."[20] Biglmaier found many dyslexics to be "often tired and apathetic."[21] Lory described the lack of initiative, the passivity, quietness, inactivity, and apathy of many of his poor readers who would either not respond at all or would respond only passively and after much prodding.[22] Kirchhoff makes an interesting, if not directly comparable quantitative statement. He found asthenia in 22% of the children he studied, and held that this proportion resembled that in the general population of children.[23]

De Hirsch had three hypoactive children among her disabled readers. "They were hypoactive, had difficulty maintaining a sitting posture, and tended to slump. Their throwing was hypotonic; some of them could hardly hold a pencil. Both hyperactive and hypoactive youngsters showed a considerable tendency to fatigue."[24] This describes very well the hypoactive as well as the hyperactive children in our sample. Clements, also depicting a hypoactive syndrome, which he said he observed less often than the hyperactive one, called these children as "tenacious as molasses," thinking and talking at a greatly reduced pace.[25]

That hypoactivity occurs less frequently than hyperactivity is confirmed by our findings and has not been questioned by any author so far. However, it might very well be that there are more hypoactive children among the slow readers than quantitative findings indicate. The hypoactive child is less likely to be noticed; he presents no disciplinary difficulties and is not disruptive in group situations. He is simply tolerated and dragged along.

It can no longer be denied that hypo- and hyperactivity are frequent and important correlates of learning disability. Questions of treatment, medically as well as educationally, of causation and of prevention need more and better investigation.

Probability formulas provided no significant disparity of frequency in our sample; there was only a statistical tendency (on the 10% level of confidence, $X^2 = 2.89$) for hypoactivity to be more frequent among the younger age group. The exact nature of the relation between hypoactivity and reading disability needs further investigation.

1.5c) Nervous Habits

A high proportion of children in the sample, namely 39.3%, displayed nervous habits, such as nail biting, tics of various kinds, restless tossing of the head or other parts of the body, thumb or finger or similar types of sucking, enuresis, encopresis (very few cases), sleep disturbances, pavor nocturnus, constant yawning, and occasional breath holding. All these disorders involve the involuntary nervous system and therefore are closely related to what might be coined obsessive behavior. Nervous habits are not accompanied by subjective feelings of illness, but, on the contrary, often provide a certain satisfaction. Parents and educators often mistakenly think the child could control these habits voluntarily if only he made an effort. This has been discussed poignantly by Dührssen.[26] Since some of these disorders are so common at certain ages that they must be considered "normal," they were included for quantitative evaluation only if they persisted beyond a specific age, or were so severe or frequent as to be abnormal. In addition to such developmental phases, as Rosen and Gregory point out, one must remember that besides disagreements in terminology and uncertainties in differential diagnostic methods there are cultural factors which make it still more difficult to decide what is normal.[27] Norms for comparison, therefore, can hardly be established. O'Connor and Franks state that approximately one out of every three English children needs psychological help, and that about 10% have severe behavior difficulties and 5%–10% mild problems. They do not consider these figures overly reliable, though.[28] Bovet studied average frequencies of onychophagy in France and found that among 6,000 unselected school children 10% had this habit, but when he broke down the group into grade levels, he found great disparities, the frequencies lying between 0% and 50%.[29] Tramer writes that the causation of nail biting can lie in somatic as well as in emotional reasons, or even in hereditary trends. "Onychophagy is, like enuresis, a somato- and psycho-functional symptom. . . ."[30] Dührrsen is convinced that tics are almost always caused by early restriction of motor activity; many of the children she examined had not been allowed to move or talk freely in their early active stages of development.[31] Tramer considers the tic "a somatic complement to psychic conflict," but he adds, and this seems important, that there exists also an "organically (brain pathologically) caused form." Jactitation in Tramer's view is caused by frustration.[32]

Whether dyslexics have more nervous habits than unselected groups of children cannot be established clearly until norms themselves have been established. Whether the nervous habits of dyslexic children are secondary consequences or primary correlates of the dyslexic condition is equally difficult to ascertain as long as all etiological questions in connection with nervous habits are unresolved. We found only one author who raised questions similar to ours. Dongier states: "Enuresis is quite often associated with other troubles of psychomotor development: dyslexia, stuttering, etc. Complementary evidence such as the EEG tend to indicate that enuresis is related, apart from its purely psychological sense (disordered mother/child relationship in particular), to a retarded maturation of the central nervous system."[33] Like Dongier we think that, at least among dyslexic children, nervous habits originate not in early emotional or environmental deprivations, as the psychoanalytical tradition maintains, but rather in organic functional or maturational disorders of the central nervous system. Thus nervous habits are another aspect of the condition which is causing the specific learning disability. In more than 1,000 first interviews with individual parents we found them to be communicative, objective, stable, and normal personalities. Yet, at least 10% of the mothers had sought psychoanalytical help to investigate their feelings of failure and guilt in connection with the child's learning failure. Exceptionally few arrived at any pertinent insight. In time most of them gave up the frustrating and painful search, feeling more guilty and frustrated than before. Schizophrenia may serve as an example here. For years, especially in the United States, psychoanalytical literature considered maternal rejection the most important causative factor in this mental disease, coining the term "schizophrenogenic mother." Scores of women went through years of agonizing psychoanalytic searches for their unconscious rejecting attitudes, only to be left with increased puzzlement and sense of failure.* Although it has long been known that schizophrenia has a hereditary component and that genogenetic as well as histogenetic forms exist, and although, with increasing progress in biochemistry, we come more and more to consider schizophrenia a chemogenetic disease, the myth of causality in the mother-child relationship is dying too slow a death. Dongier's remark about maturational delay in the central nervous system must be taken seriously.

Physiological interpretation of nervous habits gains support in the fact that many nervous habits are observed among preschool age children, i.e., before they have been exposed to failure, pressure, and frustration in the learning situation of the classroom. Linder felt that nervous habits were more obvious and frequent in unrecognized dyslexics and left open the question of which should be considered primary and which secondary.[34,35] Dührssen also cautiously summarized her experiences by stating that she would not be able to decide which came first, the learning or the emotional and nervous disturbances.[36] Our own observations lead us to believe that some day the specific learning and the neurological disorders will be identified as primary partial components, while the psychological and social disorders will be shown to be mostly of secondary order.

---

*A heart-rending, yet cognizant, rendition of one family's plight in this very context was written in book form by Louise Wilson, "This Stranger, My Son," G. P. Putnam's Sons, New York, 1968.

Examination with the chi-square method yielded a significantly higher frequency of nervous habits among the younger age group, i.e., among children between 6 and 13 years of age. As important as it is to know this for the treatment of the younger children, it is not a surprising result, in view of developmental laws. If there is any surprise, it is the fact that, in regard to nervous habits, boys are not more frequently afflicted than girls.

1.5d) Psychosomatic Symptoms

The percentage of children in our study who suffered psychosomatic symptoms was 4.6%. In comparison to other findings this is a small percentage, but it must be considered that only such cases were registered for statistical evaluation in which the symptoms had been medically diagnosed as psychological, not organic in origin. We had to rely on parents' statements in this case, and it must be assumed that not all of them were able or willing to relate all there was to be known. Among the symptoms registered, headaches and stomach aches, including nausea and vomiting, were the most frequent. Asthma and allergies were not included in these figures since diagnosis of pure psychogenic causation in such cases is medically uncertain. We found no comparable studies on the relationship between reading disability and psychosomatic disorders.

Statistically speaking there was a tendency ($\chi^2 = 2.75$, 10% level of confidence) for psychosomatic symptoms to be more frequent among boys than among girls, yet another factor pointing toward the greater biological vulnerability of boys.

1.5e) Referrals to Neurologists

Referral for neurological examination was indicated in 66% of the cases in our sample. The referrals were made either on the basis of symptoms observed during initial testing and background analysis or after prolonged observation in the classroom situation at the Institute. Symptoms leading to referral were sensory or motor disinhibition, nervous habits, hypoactivity, incoordination, poor balance, concentration problems, psychosomatic symptoms, epileptiform absences or spasms, sleep disturbances, motor dysfunctions, etc. Referrals and neurological treatment do not interfere with the child's classroom attendance at the Institute.

Of the 66% referred approximately 25% were seen by the staff neurologist* who, according to personal communication, found minimal neurological signs in almost all of them. In his experience, there have been no cases with specific reading disability and normal intelligence, which are not accompanied by neurological dysfunction—which does not include a judgment on the primary or secondary nature of these dysfunctions.

Specific correlations between minimal neurological symptoms and EEG tracings and reading disability have not yet been discovered, a fact greatly regretted by Grossman.[37] But work has begun and tendencies seem to be emerging. Reitan holds a hopeful position: "The prediction can safely be made that as neurological diagnostic methods are more thoroughly applied and improve in accuracy and validity, damage to the brain . . . will be identified in many persons who presently remain undiagnosed. . . . This situation emphasizes the urgent need for additional research aimed toward identification and classification of these children."[38] It is obvious that we need ever more interdisciplinary teamwork to progress and to develop not only diagnostic and treatment methods but preventive measures.

Probability calculations revealed that significantly more 6 to 13 than 14 to 18 year-old youngsters had to be referred to the neurologist ($\chi^2 = 10.12$, 1% level of confidence); the frequency of referral was also significantly higher for boys than for girls ($\chi^2 = 2.91$, 10% level of confidence).

1.5f) Summary

The symptoms investigated in this chapter, hyperactivity 26%, hypoactivity 18%, nervous habits 39%, and psychosomatic symptoms 4%, certainly must be considered important correlates of reading-spelling disability. How much more often they occur among dyslexics than they do among unselected popu-

---

*Ray van Meter, M.D., neurologist and psychiatrist.

lations cannot be clearly estimated until comparable norms have been developed.

Further knowledge about etiological factors depends largely on team effort and cooperation between various disciplines. The most significant contribution can probably be expected to come from neurological and psychoneurological investigations. A neurological theory of learning processes would provide insight into the various functional systems involved in the learning process. In accordance with concepts evolved in cybernetics we begin to see the nervous system as an open system of complex structure, interrelationships, functions, and organization in which communication processes (input, feedback, output, etc.) take place partially independently and partially in combinations involving alternately independent or interrelated parts of the total system. Recent studies suggest that children with learning problems show disturbances especially in the feedback mechanisms. In the predominantly visual or auditory forms of dyslexia, for instance, it is suspected that the related neurosensory systems have either disorders within themselves or in their capacity to interact with other systems, needed for flawless performance. Johnson and Myklebust, for example, speak of "semiautonomous systems," a concept on which neuropsychological theories of learning will have to be built. Such a theory would assume that the brain consists of two semiautonomous systems: each system sometimes operating semiindependently, sometimes supporting another system, and sometimes both systems working in unity.[39]

Such new insights probably indicate that the full complexity of the neuropsychological foundations of learning have not yet been recognized. Specific learning disabilities apparently have their neuropsychological equivalents in the central nervous system; the afflicted children need highly specialized help, not punishment, neglect, admonition, etc. Teachers, parents, and others concerned with the child, especially psychologists, pediatricians, and such professionals, can no longer be satisfied with the still widely used, but oversimplified labels of "laziness" and "dumbness." Linder's complaint that in Switzerland dyslexic children still go unrecognized and unassisted,[40] certainly applies to many countries. In the United States too few reading clinics are available, and German as well as French authors complain that dyslexic children are still placed in schools for retarded children. The more scientific research succeeds in discovering the neuropsychological complexities on which successful learning processes depend, the more societies will have to strive to diagnose and treat learning disorders intelligently and effectively.

1. 6 Hereditary Indications

1.6a) Review of the Literature

In 108 of our cases the necessary information on hereditary factors could not be obtained; of the remaining 392 there were 39.7% who had one or more (in the majority of the cases it was more than one) close relatives who also had related difficulties in learning, despite normal or better than average intelligence. Most of this information was obtained during initial parent conferences, and it was interesting to see how many parents had never been fully aware of the fact that their child was not the only or first one in the family to have some form of learning disability. Orton had observed that the families of his dyslexics had one factor in common, namely, that they contained two or more cases of "language disability." That there seems to be a hereditary trend, he pointed out, had been long suspected.[41] Our study further confirms this. As hereditary indications we counted: speech impediments, delayed speech development, reading-spelling difficulties, visual-perceptual and/or motor disabilities affecting written language, laterality, spatial or temporal confusion, and other functions necessary for language acquisition in the widest sense. We discovered a relatively high incidence of hereditary indications, almost 40%.

Hereditary factors have been discussed widely in connection with dyslexia. Weinschenk goes so far as to define "congenital" dyslexia as "hereditary"; among the nine cases of his first study, expanded to 13 for the revised publication, he claims 70% were apparently part of a familial trend. Weinschenk mentions that Illing and Warburg held corresponding views. Both dealt with cases of congenital word blindness; Illing's study contained 11 cases, written up in 1929, and Warburg's work, not giving any number, was published in 1911, when only a few severe, psychiatric cases came to the attention of the medical profession. Although Illing suspected localized damage, he admitted that there might be other causes for word blindness.[42]

Lory, examining 122 slow readers comparable in many ways to our sample, had 12 cases with defects which were evidently heredity and 8 more in which a hereditary factor seemed likely. This represents 9.8% and 6.5% respectively, or 16.3% total. Like many other authors he describes the difficulties investigators encounter in questioning parents: not all want to admit to other shortcomings in the family, others cannot rely on their memory. In cases of death, divorce, adoption, etc., the facts are lost or blurred. Thus, Lory concludes that the actual percentage might be higher than it appears.[43] Linder observed many families in which several members had reading difficulties and estimated their number as 40%;[44,45] this corresponds very closely with our actual quantitative findings. Schenk-Danziger had, among 100 dyslexics, 11 whose parents or siblings also suffered specific reading-spelling disabilities.[46] Kobi was aware that in several of his cases there was a familial tendency toward disturbances of speech, reading, writing ability, and/or left-handedness.[47] Kocher, after perusal of statistical figures from various countries, concluded that dyslexia was "often hereditary."[48] Similarly Kretschmer wrote that dyslexia is "very often" a hereditary phenomenon.[49]

Biglmaier finds the question of heredity too incompletely investigated as yet.[50] In the English literature we find that Morgan wrote in 1896 that the isolated reading disability called alexia or word blindness is not always due to organic brain damage, but can also occur as an inherited defect.[51] An interesting account of the early awareness and study of specific reading disabilities can be found in Critchley who discusses the classic studies conducted by Kussmaul, Berlin, Hinshelwood, Berkhan, Orton and others.[52] Critchley himself believes that the reading disability syndrome can be constitutional, can be traced to environmental inadequacies, and is often, if not always, genetically determined.[53] He emphasizes that these cases are difficult to identify and that quantitative findings are unreliable as long as no broadly based studies exist.[54] Despite his inclination toward genetic interpretation he also supports one of the newer explanatory theories, namely that of maturational delay in the nervous system.[55]

Hallgren and Hermann also represent those who support hereditary interpretations. In 1950 Hallgren published an analysis of 276 cases and concluded that "specific dyslexia" follows a dominant mode of inheritance.[56] Hermann presented evidence of hereditary influences and also found increased frequency of crossed dominance, right-left disorientation, and finger agnosia. He became convinced that heredity played a decisive part in dyslexia while environmental factors were of little importance.[57] Hermann presented a summary of studies on twins made by Hallgren in 1950 and by Norrie in 1954: in all of the 12 monozygotic pairs investigated both twins were word-blind; this constitutes 100% concordance in the cases studied. Of 33 dizygotic pairs only one third showed concordance.[58] However, twin births are often more complicated and the babies themselves are often immature, thus the likelihood of brain injury or developmental lag is increased so one must be extremely careful in drawing conclusions based on twin studies. Concordance in twins is not sufficient proof of genetic origin.

Vernon rejected Hallgren's suggestion that dyslexia follows a dominant mode, claiming this theory was not well enough tested, and advanced instead her theory of cortical maturational delay, admitting that there might be a congenital predisposition leading to a familial pattern of reading, speech, dominance, and coordination problems.[59] Similarly, Money stated that the etiology might well be primarily genetic, but, he added cautiously, increased frequency of certain symptoms within a family does not necessarily prove heredity, apparently members living in the same milieu and learning atmosphere influence each other's attitudes.[60] This, too, is a valid criticism of genetic theories.

In their studies Rabinovich,[61] Whitsell,[62] Rabkin,[63] and Blaine and McArthur[64] all observed familial tendencies, often spread over several generations. However, few quantitative findings have been presented to date.

With regard to causation two German authors made almost identical remarks within the same year. Biglmaier,[65] and Weinschenk,[66] on the basis of the observation that 70%–80% of all cases were males, concluded that a mode of inheritance typical to the male gender was involved. Since, however, boys are three to four times more frequently afflicted with birth injury, behavior disorders, etc., heredity may not necessarily be the basis of it. As we suggested earlier, greater physical and emotional vulnerability, more complex developmental patterns, different attitudes toward and expectations of boys are also possible explanatory factors.

Application of probability calculations disclosed no significant disparities of frequency; hereditary indications were equally distributed within the sex and age groups of our sample.

1.6b) Summary

The significance of heredity as a factor related to dyslexia has been under discussion for many years, but not enough exact research with quantitative findings is presently available. The few frequency data involving observed hereditary signs, gleaned from German literature, are summarized here:

Schenk-Danziger	11%
Lory	16%
Klasen	39%
Linder	40%
Weinschenk	70%

Although the English and French literature does not offer quantitative data, nobody seems to doubt that hereditary factors are clearly associated, and that there exists a genetic form of dyslexia. Since no agreement has been reached with regard to exactly which criteria should be considered as indicative of heredity, it is not surprising that the few quantitative data so far accumulated vary widely, ranging from 11% to 70%. More research in this area is needed.

2. PSYCHOPATHOLOGICAL FINDINGS*

2.1 Secondary Symptoms

Dyslexia never exists as an isolated symptom. It is always accompanied by associated and/or secondary complications. The whole person is always affected. It would be important and interesting to know which of the psychopathological difficulties of retarded readers are primary co-symptoms and which are secondary consequences, but clarification of this question is extraordinarily difficult. The dyslexic, if not very early identified, gets caught in a vicious circle leading from learning to behavior problems and from behavior problems to increased learning disability. In any individual case it is often impossible to determine where the spiral originated. Mucchielli and Bourcier described most eloquently the typical plight of these children.[1] Our own experience and impressions, gained in individual interviews with more than 1,000 families, strongly confirm their lucid description.

From our general observation we concluded that psychological difficulties increase in direct proportion to the duration of unrecognized and untreated dyslexic learning problems. Occasionally there are adult illiterates at the Raskob Institute who are socially maladjusted and suffer from severe personality disorders. Their long-term rehabilitation through psychological and educational, often also medical, therapy proves successful in most cases, at least to an appreciable extent. This seems to prove an important point, namely, dyslexia could potentially destroy a human life, whereas rehabilitation, at least to a satisfactory degree, is possible, even in most severe cases.

---

*A table summarizing all findings discussed in this chapter is presented in the appendix in Table C.

Because of the complexities of the dyslexic condition it is most difficult to decide, in individual cases as well as in regard to groups, which symptoms should be considered secondary and which primary. In the following chapter we discuss, for example, concentration problems which are such a widespread correlate of reading disability. Does the inability to concentrate cause the reading-spelling problem, is it part of the same original inability, or is it an understandable reaction to failure? Obviously, this is not necessarily an either-or proposition. Similarly, anxiety is observed in no less than 65% of our sample: is the anxiety the cause of the inability to concentrate, does this inability cause anxiety, or are they simply co-existing aspects of one basic disturbance? Only in a few cases can secondary symptoms be clearly separated from the primary condition; for example, when emotional or behavioral difficulties clearly start at the time the child first experiences learning failure in the classroom. In other cases the child might start out as a good student, but develop learning problems after some stressful situation caused emotional problems. Such clear-cut onsets of life situations are rare, however, and could easily be no more than a hypothetical construct in the mind of the observer. In reality the beginnings of these complex conditions are insidious, unnoticed at the time, and later poorly recalled and distorted by rationalizations. The child himself has little introspection and is very limited in memory as well as verbalization. Certainly, that which at one point was a reactionary and therefore secondary symptom, becomes at another point a primary one for some other problem; after several years of such increasing interlaced complications it becomes nearly impossible to untangle the situation.

On the basis of the quite large number of cases we have observed and treated, we can conclude only that clearly and exclusively psychologically caused dyslexia is extremely rare. More important than the question of origin is an inquiry into whether there are certain kinds of psychopathological disturbances which occur especially often among slow readers. Are they as a rule aggressive, maladjusted, or are they introverted, anxious, withdrawn, infantile? Are there any patterns, any characteristics that could be considered typical?

2. 2 Observed Frequencies of Psychopathological Reactions

2.2a) Anxiety

No fewer than 65.0% of the children in the sample of 500 showed symptoms of anxiety. Some of these signs could be considered "normal" in certain circumstances or to a certain degree. However, we registered only those which were abnormally frequent, persistent, or severe. We had to depend on our own psychological observations during testing and interviewing, on the reports of parents, teachers, physicians, etc., and on observations during classroom attendance at our Institute. The relatively high proportion identified in the sample appears less surprising if it is considered that this group contains many of those already previously discussed under the headings of nervous habits, psychosomatic symptoms, hyper- and hypoactivity, etc.

Anxiety constitutes by far the most frequently observed variant in our material; even the next most frequent, lack of concentration, lies about 26% lower. Burfield investigated 116 students referred to her reading clinic, and she found that the most frequently associated psychopathological symptoms were "anxiety, fear and withdrawal."[2] Marks reports that among the five complaints which most often caused parents to seek child guidance were "nervousness, sleep disturbances and anxiety."[3] Witty and Kopel estimated that about one-half of the severely retarded readers presented for psychological evaluation showed fear and anxiety to such a degree that no remediation could have been successful unless treatment was provided simultaneously to relieve the anxiety and to increase self-confidence.[4] Roudinesco and Trelat identified three groups of typical symptoms among dyslexics, one of these consisted of "anxiety, pavor nocturnus, irritability and restlessness."[5] Lory points out that speech is often affected by anxiety; one is speechless, loses one's voice, seems unable to breathe, becomes hoarse, cannot get a word out, etc., at moments of fear. Lory considers anxiety as "still the most widespread type of emotional disturbance, although we may want to believe that we live in a world where everything is orderly, clear and under control."[6]

From a psychological point of view the frequency with which anxiety occurs is more readily understood if we keep in mind that once anxious reactions have developed they are dissolved only slowly and with difficulty. Dührssen, on the basis of broad psychological experience, especially in the treatment of children, states that only slow and patiently administered psychotherapy will produce enduring results.[7]

De Hirsch, interestingly, discovered that the prematurely born children whom she studied were predisposed to anxiety for two reasons: their reduced developmental pace made their mothers anxious, and this anxiety was transmitted to the children; secondly their physiological maturational lag poorly equipped them to cope with the academic learning experience. She quotes other authors who also observed that children with defective or vulnerable nervous systems, with developmental delays, and other physiological disorders, were less able to cope with stress. She points out that this is an important finding in view of the fact that more than 4% of all American school children are born prematurely.[8]

The question has been raised whether the anxiety of the disabled reader will impede or improve learning ability. Experiments have been conducted and results were contradictory. According to our own observations the answer is dependent on the intensity or degree of anxiety. Minor anxious tension, arising from the desire to please authority figures, to excel before peers, etc. can be a valuable stimulant. Severe anxiousness, however, overriding all other feelings and making the person acutely uncomfortable, is a deterrent in the attempt to concentrate, to exert prolonged effort. Behavior observation at the Raskob Institute revealed clearly that most children suffer from a handicapping degree of anxiety, so much so that learning can take place only after it has been reduced. Anxiety reduction does not always require psychological help in the specific sense of the term, but can usually be accomplished through a therapeutic and understanding teaching-learning atmosphere, created by trained and experienced reading specialists.

In short, anxiety, usually of pathological intensity, is the most frequently observed and most important correlate in dyslexia, deserving special attention and necessitating patient therapy, either in a therapeutically oriented classroom atmosphere or in specific psychotherapy. Only after a thorough individual personality assessment of each case is it possible to determine which method should be applied.

2.2b) Poor Concentration

Lack of concentration was observed in 39.0% of our sample. Poor concentration rarely exists in isolation, but is usually found in association with motor disinhibition, anxiety, hypoactivity, etc. The inability to concentrate manifests itself as a lack either of intensity or of duration. Some, of course, cannot focus their attention either intensively or extensively; they have a short attention span, are easily distracted, are inattentive, change the subject, are careless, absentminded, or they daydream, disrupt the activity, make ready excuses, etc.

There is surprisingly little mention of concentration disability in connection with reading-spelling disorders. We were not able to find more than two quantitative studies providing comparable results. Kirchhoff studied 66 children of normal intelligence who were from 6 to 18 years old. Although he had excluded hypoactive children from his sample, he still found concentration problems in 15 boys and 4 girls. This would be 28.8% of the whole group.[9] Linder found 40% in her sample whom she characterized as "nervous, restless, distractible, unconcentrated."[10] Prechtl reports that 50% of the parents of his 50 slow readers were aware of their children's undisciplined behavior, their inability to concentrate and to persevere in any activity; this usually had started at a very early age, long before school attendance.[11]

Bennett found no outstanding psychological abnormalities among retarded readers, but did comment on their inability to concentrate for any considerable period of time; Karlsen mentioned that his "word callers" could not persist in attention; Wolfe compared nine slow readers with a group of normally reading boys and found that the slow readers had shorter attention spans and were less persistent in effort.[12]

We agree with Lory who states that it is futile to inquire whether dyslexia or the inability to concentrate appears first, and that only the fact that they are frequently associated is important.[13] Johnson and Myklebust consider inattention as manifestation of the child's inability to successfully integrate sensory information: ". . . simply a warning that the nervous system is unable to comply with its demands; the system is overloaded . . ."[14] Strang also considers distractibility as possibly organically based.[15]

The chi-square formula revealed significantly more concentration problems among our younger age group ($\chi^2 = 35.8$, 1% level of confidence). This is indicative of the number of maturational delays represented in our sample and it also tends to confirm the belief that concentration problems are closely related to, if not caused by, organic dysfunction. In our own sample lack of concentration was most pronounced in cases where there were also hyperactivity, anxiety, reduced impulse control, and nervous habits. All of these constitute the typical minimal brain damage syndrome. "Hyperactivity, distractibility, impulsiveness and emotional instability may be considered to be general personality characteristics of the brain-injured child," writes Strother.[16] Neurologists and psychologists must combine efforts in this area in order to assist teacher and child in the difficult pursuit of learning.

2.2c) Immaturity

No less than 33.2% of the poor readers in our sample were diagnosed as immature. Their comprehension, social attitudes, emotional maturity, etc. were visibly below their chronological age. This is not a unique or surprising fact; many researchers are aware of the great incidence of infantile characteristics among retarded readers. Kirchhoff identified 38 boys, 6 girls.[17] Kobi, not giving any numbers, estimates, from his experience, that up to 70% of the slow readers he works with are immature; he calls the infantile personality a "main criterion" of the dyslexic child.[18] Biglmaier saw immaturity also, but more in connection with constitutional and organic factors.[19] Kirchhoff requests that in view of the often observed developmental delay much of what appears like psychological immaturity should be seen as belonging to a primary organic syndrome.[20] Linder counted no fewer than 44% of her dyslexics as "apparently infantile."[21] Hunger-Kaindlstorfer characterized 35 out of 113 cases as "infantile";[22] this is 30.9% and thus is closest to our own percentage. Lobrot found dyslexics "generally more childish, attracted to simple activities and objects."[23]

It is psychologically easy to see why the dyslexic child would tend to regress to or to remain in the relative security of immaturity; there, less will be expected of him, he does not need to think ahead, to take on responsibility, to cope with a world which seems frightening to him, which he feels inadequate to cope with. Kleiner speaks in this connection of "psychological retardation" producing "infantile characteristics," a process which he witnessed especially often in cases with severe dyslexia.[24] Lory examined 122 dyslexics and found that 40 of them showed "disproportioned maturity"; this represents 32.8% of the group.[25]

Not all of the quantitative findings are directly comparable, yet they seem valuable enough to summarize here in tabular form:

Hunger-Kaindlstorfer	30%
Lory	32%
Klasen	33%
Linder	44%
Kirchhoff	60%

This table does not include estimates which are not based on statistical material. Although the findings range from 30% to 60%, due to varying criteria of selection, these high figures seem to support the theory held by Schenk-Danziger, as well as by Kirchhoff, that dyslexia is an "infantile symptom, a partial maturational delay."[26]

In Anglo-Saxon writings on dyslexia, infantilism finds little mention. The terms "maturational lag" and "developmental delay" are often used but have clearly neurological, organic connotations. Among the secondary symptoms anxiety, withdrawal, and aggression are frequently listed, but immaturity in a more psychological context was described only by De Hirsch who classified 5 out of her 8 "failing readers" as "infantile."[27]

She is today the most prominent representative of the theory of maturational delay. To find clear-cut correlations between physiological and psychological components of reading disability remains a wide open field for research. Kocher writes justifiably: " . . . dyslexia is usually psychophysiological in origin. It is based in the higher nervous system, located in the cerebral cortex, the seat of every form of behavior, particularly in man."[28]

2.2d) Low Frustration Tolerance

We counted 31.2% children in our sample whose frustration tolerance was lowered to the point of making it difficult for them to face even minor tasks or tensions. In testing, in learning situations, in the family and everyday life situations these children avoid any kind of confrontation that might involve or necessitate frustration tolerance. The ways and means by which they try to escape are so numerous and vary to such a degree that no general description can be given. Berna thought that these students had experienced so much frustration and failure, were so devoid of positive sensations, that they appeared indifferent, lazy, resigned, tired, discouraged, defeated.[29] Frustration intolerance indeed stifles ambition, confidence, and the ability to postpone gratification or to work toward long-distance goals. The child himself often complains of being bored at school, and it is amazing how many parents consider this sufficient explanation. Only a few seriously question why this physically healthy and mentally normal child is persistently "lazy, bored, unmotivated." Clements asks his adult readers what their frustration might look like if they were in the child's place and knew only the rudiments of reading and writing.[30] Orton discussed "frustration reactions" in the form of avoidance, self-defeat, carefully cultivated indifference, etc.[31] We are confronted here, again, with the familiar vicious circle, described eloquently by Mucchielli and Bourcier: " . . . That such determinations may well become the models of reactionary conduct, to generalize and to be transposed . . . in proportion to an excessive sensitization to frustration. . . "[32] The low frustration threshold of the retarded reader proves a resis-

tant, tenacious adversary in the remediation process. The classroom in particular apparently causes such stress for the frustration sensitized student that cooperation becomes impossible, an
observation shared by Mucchielli and Bourcier also.[33] Müller[34]
stimulated Kirchhoff into saying that the secondary emotional
overlay observed in dyslexics was based on persistent frustrations, caused during early reading classes. These frustrations
can easily lead to neurotic attitudes toward school, learning,
and life in general and may eventually cause severe personality
changes.[35] This brings to mind the well-known frustration-
aggression theory developed by Dollard and his co-workers:
the more unresolved frustration the greater the chance for
aggressive reaction.

2.2e) Withdrawal

There were 20.6% children in the sample who had to be described as withdrawn. They were reticent, evasive, unrespon-
sive, passive, distant, aloof, expressionless, uninvolved, unwill-
ing or unable to communicate, to participate, to actively interact, or to establish rapport. Many of them willing, friendly, and
well inclined, but cannot reach out of their shells. This kind of
withdrawal thrives in the fertile soil of failure at school, disapproval at home, ridicule among peers, and similar negative
reactions from the environment of the failing learner. Even in
play therapy these children are most difficult to reach. They
have no desire, no preference, no likes or dislikes, no opinion,
no feelings—apparently. They avoid any type of exposure to be
safe from negative reactions. In cases of more severe withdrawal psychotherapy must precede reading therapy.

Kobi thinks that about 70% of the retarded readers he sees
tend to be withdrawn, to avoid conflict, to hold back, to shun
friends, even tend to break existing friendships.[36] Biglmaier
also describes slow readers who keep to themselves, cannot be
challenged, tend to daydream.[37] Spache found many "autistic,
withdrawn, resisting contacts."[38] Gates had a whole group of
"loners" among 100 retarded readers. Holmes and Robinson
observed three symptoms especially frequently, "withdrawing
tendencies" was one of these.[40,41] Among 116 dyslexics Burfield

recognized that the secondary overlay consisted most often of anxiety, fear, and social isolation.[42]

As these quotations from European and American literature show, nobody doubts that withdrawal is a frequently occurring correlate of dyslexia. Not many quantitative data have been collected so far since such psychopathological traits are difficult to transfer into measurable quantitative data and agreement with regard to selective principles and terminology is hard to obtain. Nevertheless, in the individual concrete case the withdrawal symptoms must be recognized and ameliorated before the child can be expected to fully benefit from reading therapy.

2.2f) Aggression

Statistical analysis demonstrated that 14.6% of our slow readers were aggressive in a general, not a delinquent sense of the term. Their behavior was marked by forwardness, hostility, negative criticism, defiance, irritability, disruption, contradiction, threatening, verbal abuse, etc. Dührssen differentiates three kinds of aggression and all are represented in our sample: rage out of self-defense, hate out of frustrated love impulses, and mere motor disinhibition.[43] It is easily understandable that dyslexic children would tend to display all three kinds of aggression; they live in an aggression provoking situation. Their learning failure brings them under attack and they strike back; they suffer loss of affection and become hostile; they are hyperactive and therefore constantly admonished or even punished and so they react with violence. In play therapy an amazingly deep frustration-aggression reservoir is often unleashed. Frustration as well as abnormal motor activity are closely related to acting out behavior. Cohn hypothesized that motor impulses which normally are channeled into verbal and graphic expression lead to open or latent aggression in children with speech and reading-writing disabilities.[44] Mucchielli and Bourcier emphasized no less that persisting frustration often causes aggressive behavior as well as a total aggressive outlook on life, often lasting into adulthood.[45] Biglmaier[46] and Lory[47] both give further descriptions and categories of aggression observed among slow readers. Among the 100 dyslexics Linder studied, she described 6% as "active-difficult, gross, disruptive, unmanageable, strong-headed, wild, and occasionally dishonest."[48]

However, among investigators as well as casual observers, there seems to be general agreement that among retarded readers aggressive behavior disorders occur less frequently than more passive and regressive forms. Investigation into probability variations showed that aggressive behavior was equally frequent among the sex and age group of our sample population.

2.2g) Defensive Reactions

In our sample 12% of the children displayed defensive attitudes based on partially repressed and unresolved conflicts. We were not so much confronted here with defense mechanisms in the strict sense, such as occur for instance in the repression of unacceptable sexual impulses, but rather with a deep-rooted insecurity of self-concept, self-worth. This insecurity forms the nucleus of a psychological conflict that leads to defensive reactions in the form of reaction-formulation, rationalization, isolation, denial, fantasy, and related mechanisms. Dührssen writes that experiences of inadequacy and inferiority complexes often are compensated for by exaggerated forcefulness; the diametrically opposed behavior would be neurotic regression into passivity.[49] Feelings of inferiority, lack of self-confidence, ego impairment, persistent anticipation of failure, suspicious attitudes, insecurity, etc. observed in our failing readers are psycho-logically (i.e., the logic of the psyche) understandable defense reactions. In reading therapy they can be such an obstacle in cooperation that psychotherapy is needed first, or at least simultaneously. Since the children are not consciously aware of their defense mechanisms or their deeper motivation, admonition, punishment, appealing to their reason, encouragement and such educational measures remain ineffective or produce even an adverse effect. They become more and more resistant, more difficult to reach. Linder, speaking of regressive, active, and compensatory mechanisms, says of the defensive reactions that they relieve tension momentarily, but provide no way out of the basic dilemma.[50]

It appears that more specific studies of defense mechanisms among retarded readers would provide further and much needed insight which in turn would make treatment more effective.

The chi-square test indicated that in our group defensive reactions were significantly more frequent among primary than among high school students. It may be assumed that children with learning failure, and who have consequently developed defense mechanisms, which always signify severe emotional conflicts, eventually develop such serious and general disorders that they no longer get to a reading clinic. A few receive psychotherapy on the outside and come to the Institute later for specific reading help; still others are able to outgrow their difficulties with increasing maturity, self-consciousness, and motivation. One cannot help wondering how many of the inhabitants of reform schools, corrective and mental institutions were originally undiagnosed cases of learning disability who developed serious personality disorders in reaction to their unrecognized academic, social, and emotional plight.

2.2h) Depression

We found that 10.6% of our dyslexic sample showed marked depressive moods. They were discouraged, unhappy, sad, hopeless, distressed, pained, troubled, dejected, dispirited, and melancholy; some were even despondent. Only children who were chronically afflicted with these depressed moods were selected for sampling. Although many parents and educators are not aware of it, children can suffer depression, as has long been known to the psychiatric profession. Not all childhood depressions go back, as is widely assumed, to early emotional and/or oral frustration. We cannot but agree with Dührssen who considers it "a natural fact" that a positive attitude toward life can only prosper, in children as well as in adults, when confirmation and realization of one's hopes and plans seem within one's grasp.[51] Background investigation confirmed repeatedly, in the case of our children, that their depressive moods became manifest only after a certain amount of failure in the classroom had been accumulated. It would be interesting, of course, if time and methods allowed such an intensive investigation, to find out how many of the depressed children actually also suffered early emotional deprivation and thus were poorly equipped to cope with academic frustration. Punitive attitudes and measures are ineffective in the case of the depressed child. As Berna correctly remarked: unhappiness cannot be forced out of the system, just like happiness cannot be forced into it.[52] Genuine help for the depressed dyslexic can come only through psychotherapy and/or understanding, patient, cognizant reading therapy, aimed at reducing, if ever so gradually, experiences of failure and frustration.

We were not able to find comparable quantitative information on the incidence of depression in connection with reading failure, except that Linder listed 44% of her children as "withdrawn, infantile, anxious, evasive and depressed."[53] Application of the chi-square test disclosed no significant disparities in the distribution of depression among boys and girls, or among younger and older children in our sample.

2.2i) Maladjustment

Only 2.6% of the dyslexic children investigated were socially maladjusted in the sense of being chronically dishonest or guilty of theft, truancy, severe disciplinary infractions or other types of delinquent or criminal conduct. This relatively low percentage cannot be considered representative of the general population of retarded readers, however. Severe maladjustments of the types enumerated are not normally noticed until the teens have been reached and at this point the student is usually in such serious trouble that he no longer finds his way to a reading clinic, but rather to some correctional institution. A more objective picture of the relation between learning failure and social maladjustment could certainly be gained by investigating how many maladjusted youngsters are severely retarded readers with normal intelligence and relatively normal early childhood development. Fabian discovered 10% slow readers in an unselected group of schoolchildren, 33% among children referred for child guidance, 62% among foster children and 83% among a sample of maladjusted youngsters.[54] Tomkins found that 75% of the young delinquents who appear in court in New York were two or more years retarded in reading, and that 50% of these cases had a reading retardation of five or more grade levels.[55] Critchley says the same percentage applies in Paris to all 12 to 16-year-old delinquents.[56] Without mentioning quantitative data Schomburg observed a "remarkably high correlation between reading failure, truancy and delinquency."[57] Kleiner remarked that severe maladjustment is often secondarily recognized as having been caused by dyslexia.[58] Weinschenk feels that 20% of the residents in correctional institutions are dyslexics.[59]

Thus it can be seen that actual findings and general estimates of the proportion of dyslexia among asocial youngsters range from 20% to no less than 83%. Wepman warned that among the potentially criminal inner-city dwellers, reading failures are most likely to become antisocial.[60] In all highly developed civilizations reading-writing ability has become the most important basis of communication, from highly scientific literature to street and traffic signs, menus, directories, advertisements, application forms, etc.; it invades daily life. It is readily understood then that the failing reader soon comes to feel inadequate, isolated, and therefore hostile. Wolf observes that regressive study of maladjusted behavior is often traceable to the trifold complex of reading retardation, truancy, delinquency.[61] All of these observations indicate how important it is to identify and remediate reading problems in their early stages.

2.3 Psychoanalytical Theories as to Etiology

2.3a) Specific Dyslexia as Symptom of Neurotic Conflict

No specific patterns of psychopathological symptomatology in cases of dyslexia have been recognized with certainty so far. This applies especially to those psychoanalysts who consider the reading disability as a secondary symptom caused by some primary neurotic conflict. A number of psychoanalytical theories of causation have been advanced up to date, among them the fear to look (castration anxiety), identification crises (Oedipus and Electra complex), emotional deprivation (hospitalism), oral frustration, phobias, defense mechanisms (repressed aggression, sexual impulses, guilt), etc. Letters for instance may take on symbolic meaning, the "C" may look like an open mouth, ready to bite or devour; numbers may have symbolic significance to the reader, such as the "magic 3" or the "evil 7"; whole words may contain symbolic, magic, animated meaning; the book itself (vagina) and the reading eye (phallus) are not excepted. The refusal to read is thus seen as an attempt to reduce the unconscious anxieties of the neurotic reader. Psychoanalytic theory, in other words, considers reading failure a symptom of unresolved neurotic conflict, not independently caused and followed by neurotic reactions.

Since extensive discussion of these theories is beyond the framework of this study, we provide the interested reader with a list of the better known publications on the subject.*

2.3b) Psychoanalytical Versus Reading Therapy

Most authors in the field agree that only exceptionally few reading disability cases can be psychoanalytically classified and so treated. Our own observations and experiences place us with those investigators who consider the reading disability as a

---

*1. Jarvis, V.: Klinische Beobachtungen über das visuelle Problem bei Lesestörungen, Psyche, Heidelberg, 14:204–220, 1960/61; 2. Müller, R. G. E.: Die Schreib-Lese-Schwäche als neurotoide Legasthenie und als Regressionsphänomen, Schule und Psychologie, 5:266–270, 1958; 3. Blanchard, P.: Psychoanalytic Contributions to the Problem of Reading Disabilities, Psychoanal. Stud. Child, 2:163–187, 1946; 4. Fabian, A.: Reading Disability: An Index of Pathology, Americ. J. Orthopsychiatry, 25:319–329, 1955; 5. Klein, E.: Psychoanalytic Aspects of School Problems, Psychoanal. Stud. Child, 3:368–390; 6. Pearson, G.: Psychoanalysis and the Education of the Child, W. W. Norton, New York, 1954; 7. Sperry, B., et al.: Renunciation and Denial in Learning Difficulties, Americ. J. Orthopsychiatry, 13:69–76, 1943; 9. Wagenheim, L.: Learning Problems Associated with Childhood Diseases Contracted at Age Two, Americ. J. Orthopsychiatry, 29:102–109, 1959; 10. Mann, Helene P.: Some Learning Hypotheses on Perceptual and Learning Processes with Their Applications to the Causes of Reading; A Preliminary Note, The Journal of Genetic Psychology, 90, June 1957, 167–202.

primary condition which frequently causes secondary emotional problems and is potentially able to create even severe neurotic personality disorders. Purely psychogenetic forms of dyslexia are apparently extremely rare.

Lory experienced a few exceptional cases in which psychotherapeutic treatment alone sufficed to remove the dyslexic difficulties.[62] At the Raskob Institute this happened once in seven years. Joss, Leiman, and Schiffman investigated the effectiveness of various methods in the treatment of dyslexia and arrived at the following observation: 40 students were subdivided into 4 groups, Group I had psychotherapy and special reading instruction, Group II had only reading, Group III only psychotherapy, Group IV no help at all; end results indicated positive and definite results in groups I and II which had received instruction, but no definite improvement was registered for groups III and IV.[63] Rabinovitch, interestingly, reports from a psychiatric point of view that according to his experience psychotherapy remains ineffective if not accompanied by remediation efforts; he adds that parents often expect a quick discovery of the underlying concealed conflict which causes the reading failure, but that in reality the problem is a much more complex one.[64] Critchley also considers it erroneous to assume that the neurotic conflict is primary and thus will yield to psychiatric treatment alone.[65] A similar fallacy, naturally, would be to think that each and every dyslexic should have psychotherapy before being admitted for reading therapy; this would, in the majority of cases, unnecessarily postpone the needed remediation while the gap between the student and his grade level performance continued to widen. The greater this discrepancy becomes, the harder and longer the return struggle will be. Only in cases severe enough to block all communication or learning ability is psychotherapy alone indicated; and even in these cases, according to Raskob policy, simultaneous reading therapy is begun at the earliest possible time. Jampolsky agrees, however, that cases of such severity are the exception and not the rule.[66] Bond and Tinker, too, state that psychological difficulties are more frequently the consequence than the causation of reading failure.[67] That psychoanalytical interpretations of reading disability apply to but a few exceptions is even easier to see if one closely examines the readily understood development of emotional overlays. Weinschenk even thought he had found a basic common pattern: at first things go well in school, but during the second grade reading and spelling difficulties become apparent, the child falls behind, the first signs of emotional distress develop, their nature and their speed of growth depending on the individual's personality; school phobia, truancy, etc., end the pattern if the child goes undiagnosed and unaided long enough.[68]

In summary, psychoanalytical theories contribute interesting and important insights into the phenomenon of dyslexia. However, since only a minority of cases suffers from primary neurotic conflicts it must be emphasized that psychotherapeutic treatment alone, especially if initiated routinely and without the benefit of previous psychometric and neurological evaluation, is bound to remain ineffective or even to have diverse effects, resulting in one more experience of "failure." Empirical observation has shown that even in cases of neurotically based reading disability psychoanalytical treatment alone remained unsuccessful in the vast majority of cases. Again it is evident how mandatory interdisciplinary efforts are.

2.4 Psychotherapy Versus Reading Therapy

2.4a) Number of Disabled Readers Free of Emotional Disturbance

That psychotherapy plays an important part in the treatment of reading disability is apparent in view of the fact that only 8.6% of the children in our sample were free of psychopathological symptoms. As a group these excepted children showed the following characteristics:

1. The reading retardation in most cases comprised only one grade level, but in no case more than two.
2. Most of their IQ scores were above 110; quite a few were even around 130.
3. The parents were described in reports as understanding, tolerant, objective, and emotionally stable.

In other words, these children had internal as well as external advantages facilitating compensation.

Linder remarked that of the 50 children in her study only 5, i.e., 10%, were considered free of emotional disturbance.[69] Hunger-Kaindlstorfer arrived at somewhat higher figures: among 113 cases there were 21, or 18.5%, who showed no signs of psychological stress.[70] Two older American investigations, conducted by Challman[71] and Gates,[72] arrived at 25%. Very few authors say they observed no emotional disorder, another minority thinks that all dyslexic children are psychologically abnormal. In summary, there exists a general agreement that the larger proportion of disabled readers suffers from some kind and degree of psychopathology.

2.4b) Number of Disabled Readers in Need of Psychotherapy

Before discussing the various forms of psychological treatment the following summarization is presented in order to provide an overview as to the findings in our own sample:

8.6% were entirely free from psychopathology
63.2% were successfully treated by reading therapy alone
28.6% needed additional psychotherapy

Psychotherapy, the most expensive and time-consuming of the available forms of treatment, is only suggested at the Raskob Institute if tests, observation, and symptomatology indicate that the child would be unable to benefit from instruction alone, or that he would be a disruptive element even in a small group of only two to four.

The psychological measures recommended and/or initiated depend on the age, sex, and general condition of the child and his family. Psychoanalysis, group counseling, family therapy, play therapy, etc., are some of the forms available. Which will be the most effective in any given case cannot be determined by the child's learning disorder or by any one method that could be considered especially helpful in reading disability cases, but must be decided according to the type of psychological, or mental behavior disturbance, by the facilities available, the family constellation and budget, etc. No particular type of psychotherapy is especially valid in the treatment of dyslexia, but it seems clear from many observations that classic psychoanalysis is the least needed and the least effective.

Biglmaier recommends the concentration of therapeutic efforts on the disturbed relationships, the negative attitudes toward the self and toward reading.[73] Hunger-Kaindlstorfer mentions play therapy and verbal therapy as indicated for treatment and amelioration of neurotic symptoms, along with reading therapy.[74]

It is apparent that in the case of disabled readers psychotherapy is confronted primarily with secondary emotional reactions, not with repressed unconscious conflicts stemming from early childhood experience. All psychotherapy must include the parents to some degree; this will be discussed in more detail in the chapter on environmental factors.

2.4c) Reading Therapy and the Reading Therapist

We have stated that the majority of our 500 dyslexics, namely 63.2%, needed "only" remediation. This statement needs to be clarified. We agree with Lory who feels that many parents have oversimplified and unrealistic expectations; expecting that tutoring alone will enable their child to read and write well or at least better.[75] In reality matters are much more complex and complicated. Reading-writing disability almost never exists by itself. Even if approximately 10% are free from psychopathological symptoms and if 30% need and receive psychotherapy, there still remain 60% who besides their learning difficulties suffer various forms and degrees of emotional disorders which have to be included in the rehabilitation program. Therefore, it is a matter of treating the whole child, the total personality, not only the particular scholastic failing of the student. The help offered would be futile if it consisted exclusively of tutoring or even remediation. It must transcend a mere teaching process and become reading *therapy*. By definition then two important aspects are combined in reading therapy: teaching and healing. Together they serve the whole child, meeting his unique needs.

Tamm reports that the transfer of dyslexic boys and girls from regular classrooms to curative reading groups proved necessary and successful in a great number of cases.[76] While Tamm speaks of a "curative learning climate," we prefer to speak of a "therapeutic teaching-learning atmosphere." It is basic policy at the Raskob Institute that the total personality has to be understood, respected, and restored, and that the method has to suit the child, not vice versa. Just as there is no such thing as *the* type of psychotherapy for the retarded reader, there is not *the* kind of reading therapy or reading method. Prerequisite for adequate rehabilitation is the therapeutic atmosphere, free of competition, excess frustration, or pressure, offering a number of choices, methods, ways, and means, not only ready but also able to adjust to the child's particular scholastic and personality needs. All this is possible only if the reading therapist has as much data on the child as can possibly be collected before he is enrolled in the class. The teacher needs to have a file on the child providing him with information on personality, intellectual potential, family, health, school history, scholastic deficiencies, special talents, interests, and so on. Equally important, the teacher must be equipped with basic knowledge in psychology, neurology, and education; he must be familiar with a variety of methods and their implications: which is to be used with whom at what time and in what sequence. In short, the ideal reading therapist is a combination of an experienced teacher and a therapist.

Lory says for Germany that there is talk about the "reading therapist" as if he already existed, while in reality retarded readers are taught by speech therapists, teachers for the mentally retarded, part-time teachers, tutors, and the like.[77] This may still be true of most countries.

As stated, the Raskob Institute is fortunately in the position of training as well as employing reading specialists.* In addition to the qualifications already mentioned, the reading therapist must be able to relate to the child, to attain rapport with the

---

*At the time of this writing, fall 1970, the Raskob Institute has become the Special Education Department of the College of the Holy Names, offering an M.Ed. degree in Special Education.

parents, to cooperate with the interdisciplinary staff, and to
make the personal and intellectual effort to stay ahead of scientific developments in the field.

As Tamm emphasizes, reading therapy must go beyond increasing skills, it must contribute to total personality growth.[78]
Biglmaier stresses that reading therapists need qualified training, preparing each therapist to recognize and remediate scholastic as well as character disorders.[79] Kirchhoff holds that, in
addition to proper teaching techniques, the therapist's ability to
see and treat the total personality is the most decisive qualification he needs to bring to his work.[80]

2.4d) Rapport and Reading Resistance

Observation and experience prove those writers to be correct
who claim that to attain some measure of rapport during the
beginning stages of reading therapy is a most important pre-
requisite for future success. Sensitized against frustration as
most students are before they come to the therapist, they have
developed a multitude of methods and means to resist reading
as well as being taught to read. It can easily be seen how this
would require a knowledgeable and stable personality on the
part of the therapist. Some authors even think that the very
first session is the most decisive; Mucchielli and Boucier write:
"The very first session is particularly important to the fate of
the reeducation."[81]

Anxiety and reading resistance are the natural consequence
of reading failure and of parents or teachers who treat the
student as either "lazy" or "dumb." Admonition punishment,
increased pressure, deprivation, scolding, ridicule, repeating
grades, etc. have caused withdrawal, resistance, ego impairment, and other difficulties before the child finally comes to the
reading clinic. Yet, in the face of all this adversity, as Tamm
also points out,[82] it is necessary that the reading therapist
arouse the child's own initative, his self-confidence, will to
learn, desire to cooperate of his own volition. Only success
along this line will make the therapeutic teaching process
efficacious and speedy. Chassagny writes: "One should never
lose sight of the fact that success is improbable unless the child

shows himself to be cooperative."[83] And Rey says in this context: ". . . it is essential that the child himself, most often a discouraged one, assumes a new attitude toward this mystery which fluent reading is for him."[84] Kocher stresses the need for patience on the part of the therapist in attempting to replace old conditioned reflexes through new and better ones. In this he is a spokesman for many other writers with closely corresponding views on the attitudes needed by the reading therapist.[85]

2.4e) Individual or Group Instruction; Frequency and Duration

Whether reading therapy should be individual or group therapy has been disputed by a number of experts. Our own experience has made it clear that there is no conclusive resolution to this dispute. In each case the setting in which the student might have an optimum chance to benefit from instruction must be decided; and sometimes the setting must be progressively adjusted for an individual, so that he receives one form of instruction first, then, depending on progress made or not made, another. No group at Raskob contains more than four children. Individual instruction is provided for special cases which for various reasons would not be suited for group settings. Groups small enough to still allow close individual attention to each student, yet providing the support of others sharing the same struggle and progress, have proved to be ideal for the great majority of retarded readers. The child who had considered himself a sad and isolated exception now finds that he is not alone, sees others who have the same kind of problem, of feelings, of fears and hopes; these students come to encourage and help each other if the therapist is experienced in group guidance and knows how to use interpersonal relationships as a healing factor.

Just as there is no uniquely valid form of psychotherapy or teaching method, so there is no exclusively valid setting. The selection of setting must be based on each student's personality, age, intelligence, reading-writing delay, type of learning disability, etc. Thus we cannot agree with Hunger-Kaindlstorfer's recommendation that all reading therapy be initially individual.[86] A group can offer very valuable social and emotional support from the beginning. Only extremely restless, anxious, or inhibited youngsters whose symptoms would increase in a group or who would severely interfere with its proceedings should initially receive individual instruction, but always, with the goal of "promoting" them as early as possible to group attendance. In a few exceptional cases the student's chronological age may be so far above his reading level that an effort has to be made to narrow this gap in individual instruction before transfer to group participation.

Optimal length of a reading therapy session also varies with individuals. There seems to be some general agreement, however, that two to three weekly sessions, each lasting 20 to 45 minutes, yielded the best results. Relevant considerations are: the younger the child or the more disturbed he is, the more it is advisable to have him attend morning sessions; the lesson should be short enough to avoid excessive frustration or fatigue; breaks, changes in activity, often even breathing and physical exercises, should take place between short teaching-learning periods. (This is extremely necessary because most dyslexic children are quite disturbed when they first come to the reading clinic.) Older students, as a rule, can tolerate later and longer sessions.

This study may appear to neglect the significance of the didactics involved in reading therapy, because it is a psychological more than an educational investigation of the dyslexic syndrome. Although didactics are doubtlessly one of the most decisive factors in the rehabilitation of the disabled reader, they cannot be discussed within the framework of this study.

2.4f) Teamwork

Interdisciplinary cooperation is a necessity if we are to deal effectively with so complex and interwoven a syndrome as dyslexia. Mosse calls for such teamwork, listing pedagogy, linguistics, experimental psychology, clinical psychology, brain pathology, clinical neurology, psychoanalysis and child psychiatry as those scientific branches which must work together.[87] One is tempted to add pediatrics, developmental psychology, speech therapy, special education, etc. In addition, ideally, the representatives of each of these disciplines should have at least some knowledge of the others so that exchange of ideas can take place and that research can be shared.

Biglmaier rightfully includes parents as part of the team[88] and Lory considers the reading therapist as the coordinator of the various measures to be taken.[89]

A clamoring for team approach can be heard in many countries, but seems to have been realized in few places. Ellehammer does not speak only for Denmark in asking that neurologist, psychiatrist, educator, psychologist, and sociologist work together in order to get a better grasp of the complexities of reading and behavior disabilities.[90] The Raskob Institute is in the fortunate position of having had exercises in the interdisciplinary team approach under one roof for the past ten years. Whitsell's just call for greater cooperation as well as weekly staff conferences and case discussions[91] has been practiced at the Institute for an equal number of years. The team need not necessarily be assembled under one roof, but interdisciplinary teamwork is a necessity if we are to succeed with research, diagnosis, treatment, and prevention of dyslexia. Just as a whole and complex person is affected by this condition so we must direct our efforts toward a holistic approach.

2.4g) Summary

With regard to psychopathological symptoms, the controversy of secondary versus primary signs is largely futile, but a few experts doubt that dyslexia is usually associated with some emotional disturbance. The few quantitative figures available showed that only between 10% and 25% of all retarded readers are free from psychopathological symptoms. Our own sample showed that these few had internal and/or external compensatory assets.

Although there seems to be no specific emotional syndrome peculiar to dyslexia, it is apparent that anxiety is by far the most often observed symptom. Several studies confirmed this and Ephron, who treated and analyzed a variety of cases, wrote that she never encountered two identical cases, but individual dynamic constellations. An undercurrent of anxiety, however, was noticeable in all of them.[92]

According to our findings concentration problems, immaturity, and frustration intolerance followed in order of frequency. Between 10% and 20% were withdrawn, aggressive, defensive, or depressed. Only 2.6% were antisocial or delinquent.

A look at Table C in the appendix illustrates readily that aggressive reactions are less frequent among dyslexics than regressive ones. Most researchers seemed to agree on this point. While psychoanalysts tend to consider an underlying neurotic conflict the cause of reading disability, most educators, physicians, psychologists, and other experts seem convinced that most psychopathological symptoms constitute a secondary emotional overlay formed in reaction to learning failure. Individual and differential diagnosis is needed if we are to understand each case in its own right, its unique complexity, and singular needs.

Reading therapy was defined as a combination of teaching and healing, necessitating a holistic approach, a well trained and well intentioned reading therapist, the cooperation of a team of specialists and the involvement of the parents. It was pointed out that there is no uniquely valid form, group or individual, or length and frequency of instruction. As with methods and didactics, the ways and means must be selected and applied according to individual needs. The method must suit the student, not the student the method. Small groups, short and spaced sessions, interlaced with physical and breathing exercises, seem best in most cases. While psychotherapy and medication play an important part in the rehabilitation process, the majority of dyslexics can be helped significantly through reading therapy alone. The therapeutic teaching-learning atmosphere is the most decisive factor in the restoration of personality and learning ability.

3. TESTPSYCHOLOGICAL FINDINGS

3.1 Dyslexia and General Intelligence

The question is still raised repeatedly whether specific dyslexia occurs in association with mental retardation; whether it should be considered as a partial intelligence defect. General observation, however, and research figures accumulated by investigators in a variety of places and countries, clearly indicate that reading disability occurs in students with average, above, or below average degrees of intelligence. Thus there is a disparity between language ability and mental ability. It can be assumed that language acquisition in the widest sense does not depend exclusively upon general intelligence but also upon specific factors such as visual, auditory, motor, or verbal functions, and it is not contradictory at all that intelligent children present specific learning disabilities. Whether one is inclined to term reading disability a "partial and curable intelligence defect" or "unrealized intelligence," as Lory[1] does, or as something else of this kind, seems to be a semantic question and of little practical implication. Intelligence is a complex and elusive concept, definable and measurable only in terms of certain achievements, functions, skills. It cannot be observed or made tangible and cannot be tested in isolation from previous learning. In short, it would appear wise to concentrate on more operational definitions and concrete observations.

At present not all investigators agree as to the frequency of correlation between the lower extremes of intelligence and dyslexia. Opinions differ among European as well as among American investigators. We agree with Schenk-Danziger who remarked that significant reading-spelling retardation can be found in association with any intelligence degree, often also causing lower achievement in arithmetic,[2] and with Biglmaier who stated that significant disparities between general learning potential, as measured by tests, and reading ability can be found often and easily.[3] Thust also was convinced of the independence of reading retardation from the intelligence factor.[4] Lory, on the contrary, found that of 122 retarded readers 50% had below average intelligence and concluded that mental retardation was a good breeding ground for reading disability.[5]

In the United States Bills studied 22 dyslexics and found four with IQ's above 130 and four others with above average IQ's.[6] Gofman[7] confirmed the experience Malmquist[8] reported in Sweden, namely, that dyslexia can be seen in connection with all degrees of intelligence: ". . . this discovery — that poor reading ability need not necessarily be connected with subnormal intelligence — cannot be overestimated." Critchley in Great Britain wrote: "This syndrome of developmental dyslexia is . . . independent of the factor of intelligence and consequently it may appear in children of normal IQ while standing out conspicuously in those who are in the above average brackets."[9] De Hirsch in the United States found among her eight disabled readers IQ's ranging from 94 to 116.[10] Ferdinand in Germany found in a group of 18 severely retarded readers none with a full-scale Wechsler IQ of less than 100, and 13 students had IQ's higher than 100.[11] Lückert also states that the majority of disabled readers has normal intelligence.[12] Three investigators, however, obtained below or low average IQ's among dyslexics. Their samples differ from all others in the sense that the subjects were either delinquents or recipients of some kind of institutional care. All three samples were rather small. Roman worked with 21 delinquent reading failures between the ages of 13 and 16 and detected that their IQ's lay between 65 and 95.[13] Weinschenk saw among 13 delinquents referred for psychiatric evaluation IQ's between 73 and 100.[14] Among 13 eight- to eleven-year-old youngsters in institutional care Strong arrived at a mean IQ of 95.[15] These findings suggest that dyslexia, if associated with low average intelligence, tends to lead to delinquency and other serious problems, rather than that there is a direct association between dyslexia and low mental ability. How much social adjustment is threatened by severe reading retardation was expressed by Werhahn who concludes her study with the remark that she had been prepared to find behavior problems, but not *"of such degree."*[16]

There is an interesting investigation by Kaiser who studied students who despite normal intelligence were failing in school; he discovered that one-third of them were dyslexic.[17]

Efforts to analyze statistically the correlation between dyslexia and intelligence began in 1921–22 when Fildes observed among 89 disabled readers only one with an IQ higher than 89, while 50% of them had IQ's below 70; Gates, in contrast, in a much larger sample had not one reader with an IQ below 80, and the mean intelligence level of her group was above average. Fildes was convinced that there was no connection between intelligence and reading weakness; Gates, however, arrived at statistically significant positive correlations between them.[18a, b] The contradiction contained in these two pioneer studies seems to exist to this day. It appears, however, that more and more investigations lead to the conclusion that dyslexia is independent of the intelligence factor and that it is evenly distributed among all degrees of intelligence. In all such studies, of course, almost insurmountable differences exist in the representativeness of the sample selection, size of the sample, inclination and hypothesis of the researcher, methods employed, interpretation of results, etc. In addition, it is argued by some that the usual intelligence scales do not do justice to dyslexics since these tests involve verbal and visuo-motor abilities, functions especially weak in most retarded readers. Thus Biglmaier was convinced that test results often look much worse than the slow reader's actual mental potential.[19] We tend to agree with Tamm's recommendation that each child should be given a thorough examination with a standardized IQ test regardless of his specific weaknesses since most of the dyslexic children tested obtain quite good results anyway.[20] In the few cases where this is not so it is a matter of differential diagnosis anyway.

3.2 Full-Scale Intelligence Quotients

3.2a) Wechsler IQ's

In Table 1 we present the mean IQ scores, obtained on the Wechsler full scale, by as many researchers as we were able to find in the literature; omitted were findings which did not explicitly state whether or not their IQ scores had been obtained on the Wechsler scale and those samples consisting exclusively of delinquents or youngsters cared for in homes or institutions.

Table 1. Mean Wechsler full-scale IQ scores

Investigators	N	IQ
Schiffman and Clemmens[21]	240	96.0
Graham[22]	65 (WAIS)	97.1
Altus[23]	25	98.6
Kallos[24]	37	99.2
Graham[25]	31 (HAWIK)	100.3
Ferdinand[26]	18 ("minimum")	100.0
Walter[27]	52	105.0
Klasen (present study)	488	106.0
Tamm[28]	21	107.0
Robeck[29]	36	109.7

Figure 2 is a graphic illustration of the empirical IQ distribution in our sample with a theoretical frequency distribution constructed over it. This facilitates comparison between the actual distribution and the ideally expected distribution. This figure immediately brings to mind the very similar frequency distribution (Figure 3) which the test author, David Wechsler, arrived at when he tested 1,508 subjects in order to examine the reliability of his newly constructed scale.

Both empirical curves are asymmetrical and negatively skewed. As Wechsler wrote: "The distribution of our measures, however, is not Gaussian. As can be seen from the figure . . . the histogram is considerably skewed in a negative direction. . . . Some authors also believe that the resulting frequency curve ought to be Gaussian or as nearly Gaussian as possible. The last requirement seems to be a result of the widespread but mistaken belief that mental measures distribute

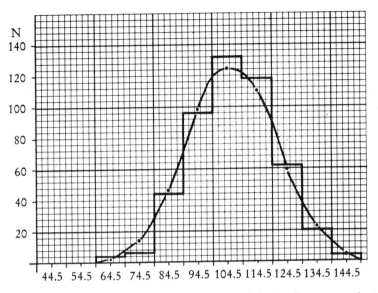

Fig. 2. Frequency distribution of full-scale Wechsler intelligence quotients of 488 slow readers with projected normal curve. Mean IQ = 106.0; standard deviation = 14.8; range = 109.

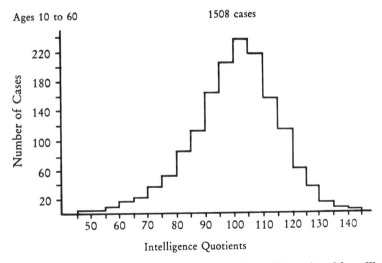

Fig. 3. Distribution of full-scale intelligence quotients. (Reproduced from Wechsler, D.: The Measurement of Adult Intelligence, The Williams and Wilkins Co., Baltimore, 1944, p. 127.)

themselves according to the normal curve of error."[30] The figure which presents the distribution of the Peabody intelligence scores also shows some skewedness to the left. The Goodenough intelligence quotients, however, form a symmetrical curve.

A comparison of the percentages of our cases which fall within the areas of ±1, ±2, or ±3 with those of a theoretical distribution makes it clear how much they resemble each other:

	Normal distribution	Dyslexics
±1	68.3%	70.9%
±2	95.5%	97.7%
±3	99.7%	99.4%

In other words: while normally 0.3% of all measures falls beyond three standard deviations, in our sample this percentage is 0.6%; this fraction does not appreciably change the total picture.

The normal curve was placed over the histogram in order to see whether the irregularities of the histogram could be considered coincidental and whether, in case an infinitely larger sample could have been used, the continuously changing values would eventually turn the histogram into a normal curve. The method used in figuring the theoretical distribution is presented, among others, by Tate,[31] Walker[32] and Hofstaetter.[33] We gained a normal curve which is similar to the Gaussian distribution but not completely symmetrical. Lobrot told the 1965 Psychological Convention on Dyslexia in Berlin, Germany, that American and French studies had long since shown that dyslexics have normally distributed IQ's, although with a slight deviation to the left.[34]

We also used the chi-square formula to test the null hypothesis and to see whether our empirical distribution could be considered a normal one. The method we used is discussed in Hofstätter[35] and Tate.[36] We arrived at a sum of $X^2 = 5.07$. If, as in our case, we have 6 degrees of freedom, a X^2 of 5.07 falls between the probability (P) values of 0.95 and 0.50. In order to reject the null hypothesis, we would have to obtain a X^2 value of at least 12.59 ($P = 0.05$). The distribution of intelligence scores of our dyslexic group, therefore, can be considered a normal distribution and this allows the assumption that dyslexics as a whole have normally distributed intelligence quotients.

To conclude the discussion on central tendency and variability figures we present Table 2. The mean scores for the total group are slightly above the mean obtained by Wechsler: 100.11; the standard deviation was in close correspondence with his: 14.69.[37] There is only a slight tendency for the boys to have higher average scores. The greatest disparity of all was a 7.3 difference in favor of high school boys as compared to high school girls. The least variation of full-scale IQ's, $S = 13.7$, was observed among elementary school age boys; the highest, $S = 17.9$, among high school age girls.

Among the boys it was the older group which obtained slightly higher mean IQ's; this was reversed for the girls. However, here too, the differences were minimal and therefore negligible.

Table 2. Wechsler scale IQ's of 488 dyslexics

Subjects	N	Verbal IQ	s	Performance IQ	s	Full-Scale IQ	s
Total group	488	104.3	14.7	105.5	15.2	106.0	14.8
Elementary school boys	275	106.0	13.9	105.8	13.9	106.5	13.7
High school boys	74	107.0	15.9	108.6	16.0	109.6	16.8
Elementary school girls	99	101.1	15.3	104.1	15.1	104.6	13.8
High school girls	40	99.7	14.3	102.2	17.9	103.0	17.8

Table 3 presents Wechsler scale IQ's as distributed among sex and age groups. This table once more confirms slightly higher scores for boys than girls and slightly higher ones for secondary than elementary school students. Again, the differences are negligible.

The full-scale IQ's are slightly higher than either verbal or performance scores; this can easily happen since the full-scale

Table 3. Distribution of Wechsler scale IQ's
among sex and age groups

Subjects	N (= 488)	Mean Verbal IQ	Mean Performance IQ	Mean Full-Scale IQ
Girls	139	100.7	103.6	104.1
Boys	349	105.8	106.2	107.1
Elementary school students	374	104.6	105.2	105.9
High school students	114	103.4	106.4	107.3

tables are constructed independently of the average values of
the two other parts, separately taking into account each of the
individual subscores. Furthermore, Wechsler himself already
pointed out that except for IQ's of about 100 the full-scale IQ
will not be the average of the two other IQ's: ". . . it should be
noted that except for the IQ's near 100, the IQ of a subject on
the full scale will seldom be equal to the exact average of his
verbal and performance IQ's calculated separately. There will
usually be a difference between them of one or two points,
which will increase as the IQ's become smaller. Thus for mean
IQ's of about 60, the difference between the IQ obtained . . .
may amount to as much as 4 or 5 points. Conversely, the full-
scale IQ above 100 will tend to be a little higher than either
verbal or performance IQ. These discrepancies result from the
fact that the IQ distribution curves for the full, performance,
and verbal scales differ somewhat in form."[38]

In summary, the mean intelligence scores of our group fall
into the upper area of the range designated as "normal average." The IQ scores are normally distributed and standard
deviations correspond with the norm. The total range of 109
presents a standard deviation of 7.3, thus conforming closely to
the $S = 8$ obtained by Wechsler on an unselected "normal"
population.[39] Neither the sexes nor the age groups showed
significant disparities among each other.

3.2b) Goodenough Draw-a-Man Test IQ's

This easy-to-administer test was developed by Goodenough[40] in 1926 and could be given to the 138 children in our group who had not yet passed the maximum age level of ten years. Test performance is scored according to detail, proportion, and coordination displayed in the drawing. In addition to intelligence and maturity factors, test performance here is influenced by body image, fine motor control, visual-perceptual, and related functions. Considering that almost one-half of the subjects in our sample were poor in these areas, it is not surprising to see that the mean IQ for the whole group — 95.5 — was appreciably lower than the Wechsler full-scale IQ of 106.0, and the Peabody IQ of 105.8. Separate calculations revealed mean Goodenough IQ's of 94.3 for boys and 95.2 for girls, a difference of less than one point.

It is interesting to compare the Goodenough mental age scores (MA) with the chronological age of children (CA):

1. MA below CA	86 cases =	62.3%
2. MA above CA	43 cases =	31.2%
3. MA and CA identical	5 cases =	3.6%
4. Extreme disparity	4 cases =	2.9%
5. Total	138 cases =	100.0%

The fourth group, looked at more closely, has this distribution:

MA 4 years 5 months above CA	1 boy
MA 4 years 5 months below CA	1 boy
MA 4 years 6 months below CA	1 boy
MA 4 years 0 months below CA	1 girl

These results show that twice as many children had mental age scores falling below their chronological ages. Disparities range from one month to four years six months in the extreme cases. Only 3.6% had totally congruent mental and chronological age scores. It is often pointed out that the Goodenough Test is not only an intelligence but also a personality test, and that the mental age scores are a truer picture of the child's development than the IQ scores obtained by it. Harris in the United

States revised the original scale. According to his findings statistically significant score differences for boys and girls occurred in the age groups between 5 and 15 years; the girls had the higher IQ scores. This fact was interpreted by Harris in terms of cultural, developmental, and personality factors.[41] Harris and Goodenough both mention that by 1905 Kerschensteiner collected almost one hundred thousand drawings which led him to conclude that the boys excelled over the girls in all drawings, except those involving decorative designs.[42]

More in accordance with our own group, Goodenough, testing 1,671 subjects, found, with the exception of 12 year olds, persistently higher results for girls, but these were not of statistical significance.[43] She found it difficult to interpret psychologically this slight edge on the part of the girls over the boys, and she concluded that it was a matter not of intellectual superiority but of personality differences. Goodenough pointed to the generally observed fact that girls develop faster in the early years, that they pay more attention to detail, want to please, and are therefore industrious, etc.[44] In the case of dyslexic children it must be assumed that their visuo-motor deficiencies and their secondary emotional and adjustment difficulties lower their performance in the drawing task. Sex, age, or intelligence level seem less decisive in this kind of test performance. Goodenough's sample of 1,671 randomly selected schoolchildren yielded a mean IQ score of 100.7. Thus, the mean score of our group lies lower by 6.1 weighted points. Her standard deviation of 18.8 was closely matched by ours which was 18.4.

3.2c) Peabody Vocabulary Test IQ's

The Peabody Picture Vocabulary Test (PPVT) can be relatively quickly and easily administered and yields, in further concordance with the previously discussed Goodenough test, an IQ score. Dunn, who in 1959 constructed and standardized this test, wrote: "The PPVT is designed to provide an estimate of a subject's *verbal intelligence* through measuring his hearing vocabulary."[45] Dunn, like Wechsler, chose an IQ of 100 as the mean and 15 as the standard deviation; he standardized the test on 4,012 subjects. The author points out that many investigations have confirmed that word understanding is one of the most reliable single factors in predicting school performance and that the Wechsler scales showed the vocabulary subtest to be the one most highly correlated with the total IQ.[46] The PPVT differs from other vocabulary tests such as the Wechsler and Binet scales in that it measures word knowledge not by verbal definitions but by having the subject point at the right picture; thus, it is more the receptive than the expressive verbal language which is assessed. Comparative investigations since have produced a mean correlation coefficient of 0.61 for Wechsler full-scale IQ's, of 0.67 for Wechsler verbal scale IQ's, and of 0.39 for Wechsler performance scale IQ's. "In terms of comparability of scores," Dunn concluded, "the PPVT and Wechsler IQ values appear to be very similar with a tendency for the PPVT (IQ's) to be one or two points higher than Wechsler (IQ's)."[47]

The PPVT was administered to 430 of the subjects in our sample. The mean IQ for the whole group was 105.8, the standard deviation 16.7. Thus, the average intelligence scores, as on the Wechsler tests, were well within the normal average range and the variability was only slightly above the norm. While Dunn found that PPVT IQ's are usually one or two weighted points higher than Wechsler scores, we found a mean IQ which fell 0.2 points below our mean Wechsler IQ. Interestingly, Neville found that for 18 retarded readers the mean Wechsler full-scale IQ was four points higher than their mean PPVT IQ; for 18 normal readers, however, it was as would have been expected, one point, and for 18 fast readers two points, higher.[48]

Separate calculations for boys and girls resulted in a mean PPVT IQ of 107.5 for the former and of 100.5 for the latter. Thus, the girls had clearly lower scores on the Peabody test, in keeping with the same trend seen on the Wechsler scale. The younger age group in our sample achieved an average Peabody IQ of 106.2, thus doing slightly better than the high school group which earned a mean IQ of 102.8. The reverse was true for the Wechsler results.

3.2d) Comparison of Wechsler, Goodenough, and Peabody IQ's

The findings to be discussed in this chapter pertain to those 138 students in our sample to whom all three of these tests had been administered. Because of the age limit on the Goodenough Test, the children, 43 girls and 95 boys, were 6 to 10 years old. Still the group is diverse and large enough to make the comparison worthwhile (see Table 4).

Table 4. Comparison of IQ's as to test

Distributions	Wechsler Full-Scale IQ	Goodenough IQ	Peabody IQ
N	138	138	138
$\overline{X}$ IQ	108.5	94.5	105.8
s	14.8	18.4	16.7
Range	79	89	99

As in the case of the larger groups, the slow readers obtained their highest IQ on the Wechsler scale, and the Goodenough IQ is distinctly lower than both other IQ results. Thus, the trend is the same for this smaller group and only six- to ten-year-old boys and girls as it is for the larger groups containing all age levels.

Figure 4 is a graphic representation, based on all three mean IQ scores obtained, of the empirical distributions, together with projected normal curves. Thus it can be seen that the accidental or chance irregularities of the empirical curve would smooth out into a normal distribution were it possible to use an infinitely large sample.

The null hypothesis was verified by the chi-square method with the following results: for the Wechsler findings the X^2 was 5.25; since we had six degrees of freedom, the X^2 would have to have been 12.59 ($P = 0.05$) for the hypothesis to be rejected. The Peabody results had a X^2 value of 7.44 and six degrees of freedom; thus, here too, the null hypothesis could not be rejected. For the Goodenough findings we had seven degrees of freedom and a X^2 of 8.60; in order to doubt the hypothesis it would have to have been a chi-square value of 14.07. Thus, the distributions of all three test results can be considered as normal (see Figure 5).

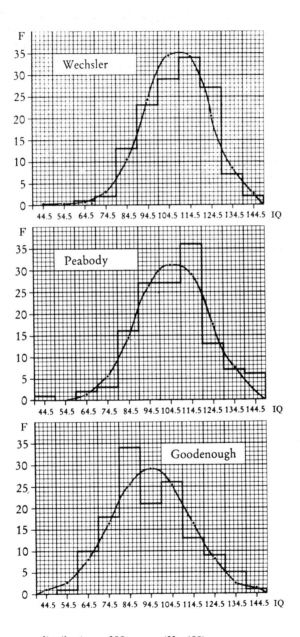

Fig. 4. Frequency distributions of IQ scores ($N = 138$).

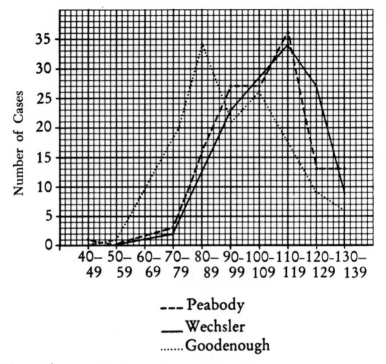

Fig. 5. Frequency distribution of IQ scores (N = 138).

This graphic presentation confirms the similarity of the distributions, and it draws attention to the fact that all three curves are close to each other in the middle section, i.e., in the IQ range between 85 and 100. In the lower range, however, the Goodenough values were higher than those of the two other tests, and in the upper ranges the Goodenough IQ's were visibly lower. Thus, children with lower Wechsler and Peabody IQ's did better on the Goodenough test and vice versa. The more intelligent children probably attributed less significance to the drawing task and their talents were possibly more in the verbal and reasoning than in the concrete and manual areas. Since the differences themselves were without statistical significance their interpretation deserves no further analysis.

Table 5 was designed to see whether the mean IQ scores on all three tests showed any disparities between age and sex

Table 5. Coefficient of correlation for IQ tests

Subjects	Wechsler $\bar{X}$ IQ $N = 488$		Goodenough $\bar{X}$ IQ $N = 138$		Peabody $\bar{X}$ IQ $N = 430$	
Boys	107.1	349	94.3	95	107.5	305
Girls	104.1	139	95.2	45	100.5	125
6 – 13 years	105.9	374	–	–	106.2	331
14 – 18 years	107.3	114	–	–	102.8	99

groups. As we expected, the Goodenough results were visibly lower, but no significant discrepancies occurred between the scores earned by boys and girls, elementary and high school students.

To obtain a quantitative measure of the degree of mutual relationships between the three mean IQ test results we determined the product-moment coefficient of correlation, using the method as described in Hofstätter[49] and Walker.[50] We arrived at the following computational values:

Tests	r_{xy}
Wechsler–Peabody	0.5898
Wechsler–Goodenough	0.5158
Peabody–Goodenough	0.2709

The highest intercorrelation existed between the Wechsler and the Peabody IQ's. Neville, who had tested 18 dyslexics with both of these tests, computed a correlation coefficient of 0.66.[51] This and our coefficient of 0.58 both correspond closely to the mean correlation of 0.61 which we calculated from various findings reported by the Peabody test author, Dunn.[52]

The degree of correlation in our Goodenough and Wechsler findings, $r_{xy} = 0.51$, is also closely related to the findings of other investigators: Harris reports four coefficients from four different authors which lie between 0.47 and 0.63.[53]

The intercorrelation between Peabody and Goodenough IQ's was considerably lower. We were unable to find material that would have been comparable to our correlation coefficient of 0.27.

We also examined our hypothesis, that in the case of dyslexics the Peabody would correlate more highly with the Wechsler verbal IQ and the Goodenough more highly with the Wechsler performance IQ. The standard product-moment formula was employed and the results were as follows:

	Wechsler Verbal IQ	Wechsler Performance IQ	Wechsler Full-Scale IQ
Goodenough	0.39	0.56	0.51
Peabody	0.58	0.48	0.59

The results confirmed our hunch retarded readers with visuo-motor deficiencies had higher correlations in the Goodenough and Wechsler performance scores; retarded readers with specific language disabilities had higher correlations between the Peabody and Wechsler verbal scores.

3. 3 Wechsler Subtest Results

3.3a) Mean Subtest Scores

In Figure 6 we present the frequency distributions of the mean standard scores obtained on 11 subtests of the Wechsler scales by the whole group. They resemble more-or-less normal distributions and need no further interpretation.

3.3b) Means, Standard Deviations, and Rank Order

In Table 6 we list the means, standard deviations, and rank order of the subtest scores obtained in our own sample for comparison with results gained by four other researchers. Graham[54] published his findings on 96 retarded readers in 1952; for reasons of simplicity we calculated the means of the three groups of results that he obtained on three Wechsler scales. In 1956 Altus[55] published his findings on 25 slow readers. Kallos, Grabow and Guarino[56] examined 37 slow reading boys with the Wechsler test and made their results public in 1961. Schiffman and Clemmens[57] had a sample of 240 failing readers and published their investigation in 1966. These latter authors and also Altus did not list the standard deviations.

These tables speak largely for themselves: The Digit Span

Table 6. Wechsler subtest scores obtained by five different investigators

Test	Klasen N = 466			Graham N = 96			Kallos et al. N = 37			Altus N = 25			Schiffman + Clemmens N = 240		
	X	s	R	X	s	R	X	s	R	X	s	R	X	s	R
I	10.5	2.9	8	7.3	2.3	9	8.5	1.5	10	8.9	–	9	8.4	–	9
C	10.9	3.0	2	9.6	2.5	5	9.6	2.3	6	10.0	–	7	9.3	–	5
A	9.4	3.4	11	5.9	2.8	11	9.3	2.4	8	8.7	–	10	8.3	–	10
S	11.4	3.3	1	8.8	1.9	6	9.5	2.0	7	9.3	–	8	9.2	–	6
V	10.9	3.1	3	7.6	2.3	8	9.6	2.0	5	10.8	–	2	9.1	–	7
DSp	9.4	2.7	10	6.8	1.9	10	–	–	–	10.7	–	3	7.3	–	11
PC	10.8	2.8	4	10.0	2.6	4	10.2	3.1	4	11.2	–	1	10.9	–	1
PA	10.7	2.7	6	10.3	2.1	2	10.7	2.1	2	10.4	–	5	10.7	–	3
BD	10.7	3.0	5	10.1	2.8	3	11.3	2.2	1	10.1	–	6	9.9	–	4
OA	10.6	2.7	7	12.1	3.0	1	10.7	2.2	3	10.7	–	4	10.8	–	2
DSy	9.8	2.8	9	7.8	3.2	7	9.0	2.3	9	8.2	–	11	8.7	–	8

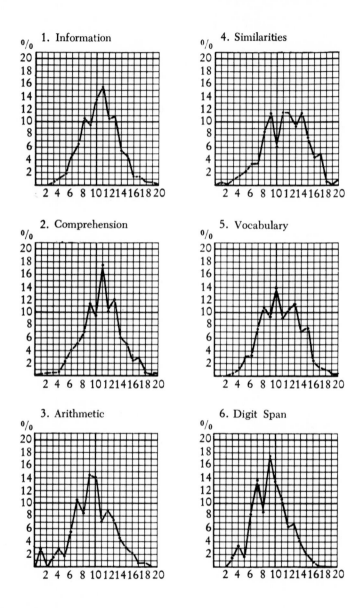

Fig. 6. Frequency distributions of the mean Wechsler verbal subscores (*N* = 466).

% 7. Picture Completion

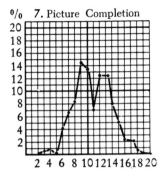

% 10. Object Assembly

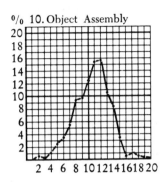

% 8. Picture Arrangement

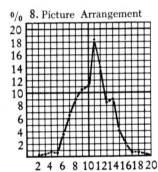

% 11. Digit Symbol

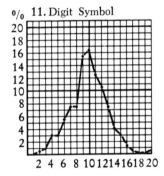

% 9. Block Design

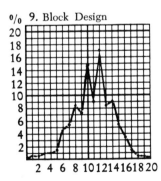

Fig. 6. *(Continued).* Frequency distributions of the mean Wechsler perform-ance subscores ($N = 466$).

(DSp), Digit Symbol (DSy), Arithmetic (A) scores are consistently low. These tendencies will be further illustrated in graphic presentations and discussed in detail in paragraph 3.3d.

3.3c) Subtest and Rank Order Profiles

Figure 7 presents the subtest scores in polygon form, first those of the boys and the girls separately, then of the elementary and secondary students separately, and then for the total group. In these graphs it is apparent once more that boys showed slightly higher scores on all but two subtests, namely, Digit Span and Digit Symbol. More striking than that is the uniformity of the profiles in all four groups. The Similarities (S), Comprehension (C), and Vocabulary (V) items of the verbal scale, as well as the Picture Completion (PC) and Block Design (BD) items on the performance scale are among the consistently higher results. Arithmetic, Digit Symbol, and Digit Span are consistently the lowest findings.

During the summer session of 1968 four adult men were enrolled at the Raskob Institute who despite regular schooling had virtually remained illiterate. Here are their most important data: Case I: A. G., 20 years old, Wechsler full-scale IQ = 99, performance IQ 10 points higher than verbal IQ; Case II: L. M., 35 years old, Wechsler full-scale IQ = 100, performance IQ 11 points higher than verbal IQ; Case III: M. M., 19 years old, Wechsler full-scale IQ 88, performance IQ 11 points higher than verbal IQ; Case IV: F. L., 42 years old, Wechsler full-scale IQ = 97, performance IQ 15 points higher than verbal IQ. The graphs in Figure 8 present the Wechsler subtest profiles of these four men. These profiles, especially those of Cases I and III, have a striking resemblance to those gained for the total group and its four subdivisions. In the individual's profiles we find again that Arithmetic, Digit Symbol, and Digit Span scores are the lowest results, whereas Comprehension, Similarities, and Object Assembly (OA) tend to be elevated.

Wechsler subtest score investigations are usually performed with the hope that a typical profile might evolve which could serve as a diagnostic and predictive tool. Wechsler himself developed such characteristic test profiles for schizophrenia,

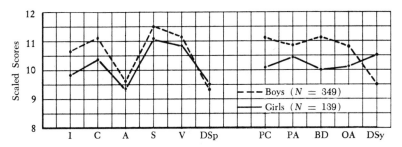

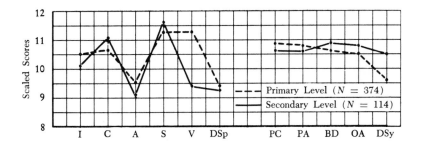

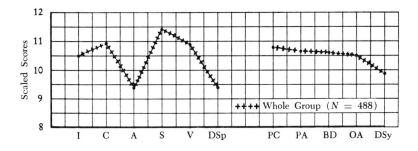

Fig. 7. Dyslexia subtest profiles on the Wechsler Intelligence Scale.

brain damage, neurosis, mental retardation, etc.[58] To date, however, the attempts to use such subject profiles as a tool in differential diagnosis have remained without the hoped for certainty and success. Nevertheless we were intrigued enough by the question of whether a typical dyslexic profile might emerge to superimpose in the graph in Figure 9 the rank order profiles

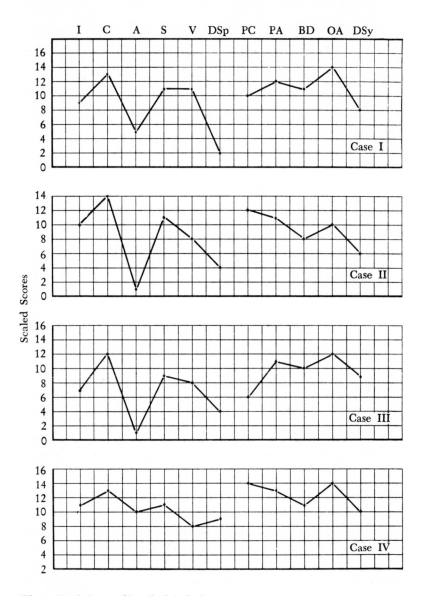

Fig. 8. Wechsler profiles of adult dyslexics.

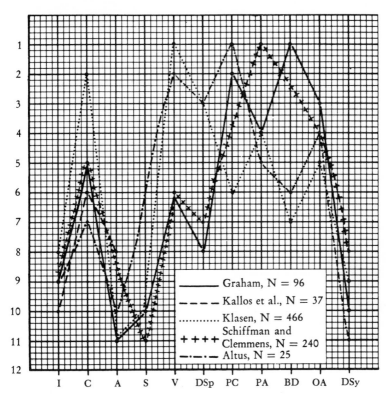

Fig. 9. Wechsler subtest profiles of retarded readers.

gained from the results of five different researchers on groups of retarded readers.

Here, again, it is immediately apparent that Arithmetic, Digit Span, and Information are generally low, while Comprehension, Vocabulary, Picture Completion, and Object Assembly are among the more or less constantly high results.

3.3d) Significant Subtest Disparities

Following the method described by Wechsler,[59] we investigated which subject's scores showed significant discrepancies from the mean of all the subscores, as calculated for each child from all 11 of his subscore results. In 466 cases of our sample all 11 subscores were available; this meant $466 \times 11 = 5,126$ subtest results, which could be broken down as follows:

$516 = 9.9\%$ were statistically significantly lower,
$551 = 9.3\%$ were statistically significantly higher than the mean of all 11 subscores,
$4,059 = 80.8\%$ showed no significant deviation from the mean.

In order to demonstrate more visually in which subtests the retarded readers were more successful and in which they were less successful, we devised the figures in Table 7.

With regard to our expectations based on previous observations, the subscores on Digit Span, Arithmetic, and Digit Symbol were far more frequently below the mean than the subscores of any other subject. While 15%–18% of these were below the mean, only 3%–7% of all the other subtests showed significantly lower results.

The subareas in which retarded readers are generally above the mean showed a more gradual decline. The ability to find similarities of concepts was clearly in the lead for 15%. Picture Arrangement, Picture Completion, Comprehension, and Vocabulary followed as a group, constituting between 10%–11% each. Block Design, Object Assembly, Digit Symbol, Arithmetic, Information, and Digit Span with 4%–9% each formed the most infrequent group.

These figures not only correspond to those of other, but also with general, i.e., not statistically determined observations. Schubenz and Böhmig observed, for instance, that poor readers were lower in Arithmetic, but better in Object Assembly than controls were. In Picture Completion and in Comprehension the slow readers were better also, but on the Information subtest they were lower. On the Block Design item these authors found no significant differences between retarded readers and normal controls.[60] Lobrot recognized that on all Wechsler tasks involving concrete knowledge, i.e., memory and orientation such as Information, Arithmetic, the first of the Block Designs, Picture Arrangement, the dyslexics were inferior; they were superior, however, in all tasks requiring concrete analysis, such as Similarities, Picture Completion, the

Table 7. Subtest scores of retarded readers

Subscores significantly below the mean	2 4 6 8 10 12 14 16 18	%
Digit Span		18.4
Arithmetic		17.8
Digit Symbol		15.8
Object Assembly		7.7
Information		7.5
Picture Completion		6.2
Block Design		6.2
Comprehension		6.0
Picture Arrangement		5.4
Vocabulary		4.8
Similarities		3.8

Subscores significantly above the mean	2 4 6 8 10 12 14 16 18	%
Similarities		15.2
Picture Arrangement		11.7
Picture Completion		11.6
Comprehension		10.8
Vocabulary		10.3
Block Design		9.4
Object Assembly		8.1
Digit Symbol		7.2
Arithmetic		5.8
Information		4.9
Digit Span		4.5

majority of the Block Designs, and Object Assembly.[61] While studying speech impediments Zuckrigl made the following interesting observation: a number of children on the intermediate level had achievement scores low enough so that one should have considered them slow and retarded learners in need of

special classes, but they earned normal average full-scale IQ's
on the Wechsler test. However, he found that subtest analysis
revealed significant qualitative disparities, most errors were
made on the Digit Symbol Test, others occurred on the Picture
Completion and Block Design items. In class these pupils happened to be poor readers, to be awkward with maps, and,
although fewer, low in math.[62] Schiffman, without mentioning
quantitative findings, pointed out that many investigators are
convinced that a high correlation exists between low Digit Symbol and Arithmetic scores on the one hand, and severe reading
retardation on the other, "Our research results with over 400
clinically referred remedial readers seem to agree with these
findings."[63] Chassagny wrote: "The children we work with are
frequently deficient in the subtests in arithmetic (except in
cases of success in computation), vocabulary, digit span, and
block design."[64]

It is a very common observation that retarded readers have
low Arithmetic scores. This seems surprising at first since one
expects their difficulties to be primarily in the verbal area.
Ellehammer in a statistical investigation of 240 students found
they were, as a group, retarded in reading, spelling, and arithmetic, but when she examined the individual achievement
scores, she found only limited agreement between reading and
arithmetic levels. She was unable to find a common factor that
could have been an impediment to both reading and arithmetic.[65] Many hypotheses have been put forward in the attempt to
explain the simultaneous weakness in reading and arithmetic.
An especially frequently mentioned factor is that of anxiety.
Thus Mussen wrote: "Anxiety undoubtedly interferes more
with conceptual learning, mathematics, and other tasks demanding abstraction and logical reasoning than it does with
routine tasks and discrimination."[66] Arithmetical reasoning requires not only the necessary skills but also prolonged concentration; this makes it particularly vulnerable to anxiety and
nervous tension. If we recall that 65% of the children in our
sample showed symptoms of anxiety, it seems rather likely that
this emotional factor contributes heavily to the low Arithmetic
scores. Furthermore, arithmetic has a strongly cumulative component: should a child, on the basis of verbal, sequencing, or

similar weaknesses, fail to master the multiplication tables or other arithmetic or geometric sequencing processes; should he miss out on the first word problems, then he could not cope adequately with any other mathematical steps building upon the ones missed. Lory drew attention to the fact that in math, as in sentence construction, much depends on the sequencing, grouping, and connecting processes.[67] Critchley pointed out that reading and arithmetic do not always go hand in hand: "Arithmetical retardation may be associated with developmental dyslexia, but not necessarily so."[68] Lückert emphasized that arithmetic repeatedly belongs to the areas in which retarded readers do considerably better.[69] These observations are confirmed by our own in that dyslexics who have no difficulty in arithmetical reasoning often show not only average, but considerably better than average scores. Mucchielli and Bourcier considered the often observed spatial confusion of dyslexics as the reason for their failure in solving mathematical problems.[70]

Investigations so far have been unsuccessful in their search for *the* common factor in the causation of the consistently low Arithmetic scores on intelligence scales. Since dyslexia apparently often occurs despite good mathematical reasoning, it is questionable whether we should think in terms of a common causative factor.

Ellehammer compared the Wechsler Digit Span scores of 21 disabled readers with those of 220 unselected controls, finding that the slow readers had considerably lower scores on this subtest; attempts to further analyze this statistically resulted in too many uncertainties for the researcher to draw any definite conclusions.[71] Our own hunch would be that the same factors are at work in both areas, the Arithmetic as well as the Digit Span items: anxiety with consequent concentration problems, memory and sequencing, auditory and similar disabilities. Messeant, comparing test findings of dyslexics, came to the conclusion that they are especially weak when expected to repeat sequences which have no apparent logic.[72]

There are also controversies with regard to whether dyslexics do poorly on the Block Design and Object Assembly subtests. Quantitative findings are contradictory. One commonly agreed upon observation, however, concerns the frequently noticed rotations; they seem to be the result of spatial and/or directional confusion among retarded readers. In our own sample the dyslexic students, despite these apparent difficulties, did not show significantly lower test scores, though; they often seemed able to compensate through speed, and many corrected their errors spontaneously within the given time limits of the tests.

All these observations and quantitative analyses show once more how much we are confronted, in the matters of intelligence, test performance, reading retardation, memory, sequencing ability, concentration, etc., with complexities tending to frustrate our desire to arrive at simple, clear, or unique explanations. In summary we say that a Wechsler Subtest Profile with significantly low scores on Information, Arithmetic, Digit Span, and Digit Symbol, together with otherwise normal or above average subscores, is indicative and confirmative as far as the presence of reading retardation is concerned, but cannot yet be considered a definitively predictive sign. To further summarize, the areas of significantly lower performance occur with more constancy than those in which dyslexics tend to show higher ability.

Table 8.* Summary of Wechsler subtest data

	Neville	Robeck	Klasen	Kallos**	Graham	Altus	Schiffman and Clemmens
I	−	−	−	−	−	−	−
C	×	+	×	×	×	×	×
A	−	−	−	−	−	−	−
S	×	+	+	×	×	×	×
V	×	+	×	×	−	+	×
DSp	−	−	−		−	+	−
PC	×	+	×	×	×	+	+
PA	+	+	×	×	×	+	+
B	+	+	×	+	×	+	×
O	×	+	×	×	+	+	+
D	−	−	−	−	−	−	−

* × = normal average, + = above average, − = below average.
** Kallos had no data on Digit Span.

Stimulated by the kind of graphic presentation utilized by Neville[73] and Robeck,[74] in Table 8 we present a simplified summary of all the Wechsler subtest data discussed in this chapter.

3.3e) Intercorrelations of Wechsler Subtest Scores

We employed the standard product-moment formula in the calculation of the intercorrelation of our own subtest scores and compared them with those which Wechsler[75] obtained on a sample with 200 unselected subjects (Table 9). Since the results on the two scales differed slightly, we treated the WISC and Wechsler-Bellevue Scale data separately. The WISC had been employed on 352 students of our sample, the Wechsler-Bellevue to 114. We also present here the subtest intercorrelations found on the WISC, given to 240 subjects by the coauthors Schiffman and Clemmens.[76]

There are no negative correlations in our sample, in contrast to Schiffman and Clemmens. It must be pointed out that the dyslexics in their sample had an *average* reading retardation of five grade levels and that their group of 240 contained only 5 girls; the mean Wechsler full-scale IQ for their sample was 96 and thus considerably lower than the mean IQ of 106 obtained for our group. These differences between the groups may account for the differences in the correlation coefficients of the two samples.

In Table 10 we present subtest findings obtained on the Wechsler-Bellevue Scale.[77] Tables 9a and b, as well as Tables 10a and b, indicate that the mutual subtest correlations in our sample of poor readers resemble very much those of the normal control group investigated by Wechsler. A few tendencies become clear: our Block Design scores correspond especially highly with those of normals on the Wechsler Children's as well as the Wechsler-Bellevue scale, all correlation coefficients on this subtest lie between 0.38 and 0.58. The intercorrelations of the Object Assembly and other WISC scores are, with only one exception, as high in our sample as they are in that of Wechsler; only between Object Assembly and Similarities was the correlation by 0.10 point higher. Our findings were thus different from

Table 9. Intercorrelations of Wechsler subscores

	I	C	A	S	V	DSp	PC	PA	BD	OA	DSy
a) Klasen, 352 dyslexics											
C	0.58										
A	.53	0.39									
S	.64	.52	0.47								
V	.69	.57	.54	0.63							
DSp	.38	.29	.43	.44	0.41						
PC	.40	,37	.31	.43	.45	0.30					
PA	.36	.31	.34	.40	.38	.25	0.34				
BD	.39	.38	.47	.44	.45	.34	.45	0.43			
OA	.30	.29	.30	.35	.35	.26	.42	.38	.52		
DSy	.21	.21	.36	.23	.25	.24	.17	.27	.29	0.28	
b) Schiffman and Clemmens, 240 dyslexics											
C	0.37										
A	.37	0.15									
S	.07	.10	0.13								
V	.59	.47	.12	0.03							
DSp	.08	− .05	.18	−.11	− 12						
PC	.13	.15	− .16	− .07	.06	0.01					
PA	.01	− .05	− .17	− .03	.04	− .12	0.14				
BD	− .21	.08	− .18	.13	.07	− .02	.22	− .11			
OA	− .29	.01	− .21	.02	− .10	.09	.26	− .12	0.58		
DSy	.01	.11	.10	.11	.17	.05	− .40	− .04	.10	− .16	
c) Wechsler's standardization, 200 children											
C	0.65										
A	.69	0.48									
S	.67	.55	0.63								
V	.75	.75	.62	0.64							
DSp	.38	.41	.45	.39	0.48						
PC	.41	.37	.32	.34	.47	0.10					
PA	.51	.48	.48	.41	.56	.33	0.35				
BD	.48	.44	.48	.38	.54	.34	.46	0.51			
OA	.28	.35	.33	.25	.41	.35	.38	.30	0.59		
DSy	.37	.32	.38	.29	.41	.30	.20	.36	.27	0.23	

Table 10. Intercorrelations of
Wechsler-Bellevue subscores

	I	C	A	S	V	DSp	PC	PA	BD	OA	DSy
a) Klasen, 114 dyslexics										
C	0.67										
A	.62	0.59									
S	.72	.66	0.65								
V	.67	.65	.61	0.60							
DSp	.37	.30	.45	.32	0.40						
PC	.42	.49	.47	.47	.45	0.19					
PA	.27	.44	.48	.40	.35	.24	0.45				
BD	.49	.53	.58	.56	.44	.39	.57	0.52			
OA	.35	.46	.44	.46	.44	.29	.58	.49	0.64		
DSy	.44	.41	.42	.39	.45	.42	.31	.33	.49	0.48	
b) Wechsler's standardization, 355 adults										
C	0.66										
A	.59	0.51									
S	.67	.72	0.60								
V	–	–	–	–							
DSp	.48	.44	.44	0.37	–						
PC	.46	.45	.40	.45	–	0.29					
PA	.38	.39	.36	.48	–	.26	0.38				
BD	.48	.46	.51	.53	–	.39	.56	0.48			
OA	.22	.28	.23	.30	–	.15	.43	.27	0.53		
DSy	.56	.47	.42	.50	–	.53	.40	.44	.53	0.31	

those obtained by Schiffman and Clemmens[78] as presented in Table 9b. On the Wechsler-Bellevue test, however, the correlation between Object Assembly and all other subtest scores turned out to be clearly higher in our population.

To conclude this chapter, we present in Table 11 the mean subtest results and standard deviations for our sample, obtained separately on the two Wechsler Test Scales.

Significant disparities among WISC and Bellevue scores were not observed. The greatest difference, not quite two weighted points, occurred on the Vocabulary subtest which was 11.3 on the Children's scale, but only 9.5 on the Bellevue scale. The tendency of the Arithmetic, Digit Span, and Digit Symbol scores to be lower, is present on both scales, just as it was present for

Table 11. Mean Wechsler subtest scores
and standard deviations

466 Dyslexics	WISC $N = 352$		Wechsler-Bellevue $N = 114$	
	χ	s	χ	s
I	10.57	2.98	10.18	2.65
C	10.64	3.02	11.66	3.08
A	9.50	3.22	9.12	4.14
S	11.32	3.24	11.65	3.51
V	11.38	3.18	9.51	2.35
DSp	9.43	2.80	9.17	2.81
PC	10.88	2.90	10.69	2.73
PA	10.81	2.60	10.69	3.01
BD	10.78	3.01	11.12	3.23
OA	10.60	2.76	10.89	2.87
DSy	9.60	2.91	10.54	2.59

the whole group, the younger and older, the male and female groups, and the four individuals, thus presenting the most constant of all our findings.

3.3f) Dyslexia Profiles on the Wechsler Scales

The search for "typical" dyslexia profiles concerns not only the subtest pattern, but also disparities between the verbal and performance scale intelligence quotients. It appears that so far all investigators found dyslexics to do more poorly on the verbal tasks of the Wechsler scales. Lückert, without presenting quantitative data, declared categorically: "... Slow readers have significantly better results on the Performance scale."[79] Schiffman and Clemmens, more cautiously, stated that the verbal IQ is significantly lower in many cases.[80] Neville observed that the mean Performance IQ for poor readers was 6.7 weighted points higher than that of normal controls and 10.6 points higher than their own mean verbal IQ.[81] Schiffman wrote that retarded readers often encounter difficulties with those test items which are similar to school subjects and with those which require concentration; thus, he considers their performance IQ a more reliable measure of their true potential than their verbal IQ.[82] Biglmaier, along the same line of reasoning, advises that estimates of a dyslexic's true mental capacity should be made on the basis of his nonverbal test scores rather than on verbal test results.[83]

Table 12.* Verbal and performance mean scores

Investigator	N	Verbal IQ	Performance IQ
Schiffman and Clemmens[21]	240	91.02	101.0
Graham[22] (WISC)	65	88.4	101.7
Altus[23]	25	97.8	100.4
Kallos et al.[24]	7	95.9	103.0
Graham[25]	31	98.9	101.7
Robeck[29]	36	106.7	111.7
Klasen	488	104.3	105.5

* The reference numbers for the bibliography are the same as those used at the beginning of this unit in Table 1.

Not all of these conclusions and suggestions are based on statistical evidence, however, and those which are, are often based on small samples or not truly significant statistical differences. Table 12 presents all of the verbal and performance mean scores of which perusal of the pertinent literature made us aware. Before we interpret this table it should be pointed out that with the exception of our own sample, which contains 139 girls, and that of Graham, who does not state the sex of his subjects, the remaining samples together contain only 10 girls. Although the findings presented in the table seem at first to confirm that dyslexics have lower verbal IQ's, a closer analysis reveals that only one sample, namely the WISC findings by Graham, shows a significantly lower mean verbal IQ, it being 13.3 points lower than the mean performance IQ. In the sample collected by Schiffman and Clemmens there is a disparity, in favor of the mean performance IQ, of exactly 10 weighted IQ points. In the remaining samples the mean verbal IQ's were only from 7 to 1 points lower. Thus, it can be said that significant disparities between mean verbal and performance

IQ's for groups are the exception rather than the rule. This observation ceases to be surprising as soon as one considers the simple, if not always immediately apparent, fact that among individuals, the equally frequent higher verbal and higher performance scores cancel out each other. Among our dyslexic children there were clearly equal numbers who earned significantly higher verbal and higher performance IQ's. The true disparities only become recognizable as we take the group findings apart and look at them individually.

Thus we decided to analyze separately the number of children in our sample with significantly higher verbal, significantly higher performance scores, those who had significant subscore disparities spread over both scales without showing either a significantly higher verbal or performance IQ, and, finally, those who had no significant disparities at all. As "significant" were considered only those differences which were greater than the mean disparity of 8.7 as calculated by Wechsler,[84] i.e., we counted as significant only disparities of 10 or more points. The results of this analysis are presented in Table 13.

Table 13. Analysis of verbal and performance IQ's

Weighted Points	Total Group	Boys 6–13 Years Old	Girls 6–13 Years Old	Boys 14–18 Years Old	Girls 14–18 Years Old
a) Significantly higher Wechsler verbal IQ's					
31–34	2	0	0	2	0
21–30	18	11	1	4	2
11–20	78	47	16	9	6
10	11	4	3	3	1
Total	109 = 22.3%	62	20	18	9
b) Significantly higher Wechsler performance IQ's					
31–36	5	4	0	0	1
21–30	18	9	5	3	1
11–20	59	33	10	10	6
10	10	3	4	1	2
Total	92 = 18.9%	49	19	14	10

Significantly higher verbal IQ's, according to these tables, occurred only slightly more often than higher performance IQ's. In the majority of cases the differences were 11 to 20 points, but in 43 cases the IQ's were even 21 to 36 points higher. Our findings confirm that many dyslexics, here approximately one fifth of the total group, have significantly higher verbal IQ's, but they show also, as has not been sufficiently emphasized by other investigators, that there are almost equally many dyslexics who earn significantly higher performance IQ's. And this is in no way a surprising result: dyslexics with visual-perceptual, fine motor control and related deficiencies would be expected to be less successful on the performance scale which involves practical problem solving, a paper-pencil task and psychomotor speed.

It would seem likely that dyslexics with a significantly higher verbal IQ are those whose reading-writing retardation began with visual-perceptual and fine muscle control problems, whereas dyslexics with significantly higher performance IQ's are those whose reading deficiencies stem primarily from specific language disability. This latter group would consist of children whose speech development was delayed, who have or had speech impediments, whose expressive or receptive language is deficient, etc. These observations and conclusions must be considered conjectural until verified by further evidence, quantitative as well as qualitative.

For practical purposes in the further discussion of profiles we designated those with a significantly higher verbal IQ as Dyslexia Profile I, those with higher performance IQ as Profile II, those with significantly differing subtest scores as Profile III and those without significant discrepancies as Profile IV. The breakdown for the whole group according to these four categories is presented in Table 14.

Some observers expressed their belief that dyslexics with higher verbal IQ's have higher general intelligence and full test scores. To test this theory we calculated the mean subtest scores for the four profile groups and included the findings in Table 14. For none of the groups was there a mean subscore disparity exceeding 0.9 weighted point. It can thus be concluded that the general intelligence as well as achievement

Table 14. Wechsler profiles of 488 dyslexic children

	Profile	N	Percent	Mean Subtest Scores
I	Verbal IQ significantly higher	109	22.3	10.7
II	Performance IQ significantly higher	92	18.9	10.0
III	Significant subtest disparities	237	48.6	10.2
IV	No significant discrepancies	50	10.2	9.8
	Total	488	100.0	

levels of the children belonging to any one group are approximately the same and that it is erroneous to assume that dyslexics with a significantly higher verbal than performance IQ are more intelligent than those with other types of test disparities.

Table 14 further demonstrates that 41.2% of the dyslexics in our sample had either significantly higher verbal or significantly higher performance IQ's, and we were interested to find how great and of what type the differences might be between students with Profile I and students with Profile II. Therefore, we figured the mean subtest scores for each of these groups separately and arrived at the data given in Table 15.

Table 15. Mean subtest scores of dyslexics with Wechsler profiles I and II

	I	C	A	S	V	DSp
Profile I	12.2	12.8	10.7	12.9	12.1	10.5
Profile II	8.7	9.6	7.9	9.7	9.4	8.8

	PC	PA	BD	OA	DSy
Profile I	10.1	9.6	10.1	9.5	9.2
Profile II	11.9	11.4	11.7	11.8	11.0

None of these mean subtest scores differs from any other by more than 3.5 (Information) or by less than 1.6 (Block Design). The discrepancies that do occur tend to be more pronounced and persistent on the verbal than on the performance scale. Dyslexics with Wechsler Profile I are especially poor on the performance tasks Digit Symbol, Object Assembly, and Picture

Arrangement. Wechsler Profile II are lowest in Arithmetic, Information, and Digit Span. A graphic presentation of the test findings for these two groups is given in Figure 10.

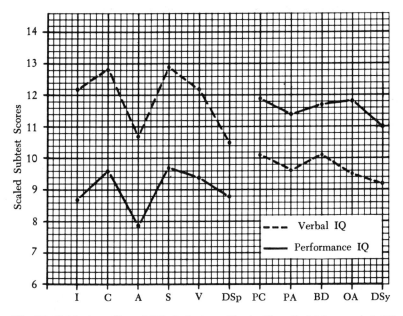

Fig. 10. Subtest profiles of 109 dyslexics with significantly higher verbal IQ's and of 92 dyslexics with significantly higher performance IQ's.

These subtest score curves for Profile groups I and II resemble closely those discussed previously for the whole group, sex groups, and age groups. Except for the significant disparities as to verbal, and performance results, these two groups, like the others, show peaks and valleys in the same subtest areas.

Going back to Table 14 we realize that Profile III occurs by far the most frequently, in our sample in nearly 50% of the cases. Here, too, we wanted to know what the disparities were when considered more individually. For each of the 237 dyslexics in this group 11 subtest results were available: $237 \times 11 = 2,607$. Of these, $279 = 9.3\%$, were significantly higher and $275 = 9.5\%$ were significantly lower than the mean score of all subtests as calculated for each child.

Table 16. Number of subscores which differed
significantly from the mean

a)

Number of Subscores	Number of Children
1	79
2	63
3	49
4	23
5	15
6	7
7	1

b) Significantly higher		c) Significantly lower	
Subtest	Number of Cases	Subtest	Number of Cases
S	46	D	58
PC	35	A	48
PA	33	DSy	45
V	30	I	19
C	29	PC	18
BD	28	C	18
OA	26	BD	18
I	14	OA	15
A	14	S	14
DSy	13	V	11
DSp	11	PA	11

As Table 16a shows, the majority of children had only one to
three subtest scores which were significantly higher or lower
than their mean subtest performance.

The observed significant inter-test variations occurred in the
order of frequency given in Tables 16b and c on the 11 subtests.
These figures demonstrate that retarded readers with Profile
III have the same test characteristics as observed previously for
the whole group, the boys and girls, the younger and older
group, those with Profile I and those with Profile II. The Profile
III group contributes heavily to the significantly low Digit Span,
Arithmetic, and Digit Symbol scores; and they stand out posi-
tively especially on the Similarities item which involves abstract
reasoning. The total picture of Tables 16b and c is very similar

to the findings presented in paragraph 3.4d and in Tables 7a, b, and c.

Our findings with regard to the three lowest subscore groups were confirmed by Robeck who examined the scores of 36 disabled readers and observed: "The reading disability group showed relative weakness, significant beyond the 0.01 level of confidence, in four subtests: Digit Span, Arithmetic, Information, and Coding."[85]

It is of some interest in this connection to take a look at similar attempts, namely those to develop a Wechsler-Subtest Profile indicative of brain injury. This kind of research was begun by Wechsler himself, who considered low results on the Arithmetic, Similarities, Block Design, and Digit Symbol items as characteristic for brain damage.[86] Morrow and Mark were able to show that patients with frank brain traumata showed persistently lower performance on the Digit Symbol, Digit Span, and Arithmetic subtests.[87] Hanvik et al. examined 148 children who had been referred for psychiatric evaluation; one-half of these children had positive electroencephalographs and were significantly low on the Wechsler Digit Symbol and the Bender Gestalt Tests, but their full test scores showed no significant deviation from those of the other half who had normal encephalographs.[88]

Inter-test variability as in our Profile III has been observed statistically or as a general impression, by several investigators who dealt with the brain injured. Capobianco, for instance, believed that test profiles vary, often even mislead, and that the only constant factor in all investigations of brain damaged patients is that of general inter-test variability.[89]

Research on the brain has repeatedly shown that language function, in the majority of people, is located in the left hemisphere and that damage to this region will impede such language functions as verbal expression, verbal understanding, reading, writing, and spelling. Damage to the right hemisphere, however, leaves developed language skills intact, but impedes, via disruption of interhemispheric connections, such nonverbal functions as spatial orientation, stability or fluency of sequencing or similar processes, and gestalt perception. It would be our guess then that dyslexics with Wechsler Profile II (= low verbal

IQ) would be those with left hemispheric damage or dysfunction, those with Wechsler Profile I (= low performance IQ) with
right hemispheric disorders, and those with Profile III (significant subtest variability) would suffer from diffuse or bilateral
brain injury, or dysfunction.

If both characteristics, significant subtest variations and significantly low Digit Symbol, Digit Span, and Arithmetic scores,
are, in fact, characteristic for the brain injured, then we must
say, in view of the so similar test characteristics observed for
our retarded readers, that this is strong support for those who
suspect that reading-spelling disability is largely due to neurological dysfunction and/or minimal brain injury. It must also be
kept in mind that a high percentage of children who come to
the attention of physicians primarily because of neurological
conditions (such as cerebral palsy, epilepsy, and lesser disorders) suffers reading-writing disabilities. A neurological explanation for dyslexia, at least for a large portion of the children
afflicted, thus finds strong support from various sides.

3.3g) Quantitative Gains after Reading Therapy

For 360 of the 500 students in our sample we have complete
initial and final achievement test scores for statistical analysis.
In 46 cases the children had not yet taken final tests. In 94
folders the test scores were incomplete for reasons beyond our
control: the families had moved, the children were ill or had
been referred elsewhere, etc. We divided the remaining 360
cases according to the number of semesters spent at the Raskob Learning Institute. Four semesters are offered per year.

The great majority, 360, attended the reading clinic for only
one semester; the 6- to 13-year-old boys are a slight exception to this rule: a relatively larger number stayed for two
and even three sessions (see Table 17). Only an exceptionally
few students remained at the Institute for five to seven semesters.

Quantitative success rates were measured by using standardized tests providing grade level scores on word recognition,
reading comprehension in silent and oral reading, rate, accuracy, fluency, word discrimination, spelling, etc. All these areas

Table 17. Breakdown of numbers of
students and semesters

Subjects	Number of Semesters							Total
	1	2	3	4	5	6	7	
Boys, 6 – 13	95	53	38	12	6	2	1	207
Girls, 6 – 13	40	13	3	3	3	1	1	64
Boys, 14–18	43	14	4	0	0	0	0	61
Girls, 14 – 18	16	9	1	2	0	0	0	28
Total	194	89	46	17	9	3	2	360

are tested at the beginning and end of each session. We figured the composite mean grade level score obtained by each student during initial and final testing. Comparing these, we could say, for instance, this child made an overall gain of ten months during the three-month session. An increase of ten months, since the school year lasts only ten months, would thus be equivalent to a whole grade level.

Table 18 presents the grade level gains first of the 194 children who attended one semester, then of the 89 who stayed for a second session. As Tables 18a and b indicate, the mean increase in reading-spelling skills after one semester of attendance for the whole group was 15.6 months, i.e., a grade level and a half. Breakdowns according to sex and age show that the high school group shows by far the greatest gain: almost two and one half grade levels in one session. The younger group, by contrast, is the only one lying distinctly below the mean for the total group. There was no significant difference for boys and girls.

Table 18b shows that the group as a whole gained an average of 26.6 months after two semesters of reading therapy; this is a 13.3 month increase for each semester and would thus lie slightly below the mean gain for the group after one semester. This decline is rather minimal in view of the fact that only the more severely handicapped learners go on for a second session. The average grade level gains after two sessions are almost equally high among both sex and age groups.

Quantitative calculations for students attending more than two semesters did not seem indicated since the groups are very small and contain extreme values which would invalidate calcu-

Table 18. Analysis of grade level gains

Gains in Terms of Months	Total Group	Number of Students		Boys	Girls
		Students 6 – 13 Years Old	Students 14 – 18 Years Old		
a) Reading-spelling gains in grade level terms after one session					
1–6	41	33	8	31	10
7–12	67	59	8	46	21
13–18	26	19	7	19	7
19–24	26	15	11	19	7
25–30	13	7	6	9	4
31–36	7	1	6	4	3
37–42	3	0	3	2	3
43–48	6	1	5	4	2
49–54	1	0	1	1	0
55–60	1	0	1	1	0
61–66	3	0	3	2	1
Total	194	135	59	138	56
Mean Gain	15.6	11.6	24.7	15.4	16.0
b) Reading-spelling gains in grade level terms after two sessions					
46–48	3	1	2	1	2
42–45	1	0	1	0	1
40–42	7	4	3	6	1
37–39	5	4	1	3	2
34–36	4	2	2	3	1
31–33	4	3	1	3	1
28–30	8	5	3	4	4
15–27	13	12	1	10	3
22–24	17	16	1	13	4
19–21	12	10	2	9	3
16–18	6	4	2	6	0
13–15	4	3	1	4	0
10–12	5	0	5	4	1
Total	89	64	25	66	23
Mean Gain	26.6	26.0	27.2	25.4	29.3

lations of central tendencies. Generally speaking, the test scores showed increases between 7 and 33 months for students attending three to seven sessions. The lowest extremes were gains of only one to three months, the highest were increases of three and one-half grade levels; and one student gained seven grade levels in seven semesters of reading therapy.

General agreement can be found in the pertinent literature with regard to the possible and actual positive benefit of reading therapy for dyslexics. We were unable, however, to find comparable statistical material. This is easily understood in view of the variability of programs offered, their ways of testing, teaching, etc., the duration of their daily sessions and total semesters, etc. It would have to be nearly impossible to find comparable criteria and methods. Observers also seem to agree that the smaller the group, the more qualified therapist and therapy, the more carefully selected and grouped the students, the more intelligent and interested they are, the better the chances for success. As certain as it is that dyslexic children will fail and stay behind in regular classes, so it also appears certain that they will overcome; at least to appreciable degrees, their learning disability if offered specific teaching-learning aid.

Last but not least it must be emphasized that quantitative gains, as intriguing as they are for statistical purposes, are only one part of the total picture. The qualitative changes, such as attitude toward self, toward learning, toward the future, toward the world around and society as a whole, cannot be expressed in numbers. Yet, in them lies the true, the essentially human gain of all the efforts centering on the dyslexic student.

3.4 Summary

Statistical evidence overwhelmingly confirms that dyslexic learning disability is independent of the intelligence factor and occurs in association with all levels of general intelligence. The intelligence quotients of retarded readers are as normally distributed as those of normal control groups. Reading-spelling dysfunctions therefore cannot be considered defects in general mental capacity.

The mean Wechsler full-scale IQ's of ten independently investigated groups of retarded readers were between 96 and 109, i.e., well within normal average limits; only samples of delinquent and institutionalized disabled readers were distinctly below average.

Our students were tested with three different intelligent scales, and we obtained a normal distribution of intelligence quotients on each of these. The full-scale Wechsler average IQ of 106 for the whole group indicated that they functioned near the upper limit of normal average intelligence. The IQ's of the boys were generally slightly higher than those of the girls. The mean Goodenough test IQ for the whole group was 94 and thus lower than the Wechsler and Peabody IQ's, yet still within the category of normal average; on this test the girls did slightly better than the boys. The mean Peabody IQ for the whole sample was 105 and thus in close correspondence with the Wechsler IQ. Analysis of differences among age or sex groups yielded no statistically significant IQ disparities. The standard deviations on all three intelligence tests were within the expected norms.

Calculations of IQ-result intercorrelations yielded coefficients of above 0.50 between Wechsler and Peabody as well as between Wechsler and Goodenough; between Peabody and Goodenough IQ's, however, the correlation coefficient was only 0.27. Employment of the product moment formula further confirmed our hypothesis that dyslexics would have Peabody scores more closely related to their Wechsler verbal IQ and Goodenough scores more closely related to their Wechsler performance IQ's.

Analysis of significant subtest variations revealed that dyslexics score particularly poorly on the Arithmetic, Digit Span, and Digit Symbol Wechsler items. Subtest profiles were surprisingly uniform: boys, girls, 6 to 13 year olds, 14 to 18 year olds, subjects with significantly higher verbal IQ's, subjects with significantly higher performance IQ's, and four adult illiterates were investigated separately, but all seven of these groups had subtest profiles with basically the same characteristics as for the whole group. In addition, they were similar to those obtained on smaller samples of retarded readers by various other researchers. In terms of specific weaknesses in the Digit Span, Digit Symbol, and Arithmetic subtests, further agreement was observed with subtest profiles gained on adults with brain injury and on children with positive EEG findings. This tends to strengthen the position of these who consider reading-spelling disability primarily a neurological problem.

We were able to differentiate four Wechsler Profiles for dyslexics:

Profile I:	Significantly higher verbal IQ	22.3%
Profile II:	Significantly higher performance IQ	18.9%
Profile III:	Significant subtest variability	48.6%
Profile IV:	No significant disparities	10.2%

It is important that significant subtest disparities which are not apparent as significantly higher verbal or performance IQ's, constitute the most frequently occurring profile among dyslexics. It is equally important that there are almost as many retarded readers with significantly higher performance IQ's as there are with significantly higher verbal IQ's. While the latter have drawn considerable attention, the former have been neglected. On the basis of our findings it is erroneous and misleading to state that the verbal IQ score is a better indicator of the dyslexic's "true" mental potential, as some authors have suggested. For just as many dyslexics the performance IQ would have to be considered the "truer" indicator. And where would be the "true" potential of the almost 50% of retarded readers who have significant subtest disparities? Speculations as to the "truer" indicator are without merit if we realize that the total mental potential is a composite of strong as well as weak intellectual properties, and that the Wechsler full-scale IQ takes each subtest result into consideration independently, thus providing an adequate indication of the overall capacity of the child tested. How true this is, even for the slow reader and his Wechsler scores, can be seen in the fact that the general intelligence of dyslexics is as normally distributed as that of control groups, and that as a group they have normal average mean IQ's on the full scales. Our concern should not be which of the IQ's is a truer reflection of the total intelligence, but in which areas the individual child with whom we are dealing has strong points to build upon and where his weak points need to be strengthened.

With regard to the significant Wechsler Verbal IQ and Wechsler Performance IQ discrepancies, we asked whether further investigations might not prove that dyslexics with low verbal scores have left hemisphere disorders and those with low performance scores right hemisphere damage or dysfunction, while those with significant overall subtest variability will prove to have diffuse or bilateral central nervous system disorders.

Measurable quantitative gains in terms of grade level scores after reading therapy, presented in our study, and reported by other investigators, show that after careful diagnosis, placement, and therapy utilizing individualized teaching as well as emotional support, retarded readers will have considerably improved skills. Greater still are the qualitative gains; and physicians as well as educators, psychologists, parents, and others concerned with the rehabilitation of disabled readers, seem to agree that none of the combined efforts are lost or in vain.

4. ENVIRONMENTAL FACTORS*

4.1 Socio-Economic Family Background

We restricted our investigation of environment largely to the child's immediate family background. School matters, such as the controversy over certain reading teaching methods, regular schooling, etc., have been explored in previous chapters. School backgrounds varied as follows: the 175 students referred to the Raskob Institute in the summer of 1968 came from 124 different schools, most of which were public, a minority parochial schools, four were adult evening schools, three military academies, and one a university. The largest number of students coming from any single school was four. This range of variability excludes automatically one-sided emphasis or selection in regard to school background.

Possible relationships between family situation and frequency of dyslexia have been considered here and there, but not yet vigorously investigated or definitely proven.

Linder remarked that dyslexia seemed to occur in all kinds of families, but most frequently in what would have to be considered "normal" settings, i.e., complete, closely-knit, well cared for families, whereas only a small portion of retarded readers seemed to come from divorced, incomplete, or constantly fighting families.[1] Schenk-Danziger also believed that the family could not be considered a decisive factor in the causation of reading disorders. She did think that the family had great influence on whether the learning disability could be overcome.[2] Bleidick felt that intellectually dull families, disturbed relationships among family members, and parents who are poor educators might have a negative influence on growth and, thus, might increase reading problems.[3] In Kobi's experience the

---

*Table D in the appendix lists all environmental data for an easier review.

parents and families of dyslexics were often described as "nervous," impatient, impulsive, tense, brutal, bragging, ambitious, unrefined, inconsequent, neglecting.[4] Biglmaier thought it quite possible that the family could be the source of reading disability, especially in cases of death, separation, divorce, illegitimacy, quarrelsome parents, etc.[5] Chassagny warned: "It is above all necessary to study the relationships between the different environments in which the child lives and how certain maladjustments, such as the educational level of the families, can inhibit normal scholarly growth."[6] Strang thought: "... there is no conclusive evidence about the influence of a broken home. The low economic status of the family and certain parent-child relationships may markedly affect a child's reading development."[7] Robinson found that reading disabilities were often associated with unfavorable family background.[8] Smith and Dechant, on the contrary, were convinced, "... cases of severe reading disability occur among children from all socio-economic levels."[9]

These quotations from the pertinent literature represent not a selection but almost a complete picture of everything that has been said on the subject. Very little quantitative data exist. Many researchers, in the face of the contradictory observations presented so far, demand more thorough research on the matter. Only a few insist that a definite and causal relationship does exist between reading disability and family background. Niemeyer for instance found among 21 dyslexics 18 whose reading problems he believed were due to family factors; only the three remaining cases did he attribute to congenital causation; he concluded: "Reading disability can be aggravated by adverse family factors, if not even caused by them."[10]

Perusal of the literature further reveals that in the discussion of family background there is often insufficient differentiation between socio-economic, educational, cultural, and psychological factors.

4.1a) Distribution of Socio-Economic Classes

In order to determine the socio-economic background of the children in our sample we had to rely on verbal statements and those given on application forms, concerning parental occupations, residential area, type of school attended, etc. Questions about exact income, property, business size, etc., could not be asked; our results therefore have to be interpreted with some degree of caution.

As "upper class" we counted parents in the professions, upper business ranks, executives, successful artists, etc. As "middle class" we designated those in secretarial, office, business, skilled vocational and similar occupations. Untrained workers, small farm operators, handymen, welfare recipients, and such constituted the "lower class." In Table 19 we present our quantitative findings, together with those gathered by Havighurst and Neugarten which are considered to be a normal distribution, representative for North America.[11]

Table 19. Distribution of socio-economic classes

	Upper Class	Middle Class	Lower Class
Our sample of 500 families of retarded readers	16.3%	68.4%	15.3%
Typical distribution for U.S., as presented by Havighurst and Neugarten	8–15%	45–75%	15–25%

Reading retardation, as well as attendance at a private institute, thus show a normal distribution among the various socio-economic groups in the population. This, and other data, to be discussed in the following chapter, seem to contradict those investigators who feel that dyslexia occurs more frequently in economically or educationally deprived families. Our statistics confirm great parental concern for their children's formal education. Parent interviews frequently reveal even an almost disturbing anxiety about the need for good grades and a college education. Parents and educators tend to equate good grades with good behavior, success in the classroom with success in life, an understandable but regrettable mistake if carried too far. At some point, the anxiety thus aroused in the child, the premature pressure to compete and to succeed, will have an adverse effect: the youngster feels that life is a threat rather than a challenge and will thus prefer, more or less consciously, to remain dependent and immature.

In any event, whether it is anxiety or healthy motivation, it must be said that parents from all socio-economic levels are ready to sacrifice, financially, in terms of time, involvement, etc. when it comes to the education of their children.

4.1b) Mother Working Outside Home

Developmental, child, and depth psychology have thoroughly emphasized the role and importance of the mother for a healthy development of the child. Prolonged physical or psychic absence of the mother, persistent marital tension, separations, pending divorces, etc. tend to have traumatic effects on the growing child, threatening his mental, emotional, and physical health. It seemed important to investigate, whether a correlation exists between maternal absence, caused by her being employed outside the home, and the occurrence of reading problems. Naturally, this question cannot be answered quantitatively alone, no matter what the numerical findings are. Whether the prolonged absence of the mother will have a negative influence on the child, depends on more than her not being there; the whole picture must be investigated: is the mother satisfied with her situation, maybe even more so than she would if she did not work, is she thus a better mother, is there a substitute mother in the house, how old are the children, is there illness, poverty, in the family, what made the mother seek employment in the first place? Even though statistics indicate frequent association of working mothers and problem children, only the study of individual situations will provide insightful answers.

The question of whether a connection exists between the employed mother and the retarded reader has been raised here and there in the literature. A partial answer was provided by Harris who found among 100 successful schoolboys only 9% whose mothers worked or whose parents had marital discords, but among 100 boys with learning difficulties he found 20% living in such families. In this latter group Harris had more eldest than youngest children which led him to believe that working mothers tend to expect more responsibility from their oldest children, making them substitute mothers, causing them to be too serious and depressed to be able to be good students. It is also interesting that he found that the intelligence quotients and the working mothers showed the same quantitative relationships for both groups.[12] De Hirsch, in a comparative study on 53 premature and 53 full term babies, found that the prematures, by the time they were from 5 to 6 years old, showed numerous learning and behavior problems; at first she felt the fact that their mothers worked was significant, but statistical analysis revealed that in both groups the percentage of working mothers was equally high, namely 24%.[13]

Our material yielded a closely corresponding ratio: 21.8% of the mothers were employed outside the home. Some of these mothers had sought employment in order to be able to meet the additional expenses caused by the child's need for special educational help. In these cases the dyslexia causes the employment, not vice versa. Exact figures as to the number of mothers currently employed in the U.S. could not be obtained. According to the 1966 census, of 71 million women 14 years of age or older, 16 million were married and employed; this would be 22.5% of all American married women and would mean that the figure for our sample lies near the national average.

It can thus be concluded that statistical evidence does not support the notion that maternal absence from the home because of employment contributes significantly to the causation of reading-writing retardation.

4.1c) Only One Parent Living With Child

In only 8.2% of our sample was the home deprived of one parent, either through divorce, separation, or death. This becomes more significant if we remind ourselves of the frequency with which child guidance and similar institutions report this variable. Dührssen wrote that all family counseling centers, child guidance clinics, and such institutions find more than 50%

of the children referred to them to come from incomplete homes or substitute families.[14] The low percentage found in our sample strengthens the impression that dyslexia and family situation are not correlated, either quantitatively or qualitatively.

4.1d) Child Not Living With His Own Family

The proportion of retarded readers living with grandparents, in foster homes, or children's institutions was with 1.4% so small that not living at home cannot be seriously taken into consideration as causal factor.

4.1e) Child Adopted

According to the 1966 U.S. census, 1% of the American population below the age of 18 was legally adopted. The ratio of adopted children in our sample, however, was 5.4%. This was considerably above the norm. Our data seem, however, to throw a light on the type of parents we are dealing with rather than on the causation of dyslexia. Only couples who are truly desirous of having and raising children will go through the expense, emotionally and financially, the adoption process brings with it. Adoptive parents probably are even more conscientiously concerned about the well-being of their children than natural parents and thus more readily inclined to seek help, even at the first sign of difficulty.

Naturally, to be adopted presents its own psychological problems and tensions, yet, so much enlightenment and professional help have been available that adoptive children now grow up with a gradually increasing awareness of their situation and few experience traumatic impacts. As a group, at our Institute, they do not evidence more, or different, or more severe emotional or social maladjustment than the rest of the children. It would be most difficult to present any basis in fact, beyond the statistical evidence of frequent numerical association, for a causal relationship between adoption and reading retardation.

4.2 Siblings

4.2a) Only Child

Statistical analysis showed 4.6% of our slow readers to be only children. As early as 1931 Anderson and Kelley had among 100 retarded readers no more than 5% only children while their control group of average students contained 17%.[15] There are psychological and educational advantages as well as disadvantages in being an only child. One hears authors here and there suggesting that dyslexia occurs less frequently among only children because they receive more attention, stimulation, and care and are thus less prone to develop learning problems. Yet, we cannot help noticing in parent conferences how depressing and frightening it must be to a child to find himself the sole object of his parents' dreams, expectations, efforts, and hopes. So often either parent will state that, because they could "not afford to get an education," they are going to make sure the child will get one. And "education" in these cases is always identical with "college degree," no more, no less. We say "no more" to point out that education comes more and more to mean "diploma" and less and less character formation and vocational training. We say "no less" since the trend is no longer the goal of a high school diploma — there are too many with that already — but a college degree. In many cases parental anxiety and ambition stubbornly resist the realization of the child's true limitations, interests, talents, etc. They try so persistently and strongly to press the child into conformity with their own expectations that emotional, adjustment, and learning problems result, and these keep the child from utilizing whatever mental abilities and vocational assets he may have. These are the cases in which parent counseling and psychotherapy are needed far more than any kind of remedial or academic help for the child. This does not exclude the realization that in certain cases being an only child can contribute to reading-writing deficiencies. If aspirations are unreasonably high and concentrated on a single child, then he may "decide" that it is safer to not learn to read, to not grow up. The only child who is spoiled, kept dependent, and overly protected, of course, will be equally prone to develop learning disabilities.

Another possible explanation as to the relatively high proportion of only children among dyslexics, is a physiological one. Only children not rarely are born to parents who married late; thus there could be biological, genetic, or traumatic (perinatal) factors involved, although such theories as "Plasmainsuffizienz" and "Produktionserschöpfung" have not yet been scientifically verified.

Among 66 dyslexics Kirchhoff had 18.1% who were only children, but he pointed out this was a normal ratio for the city of Hamburg where he conducted his research.[16] There is not enough quantitative data yet to decide whether a positive relation exists between dyslexia and being an only child.

4.2b) Oldest Child

Of our sample 24.6% were the oldest ones in their families. Anderson and Kelley in their study found 27% oldest children. These figures take on more significance if seen in relation to the number of youngest children.

4.2c) Youngest Child

Among our sample of 500 we had 36% who were the youngest children in their families. Anderson and Kelley found 34.8%.[15] The proportion of youngest children in our population appears relatively high. Harris, comparing 100 slow reading boys with 100 average or better students found among the former twice as many youngest as oldest children.[17]

Little can be found in the literature on dyslexia pertaining to the question of the low reader's position among his siblings. Other educational and psychological writings also seem to neglect this aspect. Statistical material is at a minimum. Dührssen, one of the few authors to discuss the problem at all, concentrated more on the age differences among groups of siblings and on parental attitudes toward these groups.[18] Harris was moved to write: "Despite . . . the easily noted differences between the first- and last-born, the concept of ordinal position has not taken hold."[19] It might be added that a 631-page German textbook on child psychiatry, published in 1964, as well as a book of selected readings on *The Child in Our Time*, do not mention this aspect at all. Yet it has two important kinds of influence on the child's development: one in the form of his special position among his brothers and sisters, the other in the form of the particular attitudes and expectations on the part of his parents. The youngest child certainly has problems and advantages different from those the middle or the oldest child encounter. If it is, in fact, so that youngest children, because of fewer demands made on them, grow up to be less responsible and more independent, it could be expected that their position among the siblings indirectly increases or aggravates any reading-writing disability they might be afflicted with. It cannot be concluded from the evidence available so far, that being either the youngest or the oldest child in a family contributes directly or frequently to dyslexia.

4.2d) Sibling Rivalry

In 17.6% of the cases in our dyslexia population severe and constant sibling rivalry was reported by parents or teachers. Kirchhoff had 15.1% among his 66 disabled readers.[20] He considered this proportion within normal and expected limits, provided one does not use very strict criteria as to what constitutes sibling rivalry. Since we counted only severe and persistent rivalry, and can add the impressions gained in hundreds of parent conferences, we tend to believe that sibling rivalry is stronger and more frequent in families with dyslexic children than in average homes. Our parents almost always confirm that there is one, but often there are two or more, siblings who do outstandingly well in school; being intelligent, earning good grades easily, enjoying parental approval, these favorites are often also socially well accepted, good athletes, good-looking, etc., in short, they have everything the disabled learner has not. This puts him all the more, at least in his own eyes, into the position of the outsider, the "black sheep." Most slow readers seem to accept their lot rather passively, either withdrawing or remaining immature. Some are even described by their parents as exceptionally "good around the house," eager to please, to help, to show affection, and to identify with those who suffer. It is as if these children tried to compensate socially for their scholastic failure. The majority of the "black sheep" children, however, are aggressive, negative, provocative, and openly hostile to their siblings. The question arises here, naturally, whether the reading disability has made the child a hostile, jealous loner, or whether the same condition which made him a dyslexic, as in hyperactivity for instance, is also making him the "black sheep." Whether sibling rivalry is cause, cosymptom, or consequence of dyslexia can be ascertained, if at all, only through individual case analysis. Schenk-Danziger contributed the observation, at a psychological convention in 1967, that dyslexics showed great susceptibility to behavior crises caused through sibling rivalry or marital tension in their families.[21] Kobi observed that sibling rivalry thrives especially in situations where a younger brother or sister is more mature, stable and scholastically successful than the older dyslexic child who often reacts, not in a positive manner with increased effort, but with withdrawal, regression, passivity, concealed or open hostility, aggression, etc. He noted more regressive reaction than active over-compensation,[22] a finding that coincides with overall findings on dyslexics and their emotional problems.

4. 3 Parental Attitudes

That parental attitudes are decisive in their positive or negative influence on the reading retardation of the child, that they must be helped to understand and become cognizant of the situation, that they need to be supported in their difficult position, that their active involvement in the rehabilitation program is pre-requisite to success, all have been stressed and discussed in the literature to considerable extent. But parental attitudes as po-tential causal factors in regard to dyslexia have been only mea-gerly investigated. Linder is one of the few who posed the question and she found among her 50 disabled readers almost one-third whose parents she classified as strict, nagging, im-patient and inconsistent; 10% of the mothers were described as "nervous."[23] Biglmaier wrote that labile, changing educational measures of their parents were often a source of serious frustration to retarded readers.[24] Young examined 37 boys and 4 girls with reading retardation and described how parental misunderstanding of psychological and physiological components of their reading failure further impeded the children's ability to overcome the learning difficulty.[25]

The figures presented in the following paragraphs cannot be considered complete. We selected these six categories of parental attitudes simply on the basis of most often observed characteristics. Basically, of course, this is an oversimplification, in reality there are as many parental attitudes and shades and nuances of emotions and ideas about how children should be dealt with as there are parents and individuals. That positive parental attitudes are not statistically registered, does not indicate that they do not exist; on the contrary, we find that a majority of the parents who present their children at the Institute are warm, well adjusted, communicative, cognizant, objective, understanding, eager to learn and eager to help, ready for any sacrifice, personal or financial, which might be necessary to increase the child's chances for a better life now and later.

4.3a) Overanxious Parents

The figures indicated that 22.5% of the parents interviewed were considered overanxious, overprotective, worried, and insecure. These are the parents who consult teachers, physicians, psychologists, asking for advice, changing from one to another, without opinion of their own, constantly altering their approach, their tactics, trying to follow the advice of others, always expecting a panacea, a miracle cure. This is detrimental and confusing to the child who thus remains dependent, immature, and labile. Excessively anxious and protective mothers are often those who lack true affection for the child; in this case they are unconsciously driven by guilt feelings, trying to compensate by constant demonstrations of their care and readiness to accept and follow advice. "I did all I could, you see, but nothing worked." Unconsciously these mothers need and foster the child's dependency for their own neurotic needs; as a consequence the child experiences the world as threatening, something he would rather not have to face. Such circumstances can easily lead to unconscious learning or reading resistance, or, if not directly causing, at least they aggravate learning disability where it happens to exist.

4.3b) Rejecting Parents

Almost one-fourth of our dyslexics, namely 22.8%, had at least one parent with rejecting, cold, and critical attitudes. It is amazing how many parents are able to simply label their child's scholastic failure as "lack of motivation" or "laziness"; "He doesn't want to try," "He's not interested," "He has no sense of responsibility," "He's totally indifferent, only wants to play" — these are the most frequent complaints, often expressed by the parent in such exasperated or hostile tones that the interviewer can readily identify with the child's feeling of rejection. He correctly senses that his parents have no confidence in him, no hope for him. It is important to keep in mind that such parental thoughts and feelings arise mostly on the basis of ignorance, helplessness, and long-standing defeat, not out of conscious malice. The more the child is scolded, punished, ridiculed, misunderstood, or otherwise rejected, the more he tends to feign indifference, to withdraw, to feel defeated. Parents, often unable to face their own part in the failure, blame the child exclusively and unconsciously "wash their hands of him."

Among the 22% of rejecting parents we counted only severe and persistent degrees of rejection. The important question is, here again, where the vicious circle started, with the scholastic failure or with parental disapproval of the child? Individual case studies lead us to assume that more often the parental rejection is a secondary reaction to the child's primary learning disability. Follow-up studies confirm this: matters often change much for the better once the family has been helped, either in a few sessions or over a period of counseling, to realize the underlying difficulties and their own adverse reactions. Once the vicious circle is broken, new and better ways of dealing with each other, and of coping with the child's scholastic problems, can be developed.

We see here once more how important the initial psychological evaluation of the whole child and his background is and how much the medical, psychological, and educational professions must work hand in hand.

4.3c) Overly Demanding and Punitive Parents

In 17.5% of our sample the parents had to be diagnosed as authoritarian, demanding, dominating, rigid, and overly punitive. These parents appear to be prisoners of the modern fight for existence. They live under great stress, they are in constant fear of the future; in the parent conferences they appear to be pessimistic, humorless, resentful, and bitter. They often have fixed ideas of what is good for the child's future and what is not. If the child shows even minor or temporary learning difficulties, these parents are overly alarmed and react with increased demand and rigidity. Their own security is threatened, they fear that their own expectations and plans will be interfered with by the child's shortcomings, or by any divergent interests or talents on his part. They want whatever does not meet their own picture to be ignored or erased. Constantly under pressure, forced to conform with rigid ideas, frequently corrected or punished, the child develops neurotic defenses.

Biglmaier apparently made similar observations; he said that parental attitudes toward the child's failure are to be explored and discussed; better understanding of the child must be fostered; parents must be helped to avoid at least the most obvious educational mistakes.[26]

4.3d) Cold and Critical Parents

Of the disabled readers in our sample, 4.9% had at least one emotionally detached, often neurotically perfectionist, meticulous, and overly critical parent. Cleanliness, order, tidiness, punctuality, almost blind obedience, suppression of spontaneity, etc., are the hallmarks, impeding growth and individuality. Nothing the child does is good or exact enough; if he works hard and proudly brings home a "B," the parent only says: "Make sure its going to be an "A" next time." These parents do not identify with their child's feelings, but ask, plaintively, why just *my* child?" "Why does this have to happen to *me*?" "How do I deserve this?" Neurotic self-centeredness prevents any objective or emotional involvement with the child; one is right-eously convinced that all one does and says is "only in the best interest of the child."

It is easy to see that such a parent not only cannot help effectively in cases of existing dyslexia but might well be the primary source in its causation. Dyslexics who have neurotic parents of this type can best be helped through their parents who should be gently but firmly persuaded to seek psy-chotherapeutic treatment. Reading therapy alone would not succeed; experience has proved this repeatedly at our Institute. Only after a change of attitude, a more objective and positive involvement on the part of the parent, can reading therapy be expected to be effective.

4.3e) Unrealistic Parental College Ambitions

There were no fewer than 7.0% of our parents in the sample who had unrealistic college ambitions for their slow reading children. We designated their expectations as "unrealistic" when it is obvious, and from long-standing learning failure should have been apparent to the parents, too, that this child's potential did not mark him as a candidate for college education. This relatively large proportion of parents with exaggerated expectations must be seen in context: part of the problem lies not with the individual parent but with society at large. A high school diploma is no longer sufficient for a great number of jobs. There are more high school graduates than job openings. Rapidly expanding mechanization of simple services and com-plication of higher services, increasing complexity and special-ization in technological and scientific enterprises, demand more and more education. Whether this whole development is a healthy one or not, whether we should change the economy and stop creating more college graduates than the employment market can absorb, whether we should provide better job training and more opportunities for those who are not "college material," whether we should stop equating good grades with good personality and begin to honor *all* types of work, including menial work (for which there exists a great need!), are important questions, but they lie beyond the scope of this study. It seems certain that much of the parental anxiety and consequent push for college does not result from merely personal ambition but from an attempt to cope with a situation that has become very difficult even on a national scale. Educational concerns today center primarily on job qualification, not on the formation of intellect and character. Mass education tends to be an impersonal machinery. Entrance tests are paper and pencil tasks, requiring reading, writing, speed, memory, and only some degree of reasoning. Personal qualifications, such as reliability, honesty, dedication, etc. play no part. The disabled reader, poor speller, slow but original and creative thinker, all who do not readily fit into the slot, are lost to college and to society as a whole.

Thus it is not overly surprising to find so many parents ready to deny the obvious reality of their children's limited reading capacity. They blame teachers, teaching methods, their child's illness in the first grade or some other reason for "never having caught on," anything, rather than to accept and face the child's lack of ability. To "not be college material" is the most threatening verdict to these parents; they go on looking for a panacea, a miracle, a hidden key that will suddenly unlock the child's mind. Even after twelve or more consecutive years of academic failure they still insist "the child is intelligent, able, interested, he *wants* to go to college, we only need to unlock his mind." How far parents may go in their unrealistic ambition has been demonstrated by Harris, also, who presented several extreme cases in his study.[27]

Especially interesting is the fact that the exaggerated college ambitions in our sample proved to be significantly (chi-square = 15.15, 1% level of confidence) higher for girls than for boys. That parents should try more often to force a college degree for their daughters than for their sons, probably has several psychological reasons: boys may see the need more readily anyway; the trend to give young girls a college education is still a new one; and many mothers probably still see their daughters' best chances for a "good" marriage at college.

A more specific reason for this significant finding might lie in the fact that many of the girls brought to the Raskob Institute have neither the talent nor the inclination for a college education, this is in contrast to the boys, many of whom have good learning potential but specific reading-spelling disabilities.

Here, again, one must determine through individual investigation whether it was specific learning disability which brought the student to the clinic or whether the parent wants to believe in a special problem so that he does not have to accept the child's overall lack of mental potential and/or college inclination.

4.3f) Indifferent and Distant Parents

Only 4.0% of our disabled readers had parents who remained uninvolved, indifferent to their children's needs or difficulties. These are often socially, economically, and politically highly developed and preoccupied people with shallow interpersonal relationships whose children are being raised by a succession of housekeepers and similar employees. They bring their children with the unspoken attitude: you are the expert, here is my child, now you make him function, we pay, you make him get better grades. And this is how they handle all their children's needs: trying to buy for money what they cannot provide from inner involvement. It goes without saying that these are the lonely children and that they cannot be helped academically or emotionally unless their parents can be involved in their rehabilitation. Parental cooperation, beyond the pocketbook, is very difficult to obtain in these cases, and the sad fact is that the prognosis for their children is a poor one.

4.3g) Both Parents Present for Initial Interview

It is one of the basic policies of the Raskob Institute to try to involve both parents in the rehabilitation of the child. At the time of application both parents are urged to attend the conference together which is provided after initial testing. Our statistics showed that in 55.6% of the cases both parents do, indeed, come together to the parent conference with the psychologist. If one considers that for this purpose the father has to arrange to be away from his place of business, that in 21% of the families both parents work, that 8% of the children have only one parent, that illness, military service, professional travel, etc. often make it impossible for both parents to attend, then 55% is a very good proportion. There is general agreement in the literature of dyslexia that both parents should be involved in the child's therapeutic program, especially the father who so often feels that school and other educational matters are "the wife's business." Because of the interrelatedness of family relationships, behavior and learning problems, etc. and the complexity of the whole situation, it is important to get to know both parents and to have them share the insights, responsibilities, and consequences of the initial evaluation. That, in fact, so many fathers can be involved, if only a special effort is made to gain their cooperation, is a hopeful sign and has proved a decisive factor in the therapeutic process.

4.4 Summary

In concluding this chapter, it seems important to once more emphasize that our figures concerning socio-economic status, ordinal position among siblings, and parental attitudes do not claim to be complete; they are at best a beginning, a stimulation toward more and better research in this direction.

Experience as well as the figures presented here seem to show that dyslexia occurs on all socio-economic levels and relatively independently of intellectual, cultural, social, or emotional family circumstances. Insignificantly few of the Raskob students come from broken or incomplete homes, few live outside their families; thus it can be said that family background is not even numerically related to dyslexia, much less a causative factor.

Our material confirmed the observation of other studies that there are more youngest than oldest children among the retarded readers; it is not yet clear whether this has more psychological or congenital reasons.

Severe sibling rivalry occurred relatively frequently in our sample and seemed to be a secondary complication rather than the cause of the specific reading-spelling problems.

Of parental attitudes it must be said, according to our impressions and statistical figures, that they rarely seem to be the immediate or primary cause for the reading disability, although some do seem to be inducive to learning or, in particular, reading resistance on the part of the child.

With these observations we do not intend to negate the fact that parental attitudes are of decisive influence in regard to reading disability. If the causation is not directly dependent on the parents' emotional and intellectual make-up, its treatment certainly is. The more the parents are actively and objectively able to involve themselves, the better the chances for success. That in more than 50% of the families both parents actually could be involved from the start, was an encouraging and promising sign.

III. CONCLUSIONS

1. REVIEW

Reading disability was defined in this study as a specific learning disorder occurring despite normal or better intelligence and
regular schooling. The most important criterion in the definition
was considered the incongruity between general mental capacity and schooling on the one hand and reading-spelling
deficiency on the other. Research findings showed that specific
dyslexia is far from being a rare occurrence. Estimates of prevalence ranged from 2% to 25% among regular school populations. Specific dyslexia causes numerous problems in practice
and theory many of which must be considered unexplained
and/or unresolved so far.

The survey of literature on reading disabilities showed that a
great deal has been written, but few attempts have been made
to compare and coordinate theories and findings originating in
Europe and the United States. We found little agreement with
regard to terminology, to questions of causation and treatment,
and to preventive methods. Questions remain with respect to
endogenous or exogenous origin, primary or secondary symptoms, neurological involvement, and frequency or kind of psychological correlates. Furthermore, there is little agreement
about the direction or methods further research should take.
Nevertheless, the animated controversy presently taking place
in literature leads slowly but surely toward clarification, no
matter how complex the problem of dyslexia may be. Our work
at the Institute and my personal involvement with well over
1,000 retarded readers have led me to believe that no amount
of scientific progress will ever lead to the point where a particular individual case of specific dyslexia can be reduced to a case
of simple routine diagnosis and treatment. Individual testing,
background investigation, and a personally designed treatment
plan will always be a necessity if optimal results are to be

obtained. Research on groups has to continue, though. Especially statistical analyses of larger populations are still needed. This need prompted us to study the 500 dossiers analyzed here and to compare our findings with those of other European as well as American researchers. Our study was based on the hypothesis, derived from professional experience at the Raskob Learning Institute, that it would be possible to demonstrate by empirical and statistical means an existing syndrome of dyslexia. The verification of this hypothesis included physiological, psychological, and social correlates of specific reading disability.

The results confirmed our working hypothesis and showed that dyslexia as a group phenomenon as well as in individual case analysis does show characteristic symptoms. Based on the frequency of occurrence within the group we can now list the cosymptoms of the syndrome of dyslexia:

1. Physiopsychological symptoms: primarily neurological signs, which seem to be part of the primary causative factors.
2. Specific characteristics of intelligence: probably also part of the primary causation.
3. Psychopathological symptoms: apparently more often secondary in origin.
4. Environmental symptoms: seemingly secondary and only of indirect significance.

Statistical analysis of the group showed that physiological signs, among them especially neurological dysfunctions, visual-perceptual and motoric deficiencies, inadequately developed dominance, speech impediments, delay in language development, and hyperactivity were most often present. Up to 67% of the 500 dyslexics investigated showed these correlates. Examination of statistical significance left no doubt that more boys than girls and more primary than secondary level students showed these physiological signs. While these significant differences were true in the majority of the physiological symptoms studied, they occurred only as an exception among the psychological and social correlates investigated.

The evidence of frequent neurological findings can no longer be denied. Neurological dysfunctions are usually noticed before the child enters school, that is, before his specific reading and spelling weakness becomes apparent and an issue. They occur with greater frequency among prematurely born children and among those who have a history of complicated birth, physical trauma, or illness. If the slow reader shows neurological involvement, we usually find other family members with related symptoms. All of these observations seem to indicate that we are dealing here with primary factors. It must be kept in mind, though, that in the concrete individual case it is most difficult to arrive at a differential diagnosis, clearly separating traumatic, functional, maturational or hereditary components.

Testpsychological findings from our material confirmed what had been observed in several smaller samples previously studied by some investigators, namely, no positive correlation exists between mental ability and dyslexia. Also, the distribution of intelligence quotients is as normal in dyslexics as it is in unselected groups. We calculated the mean Wechsler IQ of 1,013 dyslexics, investigated by ten different researchers (see Table 1) and found it to be 101.9, our mean IQ of 106.0 thus was somewhat higher. While the extent of intelligence can be considered an independent factor, the nature of intelligence, that is, its various dimensions, seems to be related to reading failure.

Wechsler test results were significantly lower in areas requiring arithmetical problem solving, coding, and immediate recall of digits. Dyslexics apparently fail when concrete knowledge, simple factual recall, sequencing without logical content, and practical orientation are involved. Persistently better, but not significantly higher scores were obtained by slow readers when the finding of similarities of concepts, social comprehension, auditory vocabulary, picture completion, and object assembly were concerned. Analytical thinking, thus, does not appear to be diminished in dyslexics but seems to be slightly above average. Our test profiles which demonstrate these intellectual characteristics are not isolated findings, but were observed in previous studies performed by several researchers on smaller dyslexic groups. There were frequent, significant discrepancies between verbal and performance intelligence as measured by the Wechsler scales. Statistically still more frequent were significant disparities among the eleven subscores which reflect significant discrepancies in the intellectual make-up of the students tested. Our analysis showed that only 10% of all dyslexics studied in our sample had no significant differences among the various test dimensions, but 22% had significantly higher verbal intelligence, 18% had significantly higher performance ability and no less than 48% showed significant disproportions among their subtest scores on both scales.

The obvious weakness of failing readers in the three test areas mentioned: arithmetic, digit span and digit symbol, has a parallel: the brain injured also show lowered scores on these three subtests. This parallel, of course, strengthens the hypothesis that in the case of dyslexia neurological disorders play a primary and most frequent part.

Psychopathological findings among our disabled readers were evident and anxiety was the most frequently observed symptom. No less than 65% of the whole group showed signs of anxious tension. In the majority of cases they appeared to be secondary reactions to the difficulties caused by the learning disability. The degree of anxiety suffered seemed to be directly proportional to the severity of the reading-spelling failure. In most cases anxiety did not develop until school experience caused stress and frustration and it disappeared gradually as reading therapy progressed. Only a few were in need of specific psychological help in order to overcome their anxieties.

Approximately one-third of our sample showed concentration problems, immaturity, low frustration threshold, or withdrawal. It became apparent that most reactions were of a passive, introvert nature whereas aggressive, extrovert, defensive reactions and conflicts were relatively rare. This observation probably appears unlikely at first sight, especially to teachers and educators. They have seen dyslexics in their classroom who were among the poorly adjusted, uncontrolled, disturbing, and difficult to reach students in the group. But, we must be careful here to distinguish between hyperactive children whose sensory and motor disinhibition severely reduces their self-control, and aggressive children who act out hostilities and other negative feelings. The first group must be considered as primarily neurologically handicapped while the second group is primarily emotionally disturbed.

Concentration problems, immaturity, and defensive reactions were significantly more frequent among primary schoolchildren than secondary students, a self-explanatory finding in view of normal psychophysiological maturation processes.

The facts that children with learning disabilities show a high degree of behavior disorders, that failure in school and repercussions from the environment cause anxiety, that hyperactivity is accompanied by inability to concentrate, that unpleasant consequences of the learning disability unconsciously prompt the child to hold on to the relative security of remaining immature so that he need not have to grow up and take on more responsibility — all these are "psycho-logical" consequences which are easy to understand and can be considered as secondary reactions. Only in a small minority of our cases were psycho-logical symptoms the primary and exclusive causes of the reading disorder.

Environmental factors seemed to contribute the least to the learning problems in our sample. No significant correlations were found between socio-economic family situation and specific dyslexia; none were observed with regard to working mothers, completeness of family, sibling rivalry, or birth order. Only the percentage of adopted children in our group was strikingly higher than in the general child population. This was explained, not in terms of emotional insecurity on the part of adopted children, but in terms of the particular emotional, intellectual, and economical constitution of adoptive families. These observations confirmed what several other researchers thought they had observed, namely, that environmental factors are only of indirect and secondary importance in the causation of specific dyslexia. Apparently, the influence of the family climate, of parental attitude in particular, is important only in regard to the kind and extent of the emotional overlay the child will develop. About one-fifth of our dyslexics had either overly anxious, rejecting, or demanding parents. Only between 4% and 7% of the parental attitudes had to be classified as indifferent, distant, cold, or critical. The more one-sided, exaggerated, or neurotic the parental attitude, the more difficult it becomes for the dyslexic child to outgrow his learning and behavior problems.

Generally speaking, our sample showed no characteristics of a socio-economic or cultural nature which would distinguish it clearly from any other population sample.

All the findings discussed above in connection with the whole group are largely observable in the individual dyslexic. Here too, aside from the reading-spelling problems which bring the student to the clinic, we find many neurological signs, although of minor degrees, we find specific intellectual traits in various test dimensions, we find emotional overlays of varying degrees and kinds and we observe that the family background has little or no bearing on the learning and adjustment difficulties. Of course, each case is different from any other case to some extent. The web of primary and secondary causes and reactions is complex and cannot easily be constructed. There is not just one unique syndrome of dyslexia; there are only individually different cases with varying constellations of symptoms. Each has to be diagnosed individually. No "standard" or "quick" test procedure will suffice, despite the fact that certain common characteristics do exist. As is true of human beings as a whole: we are so much alike and yet so different from each other. As in other scientific disciplines, we can only seek to describe a typical "ideal," theoretical picture of *the* dyslexic in the hopes that this picture will help to diagnose individually concrete cases, but it remains an abstract. In reality we do not meet this "ideal" dyslexic, we only find an individual with all his uniqueness who suffers from dyslexia. Anybody who keeps this point in mind will not make the mistake of looking for or proposing a complete and unique scheme of classification which could lead to neglect or overlook the uniqueness of the individual case. Our own proposal for a classification, thus, cannot be considered complete or absolutely correct, but it has been derived from broad professional experience as well as from numerous statistical data. It is based on the assumption that specific dyslexia constitutes a multietiological syndrome. According to causal relationships and frequency of occurrence we propose the following plan of classification:

1. *Somatogenetic dyslexia*
   a) *Functional:* neurological disorders in the organization or

functioning of the central nervous system without evident organic or structural changes (EEG normal or only slightly and unspecifically changed)

b) *Constitutional:* inborn weakness without pathogenetic evidence, at least as far as today's diagnostic means allow determination

c) *Hereditary:* familial tendency toward reading-spelling disorders of various manifestations in the absence of other evident causes or pathological signs

d) *Maturational:* delayed or arrested development of the nervous system, especially of its functions, often accompanied by psychological immaturity in various areas of growth (especially often observed among prematurely born children)

e) *Traumatic:* conclusively diagnosed traumata of the nervous system, organic changes, birth trauma, etc.

2. *Psychogenetic dyslexia:* Neurotic conflicts, defenses or reactions, originating in inner psychic or social tensions

3. *Sociogenetic dyslexia:* Caused by social milieu, family, school, culture, or similar social institutions and the limitations they may impose

In the concrete case that we meet in schools and clinics, of course, we will find that more often than not these various causative factors overlap, so much so, in fact, that even the most careful differential diagnosis cannot clearly differentiate them according to their chronological, their primary, and secondary origin. This complexity correlates with that of human nature in general. We see it also reflected in psychoses, neuroses, physical constitution, etc. In addition, we must remember that today's diagnostic possibilities are still limited. Future research can be expected, however, to furnish more reliable, more differentiated methods, means, and insights.

2. OUTLOOK

All our findings indicate, as has been expressed by some previous observers, that there is no such thing as *the* dyslexic. The more we learn, the more we see that we are dealing with a varied syndrome of multiple causation. This point of view corresponds with the complexities of human nature and such diseases as schizophrenia and epilepsy. It also shows future research the right direction. Attempts to characterize just one type of dyslexia and to monopolize the term can only be seen as an unjustifiable oversimplification. Our desire for clarification in terminology and simplification in diagnosis must not tempt us to ignore the complexities of the problem.

Whether we speak of polyetiology, specific configurations, multicausal, heterogeneous, or multifactorial phenomena, the insight, that dyslexia cannot be studied in pure form or in isolation, is most important. It is not just one particular symptom which characterizes the dyslexics as a group, but rather a heterogeneous syndrome of associated disorders, consisting of various physiological, and social components. It will be important to future research that each investigator study *one* aspect of dyslexia, i.e., the one with which his training and experience have familiarized him, such as intelligence, personality, speech, etc. Allergies, for instance, seem to have a high incidence among dyslexics, yet, this particular aspect has been little investigated so far. The more specific the aspect under investigation, the more it is necessary to keep the whole in mind to avoid losing sight of objectivity as well as the complexity and dignity of human nature. Our fast growing knowledge and specialization in the various scientific fields can be of service to the dyslexic only if we maintain a holistic approach. In addition, we need better teamwork and more training for reading therapists.

To collect information, to evaluate findings and methods, to develop new approaches, to coordinate efforts, to find ways of application and to stimulate further research, all amount to a difficult, yet challenging and gratifying endeavor to be carried out in a multidisciplinary effort whose home base should be in the field of special education.

IV. TRENDS IN LITERATURE PUBLISHED BETWEEN 1969 AND 1971

1. OVERVIEW

Perusal of publications on dyslexia and closely related subjects reveals that since I completed my own study there has been a tremendous increase in more or less popularized articles and booklets. "Good Gosh! My Child has Dyslexia" is a title which serves well as an example here.* Such literature renders a valuable service in familiarizing large numbers of people with a condition that might otherwise go completely unnoticed or that might maintain an aura such as is often associated with unenlightened ideas of progressive mental disease and irreversibility. The limitation, and at times danger, especially of short popularized publications, lies in oversimplified, one sided or inconsequential expositions which may be misleading and thus prevent some cases from receiving adequate attention.

Studies executed primarily with objective and statistical methods also can be found with increasing frequency. This is a natural consequence of the growing awareness, identification methods, treatment centers, number of specialists, and amount as well as duration of clinical experience with dyslexics. It is also a consequence of the rapid proliferation and growing sophistication in psycho-educational statistics. Constantly refined methods and the facilitation through computers allow for better research design and more dependable findings. A still unavoidable restriction in quantitative investigations is that they are bound to a world of exact measures, numbers, percentages, and the like. In order to get variables to work properly in a world of "objectivity," they must first be reduced to equality. Psychological entities must be converted into mathematical figures, must be isolated from the total personality context, from environmental factors, and thus are in danger of being dehydrated before they are ready for statistical investigation. The

*Dauzet, S. V., in: Reading Teacher 22:630-3, April 1969

exclusive faith that some researchers seem to have in quantification must be cautioned against as long as the hoped for ideal of social sciences — to reach the same exactitude and predictability as the natural sciences — remains an academic as well as a psychological fallacy. The numerous statistically sophisticated studies available to the reader today are needed and provide valuable information, especially on all kinds of specific questions. They need to be summarized though, according to certain fields of studies, agreeing and opposing findings, etc. They do not replace empathic reasoning or the need to see each case in its own unique constellation and individual significance. The whole is more than a summation of its parts, as the Gestaltists rightfully emphasize.

The number of extensive monographs on dyslexia seems to have decreased. Since, however, much is being done in terms of data collecting, observation, research, teaching, etc., one is inclined to consider this slowdown as a creative pause before a flood of new and more perceptive monographs.

Particularly scarce at this time are textbooks informing the student teacher and future reading specialist about the psychological, social, medical, and didactic needs as well as possibilities involved in early identification, treatment, and prevention of dyslexia. More than is presently possible could be accomplished if we had more special teachers, well enough informed through selective study of the contributions of various disciplines, to cooperate cognizantly with team experts in a multidisciplinary approach.

As to the important question of how to define dyslexia, investigators persist in a number of disagreeing views and probably even fortify their positions. Some go on trying to delineate well defined (at least theoretically) forms, such as "developmental," "specific," or "congenital" dyslexia, requesting exclusive application of these terms to cases and groups meeting the selective criteria established for their definitions. The danger of the circularity in this kind of "scientific" reasoning is obvious. In practice few if any cases fit these models of "pure" dyslexia. To claim that only definitions based on well defined, isolated symptoms deserve the connotation "scientific," not only ignores the complexity of the condition, not only denies the limitations of today's knowledge, but also attempts to capitalize on the term "scientific" which actually simply means "relating to knowledge." The principles and methods by which to obtain "scientific" knowledge must not only be well defined but also verifiable on given realities. "To identify these cases of specific developmental dyslexia . . . is no easy task. A wide experience is demanded of the diagnostician, together with a freedom from prejudice. Even so, the isolation is still a difficult matter, for there is no single clinical feature which can be accepted as pathognomic" (Bibliography No. 22, p. 74). This statement, made by Critchley, not only still holds, but might be yet closer to fact if his phrasing "no easy . . . still difficult matter" could be converted into "an as yet impossible" task. As desirable as scientific clarification, simplification, and unification of concepts and definitions may be, they must not allow any investigator to resemble the "Super-Simplifier" described in Toffler's famous "Future Shock": ". . . he needs a single neat equation that will explain all the complex novelties threatening to engulf him . . . Alas, no idea, not even mine or thine, is omni-insightful," (p. 361).

Less eloquent, but equally thoughtful and scientifically mind-ed authors can be found to speak of "The Dyslexias" or "The Dyslexic Syndrome." Aside from the authors listed in the bibliography at the end of this chapter, Gold for instance presents the implications of a regional learning disability center for pupils manifesting "the dyslexic syndrome" (In: Proceedings of the 13th Annual Convention of the International Reading Association, 1969, 13(3):82–94). In the same publication Schiffman elaborates on the provocative question: "Dyslexia: Is There Such a Thing?" (pp. 372–83). Conceptual development concerning syndromes and groups of entities can also be observed in neighboring disciplines, such as psychiatry and neurology which increasingly treat topics like "The Schizophrenias," "The Epilepsies," and "The Neurological Learning Disability Syndrome."

In the still open field of etiology, aside from already extensively researched questions of hereditary, emotional, environmental, neurological, and other potentially causative factors, growing attention is being given to metabolic, neurochemical, genetic, biochemical, and hormone imbalance as possible etiological explanations. More recent conceptualizations also include a theory of information overload. It supposes a breakdown of human cognitive performance under heavy, force-paced information processing. The accelerated pace of modern life, rapid growth of scientific data, information through mass media, mobility, confrontation with novel situations at ever shorter intervals, things to be learned, the unpredictability of the future and an individual's role in it, force us to process information to an extent and at a pace unknown to former generations. Interesting, if not yet fully conclusive experiments concerning cognitive breakdown due to information overload have been published (Udansky, G. and Chapman, L. J.: Schizophrenic-like Responses in Normal Subjects Under Time Pressure. In: The Journal of Abnormal and Social Psychology, 60:143–46, 1960, and Meier, R. L.: Information Input Overload, pp. 233–73, and Churchill, L.: Some Sociological Aspects of Message Load, pp. 274–83, both in: Massarik, F., and Ratoosh, P. (eds.): Mathematical Explorations in Behavioral Science. Homewood Ill., Irwin and Dorsey Press, 1965).

The various trends in recent literature on dyslexia as briefly exemplified in this chapter make it apparent that much has been accomplished while still more remains to be done in this field.

The bibliography that begins below presents, in the order of the year of publication, a not complete but representative sample of American and European literature. Most of the books and articles listed have bibliographies of their own which will guide the reader to further writings and information on the subject of dyslexia.

2. BIBLIOGRAPHY

1969

Adams, R. B.: Dyslexia: A Discussion of Its Definition. In: Journal of Learning Disabilities 2: 616–33, December 1969

Advisory Committee on Dyslexia. In: Elementary English 46: 679–80, May 1969

Blanche-Benveniste and Chevrel, A.: L'orthographe. Maspero, 1969

Blau, H. et al: Developmental Dyslexia and Its Remediation. In: Reading Teacher 22: 649–53, April 1969

Cratty, Bryant J.: Movement, Perception and Thought. Peek Publications, Palo Alto, Calif., 1969

Crosby, R. M. N. and Liston, Robert A.: The Waysiders. Delacorte Press, N.Y., 2nd Printing 1969

Crosby, R. M. N., and Liston, Robert A.: Dyslexia: What you can and can't do about it. In: Grade Teacher 86: 74–86, February 1969

Debray, P.: A propos de la dyslexie. In: Gazette Medicale de France 27, November 1969.

Dechant, Emerald: Diagnosis and Remediation of Reading Disability. Parker Publishing Co., West Nyack, N.Y., 3rd Printing 1969

Klasen, Edith: Der gegenwärtige Stand der Legasthenieforschung. In: Heilpädagogische Werkblätter 4:178–83, July-August 1969.

Klasen, Edith: Ein Testverfahren zur Erfassung legasthenischer Kinder. In: Heilpädagogische Werkblätter 5:237–39, September-October 1969

Schiffman, G.: Dyslexia: The Administrator's Dilemma. In: Journal of Learning Disabilities 2:566–7, November 1969

Spraings, Violet E.: The Dyslexias: A Psychoeducational and Physiological Approach. In: Tarnopol, L., Editor, Learning Disabilities 238–55, 1969

Zimmermann, K. W.: Psychodiagnostische Verfahren zur Untersuchung von Lernbehinderten. Marhold, Berlin, 1969

1970

Angermaier, Michael J. W.: Legasthenie – Verursachungsmomente einer Lernstörung. Beltz, Weinheim-Berlin, 2nd revised edition 1970

Boder, E.: Developmental Dyslexia: A New Diagnostic Approach Based on the Identification of Three Subtypes. In: The Journal of School Health 40:289–90, June 1970

Debray-Ritzen, Pierre and Melekian, Badrig: La Dyslexie de L'Enfant. Casterman, Tournai, Belgique, 1970

Hartlage, L. C.: Differential Diagnosis of Dyslexia, Minimal Brain Damage and

Emotional Disturbances in Children. In: Psychology in the Schools 7:403–6, October 1970

Klasen, Edith: Diskussion über das Zürcher Testverfahren zur Erfassung legasthenischer Kinder. In: Heilpädagogische Werkblätter 4: 192–96, July-August 1970

Klasen, Edith: Audio-Visuo-Motor Training With Pattern Cards. Peek Publications, Palo Alto, 2nd Printing, 1970

McClurg, W. M.: Dyslexia: Early Identification and Treatment in the School. In: Journal of Learning Disabilities 3:372–7, July 1970

McGuire, M. L.: Dyslexia: A Reading Specialist's Opinion. In: Journal of Learning Disabilities 3:232–3, April 1970

Michel-Smith, H.: Dyslexia in Four Siblings. In: Journal of Learning Disabilities 3:185–92, April 1970

Pearse, B. H.: Dyslexia. In: American Education 5:9–13, April 1970

Schenk-Danziger, Lotte, Editor: Handbuch der Legasthenie im Kindesalter. Beltz, Weinheim-Berlin, 2nd revised edition, 1970

Senf, G. M. and Feshbach, S.: Development of Bisensory Memory in Culturally Deprived, Dyslexic, and Normal Readers. In: Journal of Educational Psychology 61:461–70, December 1970

Tamm, Helmut: Die Betreuung legasthenischer Kinder. Beltz, Weinheim-Berlin, Bibliothekband 9, 1970

Valting, Renate: Legasthenie – Theorien und Untersuchungen, Beltz, Weinheim-Berlin, Literatur- und Forschungsberichte zur Pädagogik Band 2, 1970

Wunderlich, Ray, C.: Kids, Brains, and Learning. Johnny Reads Inc. St. Petersburg, Florida, 1970

1971

Ables, B. S., et al: Problems in the Diagnosis of Dyslexia: A Case Study. In: Journal of Learning Disabilities 4: 409–17, October 1971

Ackerman, P. T., et al: Children With Specific Learning Disabilities: WISC Profiles. In: Journal of Learning Disabilities 3:150–66, March 1971

Anapolle, L.: Vision Problems in Developmental Dyslexia. In: Journal of Learning Disabilities 4:77–83, February 1971

Black, William F.: An Investigation of Intelligence as a Causal Factor in Reading Problems. In: Journal of Learning Disabilities 3:139–42, March 1971

Lerner, J. W.: Thorn By Any Other Name: Dyslexia or Reading Disability. In: Elementary English 48:75–80, January 1971

Linder, M., and Grissemann, H.: Zürcher Lesetest – Ein Testverfahren zur Erfassung legasthenischer Kinder. Huber, Bern-Stuttgart-Wien, 1971

Silver, Larry B.: A Proposed View On The Etiology Of The Neurological Learning Disability Syndrome. In: Journal Of Learning Disabilities 3:123–33, March 1971

Tajan, Alfred, and Volard, René: Pourquoi Des Dyslexiques? – dyslexie et reeducation. Petite Bibliotheque Payot, Paris 1971

Thompson, L. J.: Mental Retardation And Dyslexia. In: Academic Therapy 6:405–6, Summer 1971

Wagner, F. R.: Symbolization Deficits in Dyslexic Conditions. In: Academic Therapy 6:359–65, Summer 1971

APPENDIX

TABLES

Table A-1. Mean frequencies of physiopsychological findings among dyslexics

	N	%	10 20 30 40 50 60 70
Speech impediments	499	22.4	
Delayed speech development	414	39.6	
Crossed dominance	500	44.2	
Left dominance	500	6.0	
Right dominance	500	49.8	
Visual-perceptual deficiencies	500	67.2	
Motor deficiencies	500	49.2	
Auditory perceptual deficiencies	500	10.2	
Impaired eye sight	473	32.1	
Hearing losses	379	9.2	
Hyperactivity	500	26.8	
Hypoactivity	500	18.4	
Nervous habits	500	39.3	
Psychosomatic symptoms	500	4.6	
Hereditary indications	392	39.7	
Referral to neurologist	500	66.0	

Table A-2. Mean frequencies of physiopsychological findings among dyslexics, according to subgroups

		Boys		Girls	
		6-13	14-18	6-13	14-18
	N	%	%	%	%
Speech impediments	499	14.0	3.8	3.8	0.8
Delayed speech development	414	25.6	4.6	8.2	1.2
Crossed dominance	500	26.6	5.0	9.8	2.8
Left dominance	500	–	–	–	–
Right dominance	500	–	–	–	–
Visual-perceptual deficiencies	500	15.2	4.6	6.4	2.4
Motor deficiencies	500	7.8	0.6	2.0	0.2
Auditory perceptual deficiencies	500	6.6	1.0	1.8	0.8
Impaired eye sight	473	18.4	3.4	7.4	2.9
Hearing losses	379	5.8	2.1	1.0	0.3
Hyperactivity	500	19.8	2.2	4.2	0.6
Hypoactivity	500	11.4	2.4	4.0	0.6
Nervous habits	500	25.9	3.6	7.6	2.2
Psychosomatic symptoms	500	3.2	0.8	0.4	0.2
Hereditary indications	392	22.4	5.6	7.9	3.8
Referral to neurologist	500	43.2	6.4	13.2	3.2

Table B. Physiophychological findings indicating statistically significant disparities between the means obtained for boys or girls, primary or secondary students

	χ^2	$(n = 1)$	Level of confidence
Speech impediments	15.18	Boys	1%
Delayed speech	7.16	Primary grades	1%
Crossed dominance	6.38	Primary grades	5%
Visual and motor deficiencies combined	6.19	Primary grades	5%
Motor deficiencies	8.01	Primary grades	1%
Hearing losses	3.99	Boys	5%
Hyperactivity	9.96 16.25	Boys Primary grades	1% 1%
Hypoactivity	2.89	Primary grades (Sign. tendency)	10%
Nervous habits	12.43	Primary grades	1%
Psychosomatic symptoms	2.75	Boys (Sign. tendency)	10%
Referral to neurologist	10.12 2.91	Primary grades Boys (Sign. tendency)	1% 10%

The Syndrome of Specific Dyslexia

Table C. Table and histogram of mean frequencies of psychopathological findings ($N = 500$)

	%	10	20	30	40	50	60
Anxiety	65.0						
Concentration problems°	39.0						
Immaturity†	33.2						
Low frustration tolerance	31.2						
Withdrawal	20.6						
Aggression	14.6						
Defensive attitudes‡	12.0						
Depressive moods	10.6						
Delinquency	2.6						

°$\chi^2 = 35.8$ (1% level)   Significantly more frequent
†$\chi^2 = 27.4$ (1% level)   at primary than at secondary
‡$\chi^2 = 4.9$ (5% level)   school age level

Table D. Mean frequencies obtained with regard to environmental factors (*N* = 500)

	10 20 30 40 50 60 70	%
Classification		
Upper class		16.3
Middle class		68.4
Lower class		15.3
Family situation		
Mother working		21.8
Only one parent		8.2
Child outside home		1.4
Child adopted		5.4
Only child		4.6
Oldest child		24.6
Youngest child		36.0
Sibling rivalry		17.6
Parental attitudes		
Overly anxious		22.5
Distant, critical		22.8
Demanding, punitive		17.5
Cold, meticulous		4.9
Unrealistic college ambitions°		7.0
Indifferent, distant		4.0
Both parents present at first interview		55.6

°Significantly more frequent for girls (1% level of confidence, $\chi^2 = 15.15$)

NOTES*

I. INTRODUCTION

1. Description and Analysis, pp. 3–6

1. LINDER, M. (91), p. 100
2. BUSEMANN, A.: Angeborene Leseschwäche (Legasthenie), 1954. Cited in: KOBI, E. (82), p. 11
3. BLEIDICK, U. (11), p. 70
4. TOMKINS, C. (140), p. 3
5. KOCHER, F. (83), p. 3
6. KOBI, E. (82), p. 12
7. MONEY, M.: Glossary. In: MONEY, J. (ed.), (99), p. 377
8. CRITCHLEY, Mc. (22), p. 2
9. MONEY, J.: Glossary. In: MONEY, J. (ed.), (99), p. 377
10. CRONIN, E. M. (23), p. 1
11. REY, A.: Préface. In: KOCHER, F. (83), p. V – VI
12. FERDINAND, W.: Über die Fehlerarten des rechtschreibschwachen Kindes. In: INGENKAMP, K. (ed.), (68), p. 88 – 95
13. BIGLMAIER, F. (8), p. 55 – 117
14. KOCHER, F. (83), p. 15

2. Survey of the Literature, pp. 7–16

1. WEINSCHENK, C. (146), p. 26
2. WEINSCHENK, C. (146), p. 26
3. WEINSCHENK, C. (146), p. 23
4. MONEY, J.: Glossary. In: MONEY, J. (ed.), (99), p. 386
5. DOYLE, P. J. (32), p. 305
6. WEINSCHENK, C. (146), p. 5
7. WEINSCHENK, C. (146), p. 29
8. CRITCHLEY, Mc. (22), p. 55
9. CRITCHLEY, Mc. (22), p. 61
10. WEINSCHENK, C. (146), p. 30
11. WEINSCHENK, C. (146), p. 5
12. HINSHELWOOD, J. (64), p. 40 – 63
13. SCHILDER, P. (119), p. 86
14. BLEIDICK, U. (11), p. 70
15. KLEINER, D.: Jugendpsychiatrische Erfahrungen. In: INGENKAMP, K. (ed), (68), p. 118

---

*The numbers in parentheses refer to the Bibliography, p. 219.

16. WEINSCHENK, C. (146), p. 30
17. WEINSCHENK, C. (146), p. 34
18. MUCCHIELLI, R. und BOURCIER, A. (103), p. 88
19. MUCCHIELLI, R. and BOURCIER, A. (103), p. 88
20. KIRCHHOFF, H. (80), p. 44-45
21. GRISSEMANN, H.: Die Legasthenie als Deutungsschwäche. In: INGEN-KAMP, K. (ed.), (68), p. 37
22. PIETROWICZ, B: Über gnostische Mängel bei Lese-Rechtschreib-Schwächen. In: KIRCHHOFF, H. and PIETROWICZ, B. (79), p. 33
23. SCHENK-DANZIGER, L.: Die Diagnose der Legasthenie nach der Wiener Methode. In: INGENKAMP, K. (ed.), (68), p. 73
24. SCHUBENZ, S.: Über einen neuen Weg in der Legasthenieforschung. In: Der Schulpsychologe. 1964, Heft X, 19-22
25. LINDER, M. (92), p. 138
26. BLEIDICK, U. (11), p. 68
27. TOMKINS, C. (140), p. 4
28. SIERSLEBEN, W.: Überblick über die vorliegenden Arbeiten zur Ätiologie. In: INGENKAMP, K. (ed.), (68), p. 6
29. BLEIDICK, U. (11), p. 11
30. MÜLLER, R. G. E. (104), p. 266-270
31. KOBI, E. (82), p. 18
32. SCHUBENZ, S.: Neuere deutsche Forschungsansätze zur Aufklärung der Legasthenieproblematik. In: INGENKAMP, K. (ed.), (68), p. 13
33. PRECHTL, H.: Reading Difficulties as a Neurological Problem in Childhood. In: MONEY, J. (ed.), (98), p. 188
34. CLEMENTS, S. et al. (18), p. 1-15
35. COHN, R. (19), p. 179-185
36. MYKLEBUST, H. (106), p. 354-360
37. WHITSELL, L.: Neurologic Aspects of Reading Disorders. In: FLOWER, R. et al. (eds.), (43), p. 45-60
38. SCHOMBURG, E.: Beiträge zur Legasthenieforschung aus Holland und England. In: INGENKAMP, K. (ed.), (68), p. 49-50
39. DOYLE, P. J. (32), p. 299
40. LÜCKERT, H.-R. (95), p. 193
41. CRITCHLEY, Mc. (22), p. 60
42. BLEIDICK, U. (11), p. 66
43. KIRCHHOFF, H. (80), p. 23
44. HALLGREN, B. (53), p. 102
45. KRETSCHMER, M. (87), p. 51
46. SCHOMBURG, E.: Beiträge zur Legasthenieforschung aus Holland und England. In: INGENKAMP, K. (ed.), (68), p. 50
47. ELLEHAMMER, M.: Überblick über Forschungen in Dänemark. In: IN-GENKAMP, K. (ed.), (68), p. 44
48. KIRCHHOFF, H.: Einführung. In: KIRCHHOFF, H. and PIETROWICZ, B. (eds.), (79), p. 3
49. CRONIN, E. M. (23), p. 1
50. GRAY, W. S. (51), p. 2
51. HANSELMANN, H. (54), p. 150-153
52. REY, A.: Préface. In: KOCHER, F. (83), p. VI
53. MONTALTA, E. (101), p. 83

3. *Aim and Method of Investigation, pp. 17–25*

1. TAMM, H.: Diskussionsprotokoll. In: INGENKAMP, K. (ed.), (68), p. 124
2. KIRCHHOFF, H. (77), p. 5
3. SCHENK-DANZIGER, L.: Diskussionsprotokoll. In: INGENKAMP, K. (ed.), (68), p. 58
4. WEINSCHENK, C. (146), p. 34–35
5. MONEY, J.: Dyslexia: A Postconference Review. In: MONEY, J. (ed.), (98), p. 31–32
6. MONEY, J.: On Learning and Not Learning to Read. In: MONEY, J. (ed.), (99), p. 38–39
7. MONEY, J.: On Learning and Not Learning to Read. In: MONEY, J. (ed.), (99), p. 39
8. CRITCHLEY, Mc. (22), p. 64–65
9. KOBI, E. (82), p. 20
10. SIERSLEBEN, W.: Überblick über die vorliegenden Arbeiten zur Ätiologie. In INGENKAMP, K. (ed.), (68), p. 7–8
11. LÜCKERT, H.-R. (95), p. 199–202
12. LÜCKERT, H.-R. (95), p. 202

II. PHENOMENOLOGY AND ETIOLOGY OF THE DYSLEXIC SYNDROME

1. *Physiopsychological Findings*

1.1 Speech, pp. 29–38

1. BLEIDICK, U.: Typologische Ordnungsgesichtspunkte der Ätiologie und Symptomatik der Lese-Rechtschreib-Schwäche. In: INGENKAMP, K. (ed.), (68), p. 11
2. SCHUBENZ, S.: Neuere deutsche Forschungsansätze zur Aufklärung der Legasthenieproblematik. In: INGENKAMP, K. (ed.), (68), p. 13
3. LOBROT, M.: Forschungen zur Legasthenie in Frankreich. In INGENKAMP, K. (ed.), (68), p. 19
4. BLEIDICK, U. (11), p. 67
5. KOBI, E. (82), p. 18
6. KOCHER, F.: Über methodologische Fragen bei der Diagnose Primärer Legastheniesymptome. In: KIRCHHOFF, H. and PIETROWICZ, B. (eds.), (79), p. 14
7. BIGLMAIER, F. (8), p. 46
8. LÜCKERT, H.-R. (95), p. 203
9. LÜCKERT, H.-R. (95), p. 197
10. LORY, P. (94), p. 49
11. LORY, P. (94), p. 50
12. LORY, P. (94), p. 50
13. CRITCHLEY, Mc. (22), p. 13
14. SMITH, H. and DECHANT, E. (124), p. 159
15. WEINSCHENK, C. (146), p. 47

16. WEINSCHENK, C. (146), p. 48
17. HARDY, W.: Dyslexia and Hearing and Speech Disorders. In: MONEY, J. (ed.), (98), p. 172
18. MOSSE, H.: Zur Symptomatik und Ätiologie der Legasthenien. In: INGEN-KAMP, K. (ed.), (68), p. 32
19. COHN, R. (19), p. 180
20. LÜCKERT, H.-R. (95), p. 196–197
21. KOCHER, F. (83), p. 3
22. SMITH, H. and DECHANT, E. (124), p. 158
23. HARRIS, A. J. (56), p. 244
24. MONROE, M. C. (100), p. 92
25. SMITH, H. and DECHANT, E. (124), p. 159–160
26. SMITH, H. and DECHANTE, E. (124), p. 160
27. BETTS, E. A.: A Physiological Approach to the Analysis of Reading Disabilities, 1934. Cited in: SIERSLEBEN, W.: Übersicht über die vorliegenden Ansichten zur Ätiologie. In: INGENKAMP, K. (ed.), (68), p. 4
28. MATEER, F. (96), p. 143
29. HARRIS, A. J. (56), p. 244
30. WHITTY, P. and KOPEL, D. (150), p. 216
31. EAMES, Th.: The Blood Picture in Reading Failures, 1953. Cited in: SMITH, H. and DECHANT, E. (124), p. 155
32. WATTS, Ph.: An Application of Clinical Diagnostic Techniques in the Classroom Situation for the Improvement of Reading at the College Level, 1949. Cited in: SMITH, H. and DECHANT, E. (124), p. 156
33. SMITH, H. and DECHANT, E. (124), p. 156
34. KOCHER, F. (83), p. 47
35. HARDY, W.: Dyslexia and Hearing and Speech Disorders. In: MONEY, J. (ed.), (98), p. 177
36. KINSBOURNE, M. and WARRINGTON, E. K.: Reading and Writing Backwardness. In: MONEY, J. (ed.), (99), p. 67 and p. 71
37. GOLDIAMOND, I. and DYRUD, J. E.: Reading as Operant Behavior. In: MONEY, J. (ed.), (99), p. 112–113, 114–115
38. LAWSON, L.: Language Disorders. The Relationship of Speech Defects and Reading Disabilities. In: FLOWER, R. et al. (eds.), (43), p. 73–79
39. LÜCKERT, H.-R. (95), p. 196
40. LÜCKERT, H.-R. (95), p. 197
41. LORY, P. (94), p. 50
42. LORY, P. (94), p. 50
43. KOBI, E. (82), p. 18
44. KOCHER, F. (83), p. 18–19
45. SAUNDERS, R. E.: Dyslexia: Its Phenomenology. In: MONEY, J. (ed.), (98), p. 36
46. ZANGWILL, O. L.: Dyslexia in Relation to Cerebral Dominance. In: MONEY, J. (ed.), (98), p. 111
47. SCHENK-DANZIGER, L.: Diskussionsprotokoll. In: INGENKAMP, K. (ed.), (68), p. 124
48. DE HIRSCH, K. (28), p. XI–XII
49. ORTON, J. L.: The Orton Story, Cited in: SCHIFFMAN, G.: Dyslexia as an Educational Phenomenon. In: MONEY, J. (ed.), (98), p. 48
50. MONEY, J.: On Learning and Not Learning to Read. In: MONEY, J. (ed.), (99), p. 33

51. CLEMENTS, S. D.: The Child with Minimal Braindysfunction – A Profile. In: CLEMENTS, S. D. et al. (ed.), (18), p. 6
52. JOHNSON, M. S.: Tracing and Kinesthetic Techniques. In: MONEY, J. (ed.), (99), p. 157
53. CRITCHLEY, Mc. (22), p. 58
54. WEPMAN, J. M.: Dyslexia: Its Relationship to Language Acquisition and Concept Formation. In: MONEY, J. (ed.), (98), p. 184
55. WEPMAN, J. M.: Conference Scriptum. In: KIRK, S. A. and BECKER, W. (eds.), (81), p. 7
56. MYKLEBUST, H.: Conference Scriptum. In: KIRK, S. A. and BECKER, W. (eds.), (81), p. 33
57. MYKLEBUST, H.: Conference Scriptum. In: KIRK, S. A. and BECKER, W. (eds.), (81), p. 26
58. JACOBSON, R.: Ciba-Symposium. In: REUCK, A. V. S. and O'CONNOR, M. (eds.), (111), p. 26
59. INGRAM, T. T. S.: Specific Learning Difficulties in Childhood. In: FRIERSON, E. C. and BARBE, W. B. (eds.), (44), p. 327
60. LORY, P. (94), p. 49
61. MONEY, J.: On Learning or Not Learning to Read. In: MONEY, J. (ed.), (99), p. 34

1.2 Laterality, pp. 38-46

1. WEGENER, H.: Linkshändigkeit und psychische Struktur, 1949. Cited in KRAMER, J. (86), p. 8
2. KRAMER, J. (86), p. 8
3. KRAMER, J. (86), p. 48–58
4. KRAMER, J. (86), p. 59
5. KRAMER, J. (86), p. 19–28
6. KRAMER, J. (86), p. 18
7. CRITCHLEY, Mc. (22), p. 51
8. SMITH, H. and DECHANT, E. (124), p. 165
9. HESS, G.: Die Linksdominanz bei Grundschulkindern in ihren Auswirkungen auf die Lese- und Rechtschreibleistungen. In: INGENKAMP, K. (ed.), (68), p. 52
10. CRITCHLEY, Mc. (22), p. 52
11. LEISER-EGGERT, A. (90), p. 265 and p. 246
12. MONROE, M. (100), p. 85
13. ZANGWILL, O. L.: Dyslexia in Relation to Cerebral Dominance. In: MONEY, J. (ed.), (98), p. 110
14. SCHONELL, F. J. (120), p. 20–27
15. HARRIS, A. J. (56), p. 254
16. KOCHER, F. (83), p. 18
17. SMITH, H. and DECHANT, E. (124), p. 168
18. WHITSELL, L.: Neurologic Aspects of Reading Disorders. In: FLOWER, R. et al. (eds.), (43), p. 47
19. WHITSELL, L.: Neurologic Aspects of Reading Disorders. In: FLOWER, R. et al. (eds.), (43), p. 47–48
20. WHITSELL, L.: Neurologic Aspects of Reading Disorders. In: FLOWER, R. et al. (eds.), (43), p. 49
21. BENTON, C. D. et al. (5), p. 55

22. DEARBORN, W. F. (27), p. 704
23. SMITH, L. C. (125), p. 324–326
24. LEAVELL, U. W. (88), p. 3 and p. 12
25. VERNON, M. D. (142), p. 107
26. ORTON, S. T. (109), p. 130 ff.
27. WEINSCHENK, C. (146), p. 49
28. KIRCHHOFF, H. (78), p. 268
29. WEINSCHENK, C. (146), p. 50
30. WEINSCHENK, C. (146), p. 52
31. HILDRETH, G. (63), p. 50
32. SPACHE, G. D. (126), p. 50–51
33. SMITH, H. and DECHANT, E. (124), p. 168–169
34. SMITH, H. and DECHANT, E. (124), p. 170
35. CRITCHLEY, Mc. (22), p. 52 and 53
36. LÜCKERT, H.-R. (95), p. 196
37. LORY, P. (94), p. 40
38. ORTON, S. T. (108), p. 286–290
39. LÜCKERT, H.-R. (95), p. 196
40. SMITH, D. E. P. and CARRIGAN, P. M. (123), p. 11
41. CRITCHLEY, Mc. (22), p. 52
42. ZANGWILL, O. L.: Dyslexia in Relation to Cerebral Dominance. In: MON-
    EY, J. (ed.), (98), p. 111–112
43. LÜCKERT, H.-R. (95), p. 196
44. LORY, P. (94), p. 40
45. VERNON, M. D. (142), p. 81 and p. 109
46. CRITCHLEY, Mc. (22), p. 53
47. DE HIRSCH, K. et al. (28), p. 70–71 and p. 59–63
48. DE HIRSCH, K. et al. (28), p. 71 and p. 73
49. ZANGWILL, O. L.: Dyslexia in Relation to Cerebral Dominance. In: MON-
    EY, J. (ed.), (98), p. 112
50. GESCHWIND, N.: The Anatomy of Acquired Disorders of Reading. In:
    MONEY, J. (ed.), (98), p. 128
51. ZANGWILL, O. L.: Dyslexia in Relation to Cerebral Dominance. In: MON-
    EY, J. (ed.), (98), p. 113
52. KRAMER, J. (86), p. 74
53. LORY, P. (94), p. 40
54. HESS, G.: Die Linksdominanz bei Grundschulkindern in ihren Auswir-
    kungen auf die Lese-Rechtschreibleistungen. In: INGENKAMP, K. (ed.),
    (68), p. 53 and p. 52
55. THIBAUT, A. (137), p. 298–299

1.3 Sensory Perception and Motor Functions, pp. 46–61

1. SPENCER, P. L. (129), p. 17–22
2. PIETROWICZ, B.: Über gnostische Mängel bei Lese-Rechtschreib-
   schwächen. In: KIRCHHOFF, H. and PIETROWICZ, B. (eds.), (79), p. 32
3. ARTLEY, A. S. (2), p. 7
4. EPHRON, B. K. (40), p. 27 and p. 282
5. SMITH, H. and DECHANT, E. (124), p. 438–439

6. BIGLMAIER, F. (8), p. 48
7. DE HIRSCH, K. et al. (28), p. 89
8. FROSTIG, M.: Teaching Reading to Children with Perceptual Disturbances. In: FLOWER, R. et al. (eds.), (43), p. 113
9. FROSTIG, M.: Teaching Reading to Children with Perceptual Disturbances. In: FLOWER, R. et al. (eds.), (43), p. 114–115
10. GETMAN, G. N. (47), p. 31
11. DE HIRSCH, K. et al. (eds.), (28), p. 89
12. THOMPSON, A. C. (138), p. 13
13. FROSTIG, M.: Teaching Reading to Children with Perceptual Disturb-
    ances. In: FLOWER, R. et al. (eds.), (43), p. 114
14. MONEY, J.: On Learning and Not Learning to Read. In: MONEY, J. (ed.),
    (99), p. 40
15. BENTON, A. L.: Dyslexia, Form Perception, and Directional Sense. In:
    MONEY, J. (ed.), (98), p. 82 and p. 87
16. BENTON, A. L.: Dyslexia, Form Perception, and Directional Sense. In:
    MONEY, J. (ed.), (98), p. 94–95
17. BIRCH, H.: Dyslexia and the Maturation of Visual Function. In: MONEY, J.
    (ed.), (98), p. 164
18. BIRCH, H.: Dyslexia and the Maturation of Visual Function. In: MONEY, J.
    (ed.), (98), p. 169
19. SILVER, A. and HAGIN, R.: Specific Reading Disability, 1960. Cited in:
    WHITSELL, L. J.: Neurologic Aspects of Reading Disorders. In: FLOWER,
    R. et al. (eds.), (43), p. 51
20. BRONNER, A. F.: The Psychology of Special Abilities and Disabilities,
    1917. Cited in: BENTON, A. L.: Dyslexia, Form Perception, and Directional
    Sense. In: MONEY, J. (eds.), (98), p. 88
21. BENTON, A. L.: Dyslexia, Form Perception, and Directional Sense. In:
    MONEY, J. (ed.), (98), p. 88–94
22. CRITCHLEY, Mc. (22), p. 46–50
23. CRITCHLEY, Mc. (22), p. 49–50
24. SCHOMBURG, E.: Beiträge zur Legasthenie-Forschung aus Holland und
    England. In: INGENKAMP, K. (ed.), (68), p. 49–50
25. LOBROT, M.: Forschungen zur Legasthenie in Frankreich. In: INGEN-
    KAMP, K. (ed.), (68), p. 22
26. DANIELS, J. C.: Kinder mit Lesestörungen. In: INGENKAMP, K. (ed.),
    (68), p. 28
27. ELLEHAMMER, M.: Überblick über Forschungen in Dänemark. In: IN-
    GENKAMP, K. (ed.), (68), p. 47
28. BIGLMAIER, F. (8), p. 47–49
29. LORY, P. (94), p. 12–15
30. BLEIDICK, U.: Über Theorien zur Ätiologie der Lese- und Schreibstör-
    ungen. In: KIRCHHOFF, H. and PIETROWICZ, B. (eds.), (79), p. 17 and p.
    24–26
31. KIRCHHOFF, H. (77), p. 45
32. MÜLLER, R. G. E. (105), p. 218
33. FERDINAND, W.: Über die Fehlerarten des rechtschreibschwächen Kin-
    des. In: INGENKAMP, K. (ed.), (68), p. 88
34. LINDER, M. (93), p. 18
35. SCHENK-DANZIGER, L. (117), p. 176

36. SCHENK-DANZIGER, L.: Die Diagnose der Legasthenie nach der Wiener Methos. In: INGENKAMP, K. (ed.), (68), p. 73–74
37. INGRAM, T. T. S.: Specific Learning Difficulties in Childhood. In: FRIERSON, E. and BARBE, W. (eds.), (44), p. 324
38. PIETROWICZ, B.: Über gnostische Mängel bei Lese-Rechtschreibschwächen. In: KIRCHHOFF, H. and PIETROWICZ, B. (eds.), (79), p. 31–33
39. KOBI, E. (82), p. 15
40. WEINSCHENK, C. (147), p. 146–147
41. LORY, P. (94), p. 17, footnote
42. KOBI, E. (82), p. 16
43. BLEIDICK, U.: Über Theorien zur Ätiologie der Lese- und Schreibstörungen. In: KIRCHHOFF, H. and PIETROWICZ, B. (eds.), (79), p. 17
44. ELLEHAMMER, M.: Überblick über die Forschungen in Dänemark. In: INGENKAMP, K. (ed.), (68), p. 47
45. TAMM, H.: Grundsätze, Methoden und Erfahrungen bei der Betreuung von lese- und rechtschreibgestörten Schülern. In: INGENKAMP, K. (ed.), (68), p. 142
46. KOCHER, F. (83), p. 4 and p. 10–11
47. BIRCH, H.: Dyslexia and the Maturation of Visual Function. In: MONEY, J. (ed.), (98), p. 167–168
48. KOBI, E. (82), p. 18
49. KOBI, E. (82), p. 14 and p. 40
50. BIGLMAIER, F. (8), p. 46
51. HUNGER-KAINDLSTORFER, M.: Über die Einzelbehandlung von Lesestörungen. In: KIRCHOFF, H. and PIETROWICZ, B. (eds.), (79), p. 56
52. BLEIDICK, U.: Über Theorien zur Ätiologie der Lese- und Schreibstörungen. in: KIRCHOFF, H. and PIETROWICZ, B. (eds.), (79), p. 18
53. LORY, P. (94), p. 36
54. KIRCHHOFF, H. (80), p. 31
55. WALTER, K.: Protokollaufzeichnung. In: INGENKAMP, K. (ed.), (68), p. 123
56. SCHENK-DANZIGER, L.: Protokoll. In: INGENKAMP, K. (ed.), (68), p. 124
57. HOHLMAN, H.: Protokollaufzeichnung. In: INGENKAMP, K. (ed.), (68), p. 130
58. KOSSAKOWSKI, A. (84), p. 46
59. LÜCKERT, H.-R. (95), p. 193
60. KEPHART, N. C.: Perceptual-Motor Aspects of Learning Disabilities. In: FRIERSON, E. and BARBE, W. (eds.), (44), p. 406
61. GETMAN, G. N. (47), p. 24–25
62. ANDERSON, R. P.: Physiologic Considerations in Learning: The Tactual Mode. In: HELLMUTH, J. (ed.), (60), p. 98
63. PRECHTL, H.: Dyslexia as a Neurological Problem in Childhood. In: MONEY, J. (ed.), (98), p. 188–191
64. ORTON, J. L.: The Orton-Gillingham Approach. In: MONEY, J. (ed.), (99), p. 127
65. JOHNSON, M. S.: Tracing and Kinesthetic Techniques. In: MONEY, J. (ed.), (99), p. 158
66. DE HIRSCH, K. et al. (eds.), (28), 47–49
67. DE HIRSCH, K. et al. (eds.), (28), p. 55
68. DE HIRSCH, K. et al. (eds.), (28), p. 33
69. KIRCHHOFF, H. (77), p. 39 and p. 56–57

70. KOCHER, F.: Über methodologische Fragen bei der Diagnose primärer Legastheniesymptome. In: KIRCHHOFF, H. and PIETROWICZ, B. (eds.), (79), p. 15-16
71. KOCHER, F. (83), p. 5-8
72. MYKLEBUST, H.-R.: Psychoneurological Learning Disorders in Children. In: KIRK, S. A. and BECKER, W. (eds.), (81), p. 29
73. BLEIDICK, U.: Über Theorien zur Ätiologie der Lese- und Schreibstörungen. In: KIRCHHOFF, H. and PIETROWICZ, B. (eds.), (79), p. 18
74. PIETROWICZ, B.: Über gnostische Mängel bei Lese-Rechtschreibschwächen. In: KIRCHHOFF, H. and PIETROWICZ, B. (eds.), (79), p. 33
75. SCHENK-DANZIGER, L.: Merkblatt. Cited in: KOBI, E. (82), p. 13
76. LORY, P. (94), p. 14, 15, 16
77. WEINSCHENK, C. (147), p. 120
78. SCHENK-DANZIGER, L.: Sitzungsprotokoll. Cited in: INGENKAMP, K. (ed.), (68), p. 56
79. CRITCHLEY, Mc. (22), p. 77-80
80. DANIELS, J. C.: Kinder mit Lesestörungen. In: INGENKAMP, K. (ed.), (68), p. 26-28
81. TAMM, H.: Die in der Schule durchführbare Fehleranalyse. In: INGENKAMP, K. (ed.), (68), p. 111
82. MÜLLER, R.: Fehleranalytische Diagnose bei Legasthenikern. In: INGENKAMP, K.: (ed.), (68), p. 101-102
83. FLOWER, R.: Auditory Disorders and Reading Disorders. In: FLOWER, R. et al. (ed.), (43), p. 81-83
84. DURRELL, D. and MURPHY, H. (36), p. 556-560
85. WEPMAN, J.: Dyslexia, Language, and Concept Formation: In: MONEY, J. (ed.), (98), p. 182
86. MYKLEBUST, H.: Psychoneurological Learning Disorders in Children. In: KIRK, S. and BECKER, W. (eds.), (81), p. 31
87. MONEY, J.: Dyslexia, A Postconference Review. In: MONEY, J. (ed.), (98), p. 12-13
88. RABINOVITCH, R.: Dyslexia: Psychiatric Considerations. In: MONEY, J. (ed.), (98), p. 75
89. HARDY, W.: Dyslexia and Hearing and Speech Disorders. In: MONEY, J. (ed.), (98), p. 172-174
90. DE HIRSCH, K. et al. (eds.), (28), p. 48 and p. 55-56
91. FLOWER, R.: Auditory Disorders. In: FLOWER, R. et al. (eds.), (43), p. 97-98
92. FLOWER, R.: Auditory Disorders. In: FLOWER, R. et al. (eds.), (43), p. 90
93. EISENBERG, L.: Epidemiology of Reading Retardation. In: MONEY, J. (ed.), (99), p. 13
94. BANNATYNE, A.: The Color Phonics System. In: MONEY, J. (ed.), (99), p. 195
95. SMITH, H. and DECHANT, E. (124), p. 100 and p. 102
96. BENTON, A.: Developmental Aplasia and Brain Damage. In: KIRK, S. and BECKER, W. (eds.), (81), p. 87 and p. 84
97. LOBROT, M.: Forschungen zur Legasthenie in Frankreich. In: INGENKAMP, K. (ed.), (68), p. 22
98. SCHUBENZ, S.: Neuere deutsche Forschungsansätze zur Aufklärung der Legasthenieproblematik. In: INGENKAMP, K. (ed.), (68), p. 14
99. BLEIDICK. U.: Über Theorien zur Ätiologie der Lese- und Schreibstörungen. In: KIRCHHOFF, H. and PIETROWICZ, B. (eds.), (79), p. 18-19

1.4 Organic Sensory Defects

1.4a) Visual-Perceptual Difficulties, pp. 61–64

1. WEINSCHENK, C. (147), p. 80
2. INGENKAMP, K. (ed.), (68), p. 123
3. BLEIDICK, U.: Über Theorien zur Ätiologie der Lese- und Schreibstörungen. In: KIRCHHOFF, H. and PIETROWICZ, B. (eds.), (79), p. 17
4. BIGLMAIER, F. (8), p. 44 – 45
5. SCHOMBURG E.: Protokoll. In: INGENKAMP, K. (ed.), (68), p. 123
6. EDSON, W. H. et al. (39), p. 451 – 457
7. JACKSON, T. and SHYE, V. (69), p. 33 – 35
8. FARRIS, L. P. (42), p. 58 – 60
9. ROBINSON, H. (114), p. 217 – 218 and p. 220 – 221
10. AUSTIN, M. C. (3), p. 112 – 117
11. TAYLOR, E. A. (136), p. 167 and p. 183
12. FARRIS, L. P. (42), p. 58 – 60
13. STROMBERG, E. L. (131), p. 70 – 78
14. SWANSON, D. E. and TIFFIN, J. (134), p. 433 – 448
15. WITTY, P. and KOPEL, D. (149), p. 449 – 459
16. ROBINSON, H. (114), p. 19
17. HARRIS, A. J. (56), p. 235
18. EAMES, T. H. (37), p. 211 – 215
19. EAMES, T. H. (38), p. 1 – 5
20. BOND, G. and TINKER, M. (12), p. 89 – 90
21. GRUBER, E. (52), p. 280 – 288
22. CRITCHLEY, Mc. (22), p. 40
23. BIGLMAIER, F. (8), p. 46
24. MOSSE, H.: Lineare Dyslexie. In: INGENKAMP, K. (ed.), (68), p. 54. Also
    in: American Journal of Psychiatry, Vol. XIII, No. 4, Oct. 1959, p. 826 – 841
25. MILES, W. R. and SEGEL, D. (97), p. 520 – 529
26. BOND, G. L. and TINKER, M. A. (12), p. 253
27. SPACHE, G. D. (128), p. 123
28. BUSWELL, G. Th. (15), p. 27 and p. 33 – 36
29. CRITCHLEY, Mc. (22), p. 45
30. MOSSE, H.: Lineare Dyslexie. In: INGENKAMP, K. (ed.), (68), p. 55
31. CRITCHLEY, Mc. (22), p. 40 – 46

1.4b) Auditory-Perceptual Deficits, pp. 64– 66

1. BLEIDICK, U.: Über Theorien zur Ätiologie der Lese- und Schreibstörungen. In: KIRCHHOFF, H. and PIETROWICZ, B. (eds.), (79), p. 18
2. BIGLMAIER, F. (8), p. 46
3. HOEKSEMA, P. E.: Over slechthoerendheid bij schoolkindern, 1958,
   Groningen. Cited in: KOBI, E. (82), p. 17
4. SILVERMAN, S. R. (122), p. 355
5. BOND, G. L. and TINKER, M. A. (12), p. 92
6. O'CONNOR, C. D. and STRENG, A. (107), p. 156
7. ROBINSON, H. (114), p. 229

8. JOHNSON, M. S. (71), p. 565–578
9. HOEKSEMA, P. E.: Over slechthoerendheid bij schoolkindern, 1958, Groningen. Cited in: KOBI, E. (82), p. 17
10. KOCHER, F. (83), p. 31
11. SHERIDAN, M. D. (121), p. 47–48
12. EWING, I. R. and EWING, A. W. G. (41), p. 245–248
13. KOBI, E. (82), p. 17
14. SHERIDAN, M. D. (121), p. 14
15. BERRY, M. F. and Eisenson, J. (7), p. 448
16. COLE, L. (20), p. 282
17. MONEY, J.: On Learning To Read and Not Learning to Read. In: MONEY, J. (ed.), (99), p. 33
18. FLOWER, R.: Auditory Disorders. In: FLOWER, R. et al. (eds.), (43), p. 98 and p. 85–87
19. DAHL, L. A. (26), p. 14
20. DAHL, L. A. (26), p. 14
21. FLOWER, R.: Auditory Disorders. In: FLOWER, R. et al. (eds.), (43), p. 98–102

1.5 Neuropsychological Symptoms, pp. 67–78

1. KLEINER, D.: Jugendpsychiatrische Erfahrungen. In: INGENKAMP, K. (ed.), (68), p. 118
2. BLEIDICK, U.: Über Theorien zur Ätologie der Lese- und Schreibstörungen. In: KIRCHHOFF, H. and PIETROWICZ, B. (eds.), (79), p. 22
3. DELACATO, J. F. and DELACATO, C. H.: A Group Approach to Remedial Reading, 1952. Cited in LÜCKERT, H.-R. (95), p. 195
4. LORY, P. (94), p. 48
5. KOBI, E. (82), p. 16
6. BIGLMAIER, F. (8), p. 47
7. KIRCHHOFF, H. (80), p. 64–66
8. CRITCHLEY, Mc. (22), p. 71
9. KLEINER, D.: Jugendpsychiatrische Erfahrungen. In: INGENKAMP, K. (ed.), (68), p. 118
10. SCHOMBURG, S.: Beiträge zur Legasthenieforschung aus Holland und England. In: INGENKAMP, K. (ed.), (68), p. 49–50
11. PRECHTL, H. F. R. and STEMMER, J. C.: Ein Choreatiformes Syndrom bei Kindern. Wiener med. Wochenschrift, 1959, 109, p. 461–463
12. PRECHTL, H. F. R. and STEMMER, J. C.: The Choreiform Syndrome in Children. Dev. Medicine and Child Neurology, 1962, 4, p. 119–127
13. PRECHTL, Heinz F. R.: Reading Difficulties as a Neurological Problem in Childhood. In: MONEY, J. (ed.), (98), p. 187–193
14. PRECHTL, Heinz F. R.: Reading Difficulties as a Neurological Problem in Childhood. In: MONEY, J. (ed.), (98), p. 192–193
15. DOYLE, P. J. (32), p. 299–306
16. DE HIRSCH, K. et al. (28), p. 47
17. GOFMAN, H.: The Identification and Evaluation of Children with Reading Disorders: A Pediatrician's View. In: FLOWER, R. et al. (eds.), (43), p. 16
18. COHN, R. (19), p. 183–184
19. BLEIDICK, U.: Über Theorien zur Ätologie der Lese- und Schreibstörungen. In: KIRCHHOFF, H. and PIETROWICZ, B. (eds.), (79), p. 21–22

20. LINDER, M.: Über das Problem sekundärer Symptome der Legasthenie. In: KIRCHHOFF, H. and PIETROWICZ, B. (eds.), (79), p. 35
21. BIGLMAIER, F. (8), p. 47
22. LORY, P. (94), p. 46–47
23. KIRCHHOFF, H. (80), p. 46
24. DE HIRSCH, K. et al. (28), p. 47
25. CLEMENTS, S. D.: The Child with Minimal Brain Dysfunction – A Profile. In: CLEMENTS, S. D. et al. (18), p. 5
26. DÜHRSSEN, A. (33), p. 185
27. ROSEN, E. and   GREGORY, I. (116), p. 493
28. O'CONNOR, N. and FRANKS, C. M.: Childhood Upbringing and Other Environmental Factors, 1960. Cited in ROSEN, E. and GREGORY, I. (116), p. 493
29. BOVET, L.: L'Onychophagie, contribution à l'étude de la pathologie de la personne, 1942. Cited in: TRAMER, M. (141), p. 410
30. TRAMER, M. (141), p. 411
31. DÜHRSSEN, A. (34), p. 278
32. TRAMER, M. (141), p. 406 and p. 407
33. DONGIER, M. (31), p. 202
34. LINDER, M.: Über das Problem sekundärer Symptome der Legasthenie. In: KIRCHHOFF, H. and PIETROWICZ, B. (eds.), (79), p. 39
35. LINDER, M.: Über das Problem sekundärer Symptome der Legasthenie. In: KIRCHHOFF, H. and PIETROWICZ, B. (eds.), (79), p. 34
36. DÜHRSSEN, A. (33), p. 319
37. GROSSMAN, H. J.: The Child, the Teacher and the Physician. In: CRUICKSHANK, W. M. (ed.), (24), p. 63–64
38. REITAN, R. M.: The Needs of Teachers for Specialized Information in the Area of Neuropsychology. In: CRUICKSHANK, W. M. (ed.), (24), p. 230
39. JOHNSON, D. J. and MYKLEBUST, H. R. (70), p. 26
40. LINDER, M.: Über das Problem sekundärer Symptome der Legasthenie. In: KIRCHHOFF, H. and PIETROWICZ, B. (eds.), (79), p. 36
41. ORTON, S. T. (109), p. 127–128
42. WEINSCHENK, C. (147), p. 94–96
43. LORY, P. (94), p. 9 and p. 32–33
44. LINDER, M. (91), p. 103
45. LINDER, M. Cited in: KOBI, (82), p. 20
46. SCHENK-DANZIGER, L. (117), p. 249
47. KOBI, E. (82), p. 20
48. KOCHER, F. (83), p. 17
49. KRETSCHMER, M. (87), p. 50
50. BIGLMAIER, F. (8), p. 43
51. MORGAN, W. P.: A Case of Congenital Word Blindness, 1896. Cited in: BIGLMAIER, F. (8), p. 42
52. CRITCHLEY, Mc. (22), p. 1–11
53. CRITCHLEY, Mc. (22), p. 18
54. CRITCHLEY, Mc. (22), p. 74
55. CRITCHLEY, Mc. (22), p. 77
56. HALLGREN, B. (53), p. 1–287
57. HERMANN, K. (61), p. 177–184 and (62), p. 87 and p. 179
58. HERMANN, K. (62), p. 87 (in the Copenhagen edition)
59. VERNON, M. D. (142), p. 81 (in the English edition)

60. MONEY, J.: On Learning and Not Learning to Read. In: MONEY, J. (ed.), (99), p. 32 and p. 34 – 35
61. RABINOVITCH, R. D.: Dyslexia. Psychiatric Considerations. In: MONEY, J. (ed.), (98), p. 77
62. WHITSELL, L. J.: Neurologic Aspects of Reading Disorders. In: FLOWER, R. et al. (eds.), (43), p. 53 and p. 56
63. RABKIN, J.: Reading Disability in Children. S. African Med. J., 1957. Cited in: KRAMER, J. (85), p. 96
64. BLAINE, G. B. and McARTHUR, C. C. (10), p. 84
65. BIGLMAIER, F. (8), p. 43
66. WEINSCHENK, C. (147), p. 95

2. Psychopathological Findings, pp. 82–106

1. MUCCHIELLI, R. and BOURCIER, A. (103), p. 114 and p. 25 – 26
2. BURFIELD, L. M. (14), p. 129
3. MARKS, P. A.: An Assessment of the Diagnostic Process in a Child Guidance Setting, 1961. Cited in: ROSEN, E. and GREGORY, I. (116), p. 492
4. WITTY, P. and KOPEL, D. (150), p. 231
5. ROUDINESCO, J. and TRELAT, M. In: LANGE-COSSACK, H. and WISSEL, M. 1956. Cited in: BIGLMAIER, F. (8), p. 50
6. LORY, P. (94), p. 45
7. DÜHRSSEN, A. (34), p. 57 and 50
8. DE HIRSCH, K. et al. (28), p. 68 – 69
9. KIRCHHOFF, H. (80), p. 13
10. LINDER, M.: Über das Problem sekundärer Symptome der Legasthenie. In: KIRCHHOFF, H. and PIETROWICZ, B. (eds.), (79), p. 36 and p. 38
11. PRECHTL, H.: Reading Difficulties as a Neurological Problem in Childhood. In: MONEY, J. (ed.), (98), p. 191 – 193
12. BENNETT, C. C.: An Inquiry into the Genesis of Poor Reading, 1938; KARLSEN, B.: A Comparison of Some Educational and Psychological Characteristics of Successful and Unsuccessful Readers, 1954; WOLFE, L. S.: Differential Factors in Specific Reading Disability, 1941; cited in: Smith, H. and DECHANT, E. (124), p. 306
13. LORY, P. (94), p. 48
14. JOHNSON, D. and MYKLEBUST, H. (70), p. 300
15. STRANG, R. (130), p. 155
16. STROTHER, Charles R.: Discovering, Evaluating, Programming for the Neurologically Handicapped Child. 1963, published by Nat. Society for Crippled Children and Adults, Inc., Chicago, p. 3
17. KIRCHHOFF, H. (77), p. 13
18. KOBI, E. (82), p. 21
19. BIGLMAIER, F. (8), p. 49
20. KIRCHHOFF, H. (80), p. 47
21. LINDER, M.: Über das Problem sekundärer Symptome der Legasthenie. In: KIRCHHOFF, H. and PIETROWICZ, B. (eds.), (79), p. 38
22. HUNGER-KAINDLSTORFER, M.: Funktionelles Üben im Rahmen der Legasthenie-Behandlung. In: INGENKAMP, K. (ed.), (68), p. 187
23. LOBROT, M.: Forschungen zur Legasthenie in Frankreich. In: INGENKAMP, K. (ed.), (68), p. 22

24. KLEINER, D.: Jugendpsychiatrische Erfahrungen. In: INGENKAMP, K. (ed.), (68), p. 118
25. LORY, P. (94), p. 36 and p. 38
26. SCHENK-DANZIGER, L.: Sitzungsprotokoll. In: INGENKAMP, K. (ed.), (68), p. 59 – 60
27. DE HIRSCH, K. et al. (28), p. 47
28. KOCHER, F. (83), p. 18
29. BERNA, J. (6), p. 25 – 26
30. CLEMENTS, S. D. et al. (18), p. 7
31. ORTON, S. (109), p. 132 – 135
32. MUCCHIELLI, R. and BOURCIER, A. (103), p. 25 – 26
33. MUCCHIELLI, R. and BOURCIER, A. (103), p. 166
34. MÜLLER, R. G. E.: Die Schreib-Lese-Schwäche als neurotoide Legasthenie und als Regressionsphänomen. Schule und Psy., 1958, H. 5
35. KIRCHHOFF, H. (80), p. 43 and p. 54
36. KOBI, E. (82), p. 22
37. BIGLMAIER, F. (8), p. 50
38. SPACHE, G. D. (127), p. 468
39. GATES, A. I. (45), p. 205
40. HOLMES, J. A. (66), p. 14
41. ROBINSON, H. M. (115), p. 122
42. BURFIELD, L. M. (14), p. 129
43. DÜHRSSEN, A. (33), p. 263 and p. 270 – 271
44. COHN, R. (19), p. 183
45. MUCCHIELLI, R. and BOURCIER, A. (103), p. 26
46. BIGLMAIER, F. (8), p. 50
47. LORY, P. (94), p. 68
48. LINDER, J.: Über das Problem sekundärer Symptome der Legasthenie. In: KIRCHHOFF, H. and PIETROWICZ, B. (eds.), (79), p. 38
49. DÜHRSSEN, A., (33), p. 23 – 24
50. LINDER, M.: Über das Problem sekundärer Symptome der Legasthenie. In: KIRCHHOFF, H. und PIETROWICZ, B. (eds.), (79), p. 37 – 38
51. DÜHRSSEN, A. (34), p. 86
52. BERNA, J. (6), p. 29
53. LINDER, M.: Über das Problem sekundärer Symptome der Legasthenie. In: KIRCHHOFF, H. and PIETROWICZ, B. (eds.), (79), p. 38
54. FABIAN, A: Reading Disability: An Index of Pathology. 1955, American Journal of Orthopsychiatry. Cited in: JAMPOLSKY, Gerald G.: Psychiatric Considerations in Reading Disorders. In: FLOWER, R. M. et al. (eds.), (43), p. 62
55. TOMKINS, C. (140), p. 3
56. CRITCHLEY, Mc. (22), p. 67 and p. 69
57. SCHOMBURG, E.: Beiträge zur Legasthenieforschung aus Holland und England. In: INGENKAMP, K. (ed.), (68), p. 50
58. KLEINER, D.: Jugendpsychiatrische Erfahrungen. In: INGENKAMP, K. (ed.), (68), p. 118 – 119
59. WEINSCHENK, C. (147), p. 8 and p. 156
60. WEPMAN, J.: Dyslexia, Language and Concept Formation. In: MONEY, J. (98), p. 185
61. WOLF, E. (151), p. 148
62. LORY, P. (94), p. 49

63. JOSS, L. W., LEIMAN, C. J. and SCHIFFMAN, G. B.: Unveröffentlichte Arbeit, 1961. Board of Education, Baltimore County, Maryland, U.S.A. Cited in: SCHIFFMAN, G. E.: Dyslexia as an Educational Phenomenon. In: MONEY, J. (ed.), (98), p. 57–58. The same work is briefly reviewed in CRITCHLEY, Mc. (22), p. 89
64. RABINOVITCH, R. D.: Dyslexia: Psychiatric Considerations. In: MONEY, J. (ed.), (98), p. 73
65. CRITCHLEY, Mc. (22), p. 71
66. JAMPOLSKY, G. G.: Psychiatric Considerations in Reading Disorders. In: FLOWER, R. et al. (43), p. 66
67. BOND, G. L. and TINKER, M. A. (12), p. 107
68. WEINSCHENK, C. (147), p. 158
69. LINDER, M.: Über das Problem sekundärer Symptome der Legasthenie. In: KIRCHHOFF, H. and PIETROWICZ, B. (eds.), (79), p. 38
70. HUNGER-KAINDLSTORFER, M.: Funktionelles Üben im Rahmen der Legastheniebehandlung. In: INGENKAMP, K. (ed.), (68), p. 187
71. CHALLMAN, R. (16), p. 7–11
72. GATES, A. I. (46), p. 83
73. BIGLMAIER, F. (8), p. 172
74. HUNGER-KAINDLSTORFER, M.: Über die Einzelbehandlung von Lesestörungen. In: KIRCHHOFF, H. and PIETROWICZ, B. (eds.), (79), p. 57
75. LORY, P. (94), p. 72
76. TAMM, H.: Über die Arbeit in den Hamburger LRS-Klassen. In: KIRCHHOFF, H. and PIETROWICZ, B. (eds.), (79), p. 50
77. LORY, P. (94), p. 77
78. TAMM, H.: Grundsätze, Methoden und Erfahrungen bei der Betreuung von lese- und rechtschreibgestörten Schülern. In: INGENKAMP, K. (ed.), (68), p. 143
79. BIGLMAIER, F. (8), p. 131
80. KIRCHHOFF, H. (80), p. 47
81. MUCCHIELLI, R. and BOURCIER, A. (103), p. 128–129
82. TAMM, H.: Über die Arbeit in den Hamburger LRS-Klassen. In: KIRCHHOFF, H. and PIETROWICZ, B. (eds.), (79), p. 55
83. CHASSAGNY, C. (17), p. 74
84. REY, A.: Préface. In: KOCHER, F. (83), p. VI
85. KOCHER, F. (83), p. 44
86. HUNGER-KAINDLSTORFER, M.: Über die Einzelbehandlung von Lesestörungen. In: KIRCHHOFF, H. and PIETROWICZ, B. (eds.), (79), p. 57
87. MOSSE, H: Zur Symptomatik und Ätiologie der Legasthenien. In: INGENKAMP, K. (ed.), (68), p. 30
88. BIGLMAIER, F. (8), p. 178
89. LORY, P. (94), p. 74
90. ELLEHAMMER, M.: Über die Behandlung von Lesestörungen in Kopenhagen. In: KIRCHHOFF, H. and PIETROWICZ, B. (eds.), (79), p. 63
91. WHITSELL, L. J.: Neurologic Aspects of Reading Disorders. In: FLOWER, R. et al. (eds.), (43), p. 55
92. EPHRON, B. (40), p. 3–7

3. Testpsychological Findings, pp. 107–152

1. LORY, P. (94), p. 64

2. SCHENK-DANZIGER, L.: Diskussionsprotokoll. In: INGENKAMP, K. (ed.), (68), p. 58
3. BIGLMAIER, F.: Diskussionsprotokoll. In: INGENKAMP, K. (ed.), (68), p. 59
4. THUST: Diskussionsprotokoll. In: INGENKAMP, K. (ed.), (68), p. 59
5. LORY, P. (94), p. 64
6. BILLS, R. E. (9), p. 140–149
7. GOFMAN, H. F.: The Identification and Evaluation of Children with Reading Disorders: A Pediatrician's View. In: FLOWER, R. M. et al. (eds.), (43), p. 6
8. MALMQUIST, R.: Factors Related to Reading Disabilities in the First Grade of the Elementary School, 1960. Cited in: GOFMAN, H. F.: The Identification and Evaluation of Children with Reading Disorders: A Pediatrician's View. In: FLOWER, R. M. et al. (eds.), (43), p. 6
9. CRITCHLEY, Mc (22), p. 18
10. DE HIRSCH, K. et al. (28), p. 46
11. FERDINAND, W.: Über die Fehlerarten des rechtschreibschwachen Kindes. In: INGENKAMP, K. (ed.), (68), p. 94 and 95
12. LÜCKERT, H.-R. (95), p. 193
13. ROMAN, M.: Tutorial Group Therapy, 1955. Cited in: SMITH, H. P. and DECHANT, E. V. (124), p. 310
14. WEINSCHENK, C. (147), p. 82 and p. 83
15. STRONG, K. (132), p. 19–20
16. WERHAHN, M. (148), p. 136
17. KAISER, L. (73), p. 94
18. a) FILDES, L. G.: A Psychological Inquiry into the Nature of the Condition Known as Congenital Word-Blindness, 1921, and b) GATES, A. I.: The Psychology of Reading and Spelling with Special Reference to Disability, 1922. Cited in BENTON, A. L.: Dyslexia, Form Perception, and Directional Sense. In: MONEY, J. (ed.), (98), p. 89–90
19. BIGLMAIER, F. (8), p. 124
20. TAMM, H.: Diskussionsprotokoll. In: INGENKAMP, K. (ed.), (68), p. 124
21. SCHIFFMAN, G. and Clemmens, R.: Observations on Children with Severe Reading Problems. In: HELLMUTH, J. (ed.), (60), p. 306
22. GRAHAM, E. E. (50), p. 268–271
23. ALTUS, G. T. (1), p. 155–156
24. KALLOS, G. L. et al. (74), p. 477
25. GRAHAM, E. E. (50), p. 268–271
26. FERDINAND, W.: Über die Fehlerarten des rechtschreibschwachen Kindes. In: INGENKAMP, K. (ed.), (68), p. 94
27. WALTER, K.: Die Duisburger Sondergruppen für Legastheniker. In: INGENKAMP, K. (ed.), (68), p. 195
28. TAMM, H.: Die in der Schule durchführbare Fehleranalyse. In: INGENKAMP, K. (ed.), (68), p. 110
29. ROBECK, M. C. (113), p. 111
30. WECHSLER, D. (144), p. 127 and p. 126
31. TATE, M. W. (135), p. 111–114
32. WALKER, H. M. (143), p. 195–197
33. HOFSTÄTTER, P. R. (65), p. 61
34. LOBROT, M.: Forschungen zur Legasthenie in Frankreich. In: INGENKAMP, K. (ed.), (68), p. 18
35. HOFSTÄTTER, P. R. (65), p. 61 and p. 62

36. TATE, M. W. (135), p. 300 –301
37. WECHSLER, D. (144), Footnote p. 127
38. WECHSLER, D. (144), p. 138
39. WECHSLER, D. (144), p. 126
40. GOODENOUGH, F. L. (49)
41. HARRIS, D. B. (57), p. 126 –129
42. KERSCHENSTEINER, D. G.: Die Entwicklung der zeichnerischen Bega-
    bung, 1905. Cited in: HARRIS, D. B. (57), p. 15, and in GOODENOUGH, F.
    L. (49), p. 4 –5
43. GOODENOUGH, F. L. (49), p. 46 (Table) and p. 56 (Text)
44. GOODENOUGH, F. L. (49), p. 56 –57
45. DUNN, L. M. (35), p. 25
46. DUNN, L. M. (35), p. 32
47. DUNN, L. M. (35), p. 35 and p. 41 (Text), and p. 34 –40 (Tables)
48. NEVILLE, D.: The Relationship between Reading Skills and IQ Test
    Scores, 1964. Cited in: DUNN, L. M. (35), p. 38
49. HOFSTÄTTER, P. R. (65), p. 92–94
50. WALKER, H. M. (143), p. 246 –248
51. NEVILLE, D.: The Relationship between Reading Skills and IQ Test
    Scores, 1964. Cited in: DUNN, L. M. (35), p. 38
52. DUNN, L. M. (35), p. 33
53. HARRIS, D. B. (57), p. 97
54. GRAHAM, E. E. (50), p. 268 and p. 270
55. ALTUS, G. (1), p. 155
56. KALLOS, G. L. et. al. (74), p. 477
57. SCHIFFMAN, G. and CLEMMENS, R. L.: Observations on Children with
    Severe Reading Problems. In: HELLMUTH, J. (ed.), (60), p. 306
58. WECHSLER, D. (144), p. 150 –152
59. WECHSLER, D. (144), p. 148 –149
60. SCHUBENZ, S. and BÖHMIG, S.: Legasthenie und Intelligenz, 1964. Cited
    in: INGENKAMP, K.: Diskussionsprotokoll. In: INGENKAMP, K. (ed.),
    (68), p. 125
61. LOBROT, M.: Forschungen zur Legasthenie in Frankreich. In: INGEN-
    KAMP, K. (ed.), (68), p. 18
62. ZUCKRIGL, A.: (153), p. 143
63. SCHIFFMAN, G.: Dyslexia as an Educational Phenomenon. In: MONEY, J.
    (ed.), (98), p. 52
64. CHASSAGNY, C. (17), p. 48
65. ELLEHAMMER, M.: Überblick über Forschungen in Dänemark. In: IN-
    GENKAMP, K. (ed.), (68), p. 47
66. MUSSEN, P. H.: Individual Differences in Development. In: FLOWER,
    R. M. et al. (eds.), (43), p. 37
67. LORY, P. (94), p. 75, 66, and p. 50
68. CRITCHLEY, Mc (22), p. 59 and p. 38
69. LÜCKERT, H.-R. (95), p. 195
70. MUCCHIELLI, R. and BOURCIER, A. (103), p. 167
71. ELLEHAMMER, M.: Überblick über Forschungen in Dänemark. In: IN-
    GENKAMP, K. (ed.), (68), p. 47
72. MESSEANT, G.: Unveröffentlichte Arbeit. Cited in: LOBROT, M.: For-
    schungen zur Legasthenie in Frankreich. In: INGENKAMP, K. (ed.), (68),
    p. 19

216   *Notes, pp. 135–160*

73. NEVILLE, D.: The Intellectual Characteristics of Severely Retarded Readers. In: HELLMUTH, J. (ed.), (60), p. 286
74. ROBECK, M. C. (113), p. 113
75. WECHSLER, D. (145), p. 11
76. SCHIFFMAN, G. and CLEMMENS, R. L.: Observations on Children with Severe Reading Problems. In: HELLMUTH, J. (ed.), (60), p. 305
77. WECHSLER, D. (144), p. 223
78. SCHIFFMAN, G. and CLEMMENS, R. L.: Observations on Children with Severe Reading Problems. In: HELLMUTH, J. (ed.), (60), p. 304
79. LÜCKERT, H.-R. (95), p. 204
80. SCHIFFMAN, G. and CLEMMENS, R. L.: Observations on Children with Severe Reading Problems. In: HELLMUTH, J. (ed.), (60), p. 305
81. NEVILLE, D.: The Intellectual Characteristics of Severely Retarded Readers. In: HELLMUTH, J. (ed.), (60), p. 284–285
82. SCHIFFMAN, G.: Dyslexia as an Educational Phenomenon. In: MONEY, J. (ed.), (98), p. 51–52
83. BIGLMAIER, F. (8), p. 48
84. WECHSLER, D. (144), p. 125 and p. 147
85. ROBECK, M. C. (113), p. 115
86. WECHSLER, D. (144), p. 150
87. MORROW, R. S. and MARK, J. C. (102), p. 283–289
88. HANVIK, L. et al. (55), p. 364–375; and in: FRIERSON, E. C. and BARBE, W. B. (ed.), (44), p. 262–278
89. CAPOBIANCO, R. F.: Diagnostic Methods Used with Learning Disability Cases. In: FRIERSON, E. C. and BARBE, W. B. (eds.), (44), p. 248

4. Environmental Factors, pp. 153–170

1. LINDER, M. (92), p. 137
2. SCHENK-DANZIGER, L.: Diskussionsprotokoll. In: INGENKAMP, K. (ed.), (68), p. 122
3. BLEIDICK, U.: Über Theorien zur Ätiologie der Lese- unde Schreibstörungen. In: KIRCHHOFF, H. and PIETROWICZ, B. (eds.), (79), p. 22
4. KOBI, E. (82), p. 24
5. BIGLMAIER, F. (8), p. 50 and p. 51
6. CHASSAGNY, C. (17), p. 7
7. STRANG, R. (130), p. 268
8. ROBINSON, H. M. (114), p. 40
9. SMITH, H. P. and DECHANT, E. V. (124), p. 97–98
10. NIEMEYER, W.: Legasthenie und Anpassung. In: Schule und Psychologie, 1964, Heft 3
11. HAVIGHURST, R. J. and Neugarten, B. L. (59), p. 20 and p. 21
12. HARRIS, I. D. (58), p. 188, 57, and p. 21
13. DE HIRSCH, K. (28), p. 12 and p. 100
14. DÜHRSSEN, A. (33), p. 214
15. ANDERSON, M. and KELLEY, M.: An Inquiry into Traits Associated with Reading Disability, 1931. Cited in: MONROE, S. (100), p. 100, and in CRITCHLEY, Mc. (22), p. 65
16. KIRCHHOFF, H. (80), p. 12
17. HARRIS, I. D. (58), p. 54
18. DÜHRSSEN, A. (33), p. 210 and p. 211

19. HARRIS, I. D. (58), p. 177 and p. 178
20. KIRCHHOFF, H. (80), p. 12
21. SCHENK-DANZIGER, L.: Diskussionsprotokoll. In: INGENKAMP, K. (ed.), (68), p. 122
22. KOBI, E. (82), p. 22
23. LINDER, M.: Über Legasthenie (Spezielle Leseschwäche). In: Zeitschrift für Kinderpsychiatrie, 1951, 18. Jg., Heft. 4, p. 110 ff.
24. BIGLMAIER, F. (8), p. 51
25. YOUNG, R. A. (152), p. 247
26. BIGLMAIER, F. (8), p. 173
27. HARRIS, I. D. (58), p. 42

BIBLIOGRAPHY

1. ALTUS, Grace T.: A WISC Profile for Retarded Readers. In: Journal of Consulting Psychology. April 1956, 20, No. 2, p. 155 -156
2. ARTLEY, A. Sterl: Your Child Learns to Read. Scott, Foresman and Co., Glenview, 1953
3. AUSTIN, Mary C.: Personal Characteristics that Retard Progress in Reading. Keeping Reading Programs Abreast of the Times. In: Supplementary Educational Monographs, No. 72. University of Chicago Press, Chicago, 1950, p. 112–117
4. BATEMAN, Barbara D.: Learning Disabilities – Yesterday, Today and Tomorrow. In: Exceptional Children. Dec. 1964, Vol. 31, No. 4, p. 167–177
5. BENTON, C. D.; McCANN, J. W.; LARSEN, M.: Dyslexia and Dominance. In: Journal of Pediatric Ophthalmology. July 1965, Vol. 2, No 3
6. BERNA, Jacques: Schulschwierigkeiten als Folge seelischer Störungen. 3. Aufl. Ernst Reinhardt Verlag, München 1965
7. BERRY, Mildred F.; EISENSON, Jon: Speech Disorders: Principles and Practices of Therapy. Appleton-Century-Crofts, New York 1956
8. BIGLMAIER, Franz: Lesestörungen. Diagnose und Behandlung. 2. Aufl. Ernst Reinhardt Verlag, München/Basel 1965. (Erziehung und Psychologie, Beihefte der Zeitschrift Schule und Psychologie. Hrsg.: Lückert, H.-R., Heft 14)
9. BILLS, Robert E.: Nondirective Play Therapy with Retarded Readers. In: Journal of Consulting Psychology, April 1950, 14, p. 140–149
10. BLAINE, Graham B.; McARTHUR, Charles C. and Others: Emotional Problems of the Student. Anchor Books, Doubleday & Co., Garden City 1966
11. BLEIDICK, Ulrich: Der Gegenwärtige Stand der Lese- und Schreibschwäche-Forschung. In: Schule und Psychologie, 1960, Heft 3, p. 65–82
12. BOND, Guy L.; TINKER, Miles, A.: Reading Difficulties: Their Diagnosis and Correction. Appleton-Century-Crofts, New York 1957
13. BOURCIER, A.: Traitement de la Dyslexie. Les Editions Sociales Françaises, Paris 1966
14. BURFIELD, Leone M.: Emotional Problems of Poor Readers among College Students. Clinical Studies in Reading I. Supplementary Educational Monographs, No. 68, University of Chicago Press, Chicago 1949, p. 123–129
15. BUSWELL, Guy Th.: Fundamental Reading Habits. A Study of Their Development. In: Supplementary Educational Monographs, No 21, University of Chicago Press, Chicago 1922
16. CHALLMAN, Robert: Personality Maladjustments and Remedial Reading. In: Journal of Exceptional Children, October 1939, 6, p. 7–11
17. CHASSAGNY, Claude: Manuel pour la rééducation de la lecture et de l'orthographe. 3e éd., Editions Néret, Paris 1966

18. CLEMENTS, Sam D.; LEHTINEN, Laura E.; LUKENS, Jean E.: Children with Minimal Brain Injury. A Symposium. National Society for Crippled Children and Adults, Inc., Chicago, Ill., Copyright 1964
19. COHN, Robert: The Neurological Study of Children with Learning Disabilities. In: Journal of Exceptional Children, December 1964, Vol. 31, No 4, p. 179–185
20. COLE, Luelle: The Improvement of Reading with Special Reference to Remedial Instruction. Farrar & Rinehart, New York 1938
21. COLEMAN, James C.: Perceptual Retardation in Reading Disability Cases. In: Journal of Educational Psychology, December 1953, 44, p. 497–503
22. CRITCHLEY, Macdonald: Developmental Dyslexia. Reprint. William Heinemann Medical Books, London 1966
23. CRONIN, Eileen M.: For the Problem Reader of Any Age. Sounds and Symbols in Reading. Academy Guild Press, Fresno, 1966
24. CRUICKSHANK, William M. (ed.): The Teacher of Brain-Injured Children – a Discussion of the Bases for Competency. Syracuse University Press, Syracuse 1966
25. CRUICKSHANK, William M.: The Brain-Injured Child in Home, School and Community. Syracuse University Press, Syracuse 1967
26. DAHL, L. A.: Public School Audiometry, Principles and Methods. The Interstate Printers and Publishers, Danville 1949
27. DEARBORN, Walter F.: Ocular and Manual Dominance in Dyslexia. In: Psychological Bulletin, 1931, Vol. 28, p. 704–715
28. DE HIRSCH, Katrina; JANSKY, Jeannette J., LANGFORD, William S.: Predicting Reading Failure. A Preliminary Study. Harper & Row Publishers, New York, Evanston and London 1966
29. DELACATO, Carl H.: The Treatment and Prevention of Reading Problems. Charles C. Thomas, Springfield, Ill., 1959
30. DELACATO, J.; DELACATO, Carl H.: A Group Approach to Remedial Reading, Part I. In: Elementary English, March 1952, Vol. 29, und Part II, Jan. 1953, Vol. 30
31. DONGIER, Maurice: Nevroses et troubles psychosomatiques. Charles Dessart, Bruxelles 1966
32. DOYLE, P. J.: The Organic Hyperkinetic Syndrome. In: The Journal of School Health, October 1962, Vol. XXXII, No. 8, p. 299–306
33. DÜHRSSEN, Annemarie: Psychotherapie bei Kindern und Jugendlichen. Biographische Anamnese und therapeutische Verfahren. 2. Aufl. Verlag Für Medizinische Psychologie, Göttingen 1963
34. DÜHRSSEN, Annemarie: Psychogene Erkrankungen bei Kindern und Jugendlichen. Eine Einführung in die allgemeine und spezielle Neurosenlehre. 5. Aufl. Verlag für Medizinische Psychologie, Göttingen 1965
35. DUNN, Lloyd, M.: Peabody Picture Vocabulary Test. Expanded Manual. American Guidance Service, Minneapolis 1965
36. DURRELL, Donald D.; MURPHY, Helen, A.: The Auditory Discrimination Factor in Reading Readiness and Reading Disability. In: Education, May 1953, 73, p. 556–560
37. EAMES, Thomas H.: A Comparison of the Ocular Characteristics of Unselected and Reading Disability Groups. In: Journal of Educational Research, March 1932, 25, p. 211–215
38. EAMES, Thomas H.: A Frequency Study of Physical Handicaps in Read-

ing Disability and Unselected Groups. In: Journal of Educational Research, Sept. 1935, 29, p. 1–5

39. EDSON, William H.; BOND, Guy L.; COOK, Walter W.: Relationships between Visual Characteristics and Specific Silent Reading Abilities. In: Journal of Educational Research, Febr. 1953, 46, p. 451–457
40. EPHRON, Beulah, K.: Emotional Difficulties in Reading. A Psychological Approach to Study Problems. The Julian Press, New York 1953
41. EWING, Irene R.; EWING, A. W. G.: Speech and the Deaf Child. The Volta Bureau, Washington 1954
42. FARRIS, L. P.: Visual Defects as Factors Influencing Achievement in Reading. In: Journal of Experimental Education, Sept. 1936, 5, p. 58–60
43. FLOWER, Richard M.; GOFMAN, Helen F.; LAWSON, Lucie I. (eds.),: Reading Disorders. A Multidisciplinary Symposium. F. A. Davis Company, Philadelphia 1965
44. FRIERSON, Edward C.; BARBE, Walter B. (eds.),: Educating Children with Learning Disabilities. Selected Readings. Appleton-Century-Crofts, New York 1967
45. GATES, Arthur I.: Failure in Reading and Social Maladjustment. In: Journal of the Nat. Education Ass., October 1936, 25, p. 205–206
46. GATES, Arthur I.: The Role of Personality Maladjustment in Reading Disability. In: Journal of Genetic Psychology, Sept. 1941, 59, p. 77–83
47. GETMAN, Gerald N.: How to Develop Your Child's Intelligence. The Announcer Press, Luverne, Minnesota, 1962
48. GILLINGHAM, Anna; STILLMAN, B. W.: Remedial Training for Children with Specific Disability in Reading, Spelling and Penmanship. 5th ed. 1956, 6th ed. 1960, both published by the Educators Publishing Service, Cambridge, Mass.
49. GOODENOUGH, Florence, L.: Measurement of Intelligence by Drawings. World Book Co., Yonkers, Hudson, N.Y., World Book Co., Chicago 1926
50. GRAHAM, Ellis E.: Wechsler-Bellevue and WISC Scattergrams of Unsuccessful Readers. In: Journal of Consulting Psychology, Aug. 1952, 16, p. 268–271
51. GRAY, William S.: The Teaching of Reading. Burton Lecture, Harvard, Cambridge, Mass., 1957
52. GRUBER, E.: Reading Ability, Binocular Coordination and the Ophthalmograph. In: Arch. Oph., 1962, Vol. 67, p. 280–288
53. HALLGREN, Bertil: Specific Dyslexie. (Congenital Word-Blindness): A Clinical and Genetic Study. In: Acta Psychiatrica et Neurologica Suppl., (Kopenhagen) 1950, No 65, p. 1–287
54. HANSELMANN, H.: Einführung in die Heilpädagogik. Rotapfelverlag, Zürich 1958
55. HANVIK, Leo et al.: Diagnosis of Cerebral Dysfunction in Children. In: American Journal of Diseases of Children, March 1961, Vol. 101, p. 364–375
56. HARRIS, A. J.: How to Increase Reading Ability, 3rd ed. Longmans, Green and Company, New York 1956
57. HARRIS, Dale B.: Children's Drawings as Measures of Intellectual Maturity. Harcourt, Brace & World, Inc., New York 1963
58. HARRIS, Irving D.: Emotional Blocks to Learning. A Study of the Reasons for Failure in School. The Free Press, New York, and Collier-Macmillan Ltd., London 1961

59. HAVIGHURST, Robert J.; NEUGARTEN, Bernice L.: Society and Education. Allyn and Bacon, Inc., Boston 1962
60. HELLMUTH, Jerome: Learning Disorders, Vol. II. Special Child Publications, Seattle 1966
61. HERMANN, Knud: Congenital Word-Blindness. Poor Readers in the Light of Gerstmann's Syndrome. In: Acta Psychiatr. et Neurol., Suppl., 1956, 103, p. 117-184
62. HERMANN, Knud: Reading Disability, A Medical Study of Word-Blindness and Related Handicaps. Forum, Copenhagen 1959
63. HILDRETH, G.: The Development and Training of Hand Dominance. In: Journal of Genetic Psychology, March 1950, 76, p. 39 – 144
64. HINSHELWOOD, James: Congenital Word-Blindness. H. K. Lewis & Co., Ltd., London 1917
65. HOFSTÄTTER, Peter R.: Einführung in die quantitativen Methoden der Psychologie. Johann Ambrosius Barth, München 1953
66. HOLMES, Jack A.: Emotional Factors and Reading Disabilities. In: The Reading Teacher, 1955, 9, p. 11 – 17
67. HUNGER-KAINDLSTORFER, Maria: Ein prägnanter Fall einer echten Legasthenie. In: Schule und Psychologie, 1960, 7. Jg., Heft 5, p. 154 – 159
68. INGENKAMP, Karlheinz: Lese- und Rechtschreibschwäche bei Schulkindern. Veröffentlichung des Pädagogischen Zentrums, Reihe C: Berichte, Band 2, Verlag Julius Beltz, Weinheim und Berlin, 1966
69. JACKSON, Thomas; SHYE, Virginia: A Comparison of Vision with Reading Scores of Ninth Grade Pupils. In: Elementary School Journal, Sept. 1945, 46, p. 33 – 35
70. JOHNSON, Doris J.; MYKLEBUST, Helmer R.: Learning Disabilities. Educational Principles and Practices. Grune & Stratton, New York and London 1967
71. JOHNSON, Marjorie S.: A Study of Diagnostic and Remedial Procedures in a Reading Clinic Laboratory School. In: Journal of Educational Research, April 1955, 48, p. 565 –578
72. JOHNSON, Marjorie S.: Factors Relating to Disability in Reading. In: Journal of Experimental Education, 1957, Vol. 26, No 16, p. 1 – 26
73. KAISER, Lothar: Ursachen des Schulmisserfolges bei normaler Intelligenz. Unveröffentlichte Diplomarbeit. Heilpädagogisches Institut der Universität Freiburg, Schweiz, 1965
74. KALLOS, George L.; GRABOW, John M.; GUARINO, Eugene A.: The WISC Profile of Disabled Readers. In: Personnel and Guidance Journal, 1961, 39, p. 476 –478
75. KEPHART, Newell C.: The Brain Injured Child in the Classroom. National Society for Crippled Children and Adults, Inc., Chicago 1963
76. KETCHUM, Gillet E.: Neurological and Psychological Trends in Reading Diagnosis. In: The Reading Teacher, May 1964, Vol. 17, No 8, p. 589 – 592
77. KIRCHHOFF, Hans: Lese- und Rechtschreibschwäche bei Schulkindern. S. Karger Verlag, Basel/New York, 1954 (14. Heft, Psychologische Praxis)
78. KIRCHHOFF, Hans: Erfahrungen mit Legasthenikerklassen in Hamburg. In: Die Schulwarte, 1958, Heft 11
79. KIRCHHOFF, Hans; PIETROWICZ, Bernard: Neues zur Lese- und Rechtschreibschwäche. S. Karger Verlag, Basel/New York, 1963 (34. Heft, Psychologische Praxis)
80. KIRCHHOFF, Hans: Verbale Lese- und Rechtschreibeschwäche im

Kindesalter. S. Karger, Basel/New York, 1964 (14. Heft, Psychologische Praxis)

81. KIRK, S. A.; BECKER, W. (eds.): Conference on Children with Minimal Brain Impairment. Scriptum of Conference Held at University of Illinois, Urbana, Illinois, January 1963

82. KOBI, Emil: Das legasthenische Kind. Schriften zur Psychologie, Pädagogik, Heilpädagogik und Sozialarbeit, Heft 22, Verlag des Instituts für Heilpädagogik, Luzern 1965

83. KOCHER, Francis: La Rééducation des Dyslexiques. 3e éd. Presses Universitaires de France, Paris 1966

84. KOSSAKOWSKI, A.: Wie überwinden wir die Schwierigkeiten beim Lesen- und Schreibenlernen, insbesondere bei Lese-Rechtschreib-Schwäche? Volk and Wissen, volkseigener Verlag, Berlin 1961

85. KRAMER, Josefine: Intelligenztest. Mit einer Einführung in Theorie und Praxis der Intelligenzprüfung. 2 Aufl. St. Antonius-Verlag, Solothurn, Schweiz, 1959. (Arbeiten zur Psychologie, Pädagogik und Heilpädagogik, Band 5, Hrsg.: Professoren Dr. Dupraz und Dr. Montalta)

86. KRAMER, Josefine: Linkshändigkeit. St.-Antonius-Verlag, Solothurn, Schweiz, 1961. (Arbeiten zur Psychoiogie, Pädagogik und Heilpädagogik, Band 19, Hrsg.: Professoren Dr. Dupraz und Dr. Montalta)

87. KRETSCHMER, Maria: Was ist Legasthenie? Schweizerische Erziehungsrundschau, Juni 1962, Heft 3, p. 49–52

88. LEAVELL, U. W.: The Problem of Symbol Reversals and Confusions, Their Frequency and Remediation. In: Peabody Journal of Education, November 1954

89. LEHTINEN, Laura E.: Have You Ever Known a Perceptually Handicapped Child. A C.A.N.H.C. special printing of this article which originally appeared in: A Bulletin of the Fund for Perceptually Handicapped Children, Inc. "Learn," Box 656, Evanston, Ill.

90. LEISER-EGGERT, A.: Methodische und Statistische Untersuchungen zum Problem der Lateralisation. In: Zeitschr. f. exp. u. angew. Psychologie, 1954, H. 2, p. 239–267

91. LINDER, Maria: Über die Legasthenie (spezielle Leseschwäche), 50 Fälle. Erscheinungsbild und Möglichkeiten der Behandlung. In: Zeitschrift für Kinderpsychiatrie, 1951, 18. Jg., Heft 4, p. 97–143

92. LINDER, Maria: Das Problem der Legasthenischen Kinder in der deutschen Schweiz. In: Schweizer Erziehungsrundschau, Okt. 1961, Heft 7, p. 137–160

93. LINDER, Maria: Lesestörungen bei normalbegabten Kindern. Schweizer Lehrerverein, Zürich 1962

94. LORY, Peter: Die Leseschwäche. Entstehung und Formen, ursächliche Zusammenhänge, Behandlung. Reinhardt Verlag, München/Basel 1966. (Band 44, Erziehung und Psychologie, Beihefte der Zeitschrift Schule und Psychologie, Lückert, H.-R., Hrsg.)

95. LÜCKERT, Heinz-Rolf: Behandlung und Vorgeugung von Leseschwierigkeiten. In: Schule und Psychologie, Juli 1966, 13. Jg., Heft 7, p. 193–207

96. MATEER, Florence: The Constitutional Basis of Alexia. Physiological Factors Affecting the Reading Process. 11th Yearbook of the Claremont College Reading Conference, Claremont 1946

97. MILES, W. R.; SEGEL, D.: Clinical Observation of Eye-Movements in the

Rating of Reading Disability. In: Journal of Educational Psychology, Oct. 1929, 20, p. 520–529

98. MONEY, John (ed.),: Reading Disability. The Johns Hopkins Press, Baltimore 1962

99. MONEY, John (ed.): The Disabled Reader. Education of the Disabled Child. The Johns Hopkins Press, Baltimore 1966

100. MONROE, Marion C.: Children Who Cannot Read. The Analysis of Reading Disabilities and the Use of Diagnostic Tests in the Instruction of Retarded Readers. The University of Chicago Press, Chicago 1932

101. MONTALTA, Eduard: Die Ausbildung der Heilpädagogen. In: Heilpädagogische Werkblätter, 1964–65, p. 33–34

102. MORROW, R. S.; MARK, J. C.: The Correlation of Intelligence and Neurological Findings on 22 Patients Autopsied for Brain Damage. In: Journal of Consulting Psychology, 1951, 19, p. 283–289

103. MUCCHIELLI, Roger; BOURCIER, Arlette: La Dyslexie, Maladie du Siècle. 2e éd. Les Editions Sociales Françaises, Paris 1964

104. MÜLLER, Richard G. E.: Die Schreib-Lese-Schwäche als neurotoide Legasthenie und als Regressphänomen. In: Schule und Psychologie, 1958, Heft 5, p. 266–270

105. MÜLLER, Richard G. E.: Zur Problematik der "Legasthenie" Diagnose. Differenzierung von "Typen" der Lese-Rechtschreibschwäche. In: Psychologische Beiträge, 1961, Bd. 6, p. 218–236

106. MYKLEBUST, Helmer: Learning Disorders, Psychoneurological Disturbances in Childhood. Rehabilitation Literature, 1964, Vol. 25, No 12, p. 354–360

107. O'CONNOR, Clarence D.; STRENG, Alice: Teaching the Acoustically Handicapped. In: The Education of Exceptional Children, 49th Yearbook of the National Society for the Study of Education, Part II. University of Chicago Press, 1950, p. 152–176

108. ORTON, Samuel T.: An Impediment to Learning to Read – A Neurological Explanation of the Reading Disability. In: School and Society, Sept. 1928, 28, p. 286–290

109. ORTON, Samuel T.: Reading, Writing and Speech Problems in Children. A Presentation of Certain Types of Disorders in the Development of the Language Faculty. W. W. Norton & Co., New York 1937

110. RABKIN, J.: Reading Disability in Children. In: S. Afr. Med. Journal, cited in: Ztbl. ges. Neurol.-Psychol., 1957, p. 678-681

111. REUCK, de, A. V. S.; O'CONNOR, Maeve (eds.): Disorders of Language, Ciba-Foundation Symposium. Little, Brown & Co., Boston 1964

112. REY, André: Monographies de Psychologie Clinique. Edition Delachaux-Niestlé, Paris 1952

113. ROBECK, Mildred C.: Subtest Patterning of Problem Readers on WISC. In: California Journal of Educational Research, May 1960, Vol. XI, No 3, p. 110–115

114. ROBINSON, Helen M.: Why Pupils Fail in Reading. University of Chicago Press, Chicago 1946

115. ROBINSON, Helen M.: Manifestations of Emotional Maladjustments. In: Clinical Studies in Reading, I, Supplementary Educational Monographs, No 68, University of Chicago Press, Chicago 1949, p. 114–122

116. ROSEN, Ephraim; GREGORY, Ian: Abnormal Psychology. W. B. Saunders Co., Philadelphia and London 1966

117. SCHENK-DANZIGER, Lotte: Der Zusammenhang der Legasthenie mit anderen psychischen Faktoren. In: Bericht des 3. Internationalen Kongresses für Heilpädagogik, Wien 1954, p. 249

118. SCHENK-DANZIGER, Lotte: Was ist Legasthenie? In: Schweiz. Erziehungsrundschau, 1960, Heft 1, p. 18 – 20

119. SCHILDER, P.: Congenital Alexia and Its Relation to Optic Perception. In: Journal of Genetic Psychology, Sept. 1944, 65, p. 67 – 88

120. SCHONELL, Fred J.: The Relation of Reading Disability to Handedness and Certain Ocular Factors. In: British Journal of Educational Psychology, Feb. 1941, 11, p. 20 – 27

121. SHERIDAN, Mary D.: The Child's Hearing for Speech. Methuen & Co., London 1948

122. SILVERMAN, S. R.: Hard-of-Hearing Children. In: Hearing and Deafness: A Guide for Laymen, Davis & Hallowell, eds. Murray Hill Books, Inc., New York 1947, p. 352 – 356

123. SMITH, D. E. P.; CARRIGAN, P. M.: The Nature of Reading Disability, Harcourt, Brace & Company, New York/Chicago 1959

124. SMITH, Henry P.; DECHANT, Emerald V.: Psychology in Teaching Reading. Prentice-Hall, Englewood Cliffs 1961

125. SMITH, Linda C.: A Study of Laterality Characteristics of Retarded Readers and Reading Achievers. In: Journal of Experimental Education, June 1950, Vol. 18, No 4, p. 327

126. SPACHE, George D.: Factors Which Produce Defective Reading. Corrective Reading in Classroom and Clinic. In: Supplementary Educational Monographs, No 79, University of Chicago Press, Chicago 1953, p. 49 – 57

127. SPACHE, George D.: Personality Patterns of Retarded Readers. In: Journal of Educational Research, Feb. 1957, 50, p. 461 – 469

128. SPACHE, George D.: A Rationale for Mechanical Methods for Improving Reading. Significant Elements in College and Adult Reading Improvement. In: Seventh Yearbook of the National Reading Conference for Colleges and Adults. Texas Christian University Press, Fort Worth 1958, p. 115 – 132

129. SPENCER, P. L.: The Reading Process and Types of Reading; In: Claremont College Reading Conference, 11th Yearbook, Claremont 1946, p. 17 – 22

130. STRANG, Ruth: Diagnostic Teaching of Reading. McGraw-Hill Book Company, New York 1964

131. STROMBERG, E. L.: The Relationship of Measures of Visual Acuity and Ametropia to Reading Speed. In: Journal of Applied Psychology, Feb. 1938, 22, p. 70 – 78

132. STRONG, Katherine: Recherche multifactorelle sur quelques cas de dyslexie. Unveröffentlichte Diplomarbeit. Heilpädagogisches Institut der Universität Freiburg, Schweiz, 1965

133. STROTHER, Charles, R.: Discovering, Evaluating, Programming for the Neurologically Handicapped Child. National Society for Crippled Children and Adults. An Easter Seal Publication, Chicago 1963

134. SWANSON, Donald E.; TIFFIN, Joseph: Bett's Physiological Approach to the Analysis of Reading Disabilities as Applied to the College Level. In: Journal of Educational Research, Feb. 1936, 29, p. 433 – 448

135. TATE, Merle W.: Statistics in Education and Psychology. A First Course. 3rd printing. Copyright 1955. The Macmillan Company, New York and Collier-Macmillan Ltd., London 1967

136. TAYLOR, Earl A.: Controlled Reading: A Correlation of Diagnostic Teaching and Corrective Techniques. University of Chicago Press, Chicago, 1937
137. THIBAUT, A.: Le langage et la prévention de la dyslexie. Le Gaucher. In: La nouvelle revue pédagogique, 1967, 22e année, Tome XXII, No 5, p. 298–301
138. THOMPSON, Alice C.: Educational Handicap. Some Questions and Some Partial Answers. Special Publication of Escalon Inc., Monterey Park, Calif., 1964
139. THOMPSON, Lloyd J.: Reading Disability. Developmental Dyslexia. Charles C. Thomas, Publisher, Springfield 1966
140. TOMKINS, Calvin: A Reporter at Large. The Last Skill Acquired. In: The New Yorker, Sept. 14, 1963, special printing of the Children's Neurological Development Program
141. TRAMER, Moritz: Lehrbuch der allgemeinen Kinderpsychiatrie einschliesslich der allgemeinen Psychiatrie der Pubertät und Adoleszenz. 4. Aufl. Schwabe & Co. Verlag, Basel/Stuttgart 1964
142. VERNON, Magdalen, D.: Backwardness in Reading. A Study of Its Origin and Nature. The University Press, Cambridge, Eng. 1957. Also Cambridge University Press, New York 1958
143. WALKER, Helen M.: Statistische Methoden für Psychologen und Pädagogen. Eine Einführung. 6./7. Aufl. Julius Beltz, Weinheim/Bergstrasse, Germany, 1964
144. WECHSLER, David: The Measurement of Adult Intelligence. 3rd ed. The Williams & Wilkins Company, Baltimore, 1944, Reprinted 1950
145. WECHSLER, David: WISC Manual. Wechsler Intelligence Scale for Children. The Psychological Corporation, New York, N.Y., 1949
146. WEINSCHENK, Curt: Die erbliche Lese-Rechtschreibschwäche und ihre sozialpsychiatrischen Auswirkungen. Verlag Huber, Bern 1962, (Heft 44 der Beihefte zur Schweizerischen Zeitschrift für Psychologie und ihre Anwendungen)
147. WEINSCHENK, Curt: Die erbliche Lese-Rechtschreibschwäche und ihre sozialpsychiatrischen Auswirkungen. Ein Lehrbuch für Ärzte, Psychologen und Pädagogen. 2 Aufl. Verlag Hans Huber, Bern und Suttgart 1965
148. WERHAHN, Maria: Legasthenie, Diagnose und Therapie eines Falles. Unveröffentlichte Diplomarbeit. Heilpädagogisches Institut der Universität Freiburg, Schweiz, 1966
149. WITTY, Paul; KOPEL, David: Factors Associated with the Etiology of Reading Disability. In: Journal of Educational Research, Feb. 1936, 29, p. 449–459
150. WITTY, Paul; KOPEL, David: Reading and the Educative Process. Ginn and Company, Boston 1939
151. WOLF, E.: Diagnostische Untersuchungsstelle im Bereich der Massnahmen zur Bekämpfung der Jugendkriminalität in den USA. In: Praxis der Kinderpsychologie und Kinderpsychiatrie, 1956, 5. Jg., p. 181–187
152. YOUNG, Robert A.: Case Studies in Reading Disability. In: American Journal of Orthopsychiatry. April 1938, 8, p. 230–254
153. ZUCKRIGL, Alfred: Sprachschwächen. Der Dysgrammatismus als sprachheilpädagogisches Problem. Neckarverlag, Villingen, 1964

AUTHOR INDEX

SUBJECT INDEX